D0078218

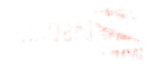

Captives of the Cold War Economy

Captives of *the* Cold War Economy

The Struggle for Defense Conversion in American Communities

JOHN J. ACCORDINO

Westport, Connecticut
London

Library of Congress Cataloging-in-Publication Data

Accordino, John J.
  Captives of the Cold War economy : the struggle for defense conversion in American communities / John J. Accordino.
    p. cm.
  Includes bibliographical references and index.
  ISBN 0-275-96561-9 (alk. paper)
  1. Military base conversion—United States. 2. Economic conversion—United States.
  3. Defense industries—United States. I. Title.
  HC110.D4 A58 2000
  338.4'76233'0973—dc21   99-088486

British Library Cataloguing in Publication Data is available.

Library of Congress Catalog Card Number: 99-088486
ISBN: 0-275-96561-9

First published in 2000

Praeger Publishers, 88 Post Road West, Westport, CT 06881
An imprint of Greenwood Publishing Group, Inc.
www.praeger.com

Printed in the United States of America

∞™ The paper used in this book complies with the
Permanent Paper Standard issued by the National
Information Standards Organization (Z39.48-1984).

10 9 8 7 6 5 4 3 2 1

To my patient and loving family

ANNE-MARIE, JOEY, and MARIO

Contents

Maps

Preface

This project began in 1990, when the Richmond Peace Education Center, a small volunteer organization that promotes nonviolent conflict resolution, established a task force on Economic Conversion.[1] Although I was not a member of the Peace Education Center, as a local academic with expertise in community economic development I was asked to join the task force. Inspired by a defense-conversion study that had just been completed by a peace-advocacy group in Charlottesville (west of Richmond), our task force decided to ascertain which Virginia communities were most dependent on defense spending and how, if at all, they were planning to respond to defense downsizing.

The fall of the Berlin Wall was still fresh in everyone's mind. Although defense spending had already declined from its mid-1980s high mark, we felt certain that, despite the Persian Gulf War, it would continue to fall. Indeed, like many Americans, we assumed that the tacit national consensus was that defense spending would, and should, now be reduced to a peacetime level. Our concern was whether the Commonwealth of Virginia would plan for these anticipated spending cutbacks, would assist companies wishing to convert to commercial markets, and assist communities where bases were closing and workers were losing their jobs.

Virginia is one of the three most defense-dependent states in the nation. It is home to the Pentagon as well as to the largest naval base in the world; a plethora of navy, air force, and army command, control, and operations centers; extensive combat-training grounds; and supply depots. Its defense manufacturers make explosives, nuclear carriers, submarines and other military ships, night-vision goggles, and a wide variety of other hardware. Its software and communications-systems developers work on the National Missile Defense project (aka Star Wars), on high-tech warfare-simulation modeling, and on other military projects ranging from the routine to the exotic. Virginia also is home to an electronic eavesdropping station—now closed—and a federal research laboratory. Like many other states in the so-called Gunbelt it is politically conservative, with a tradition of aversion to taxes, environmental regulations, unions, and industrial policy.[2]

The task force's role, we optimistically envisioned, would be to bring information and ideas on state and local conversion and adjustment policies, gleaned from the practices of other defense-dependent states and localities, to state and local governments and grass-roots groups in Virginia. However, we quickly found that grass-roots peace-advocacy groups in Virginia's most defense-dependent communities were either tiny or nonexistent.[3] Being short of funds and staff, we decided to focus our efforts on state policy. We participated in state-sponsored meetings and conferences and spoke often with state staff working on economic development or defense downsizing. We became alarmed by a seeming lack of urgency in the state's response to the prospect of defense downsizing and therefore recommended more initiatives. It was gratifying when, late in 1992, Governor L. Douglas Wilder named a Commission on Defense Conversion and Economic Adjustment; we testified before the commission and participated to some extent in its work. Even those modest initiatives, however, ended when Governor George Allen took office in January 1994. Like many of his fellow governors, he championed resistance to base closures and he ignored the concept and practice of defense conversion entirely. In 1995, as the federal Base Realignment and Closure process finished and as Congress began to increase defense spending, the task force stopped meeting.

Clearly, conversion and adjustment policies had not won the day in Virginia, but neither were they opposed in all quarters. Rather, the responses to defense-spending cutbacks had been mixed and, above all, fragmented. Some had welcomed defense reductions as an opportunity, some had accepted and sought to adjust to them, and others had resisted them. What factors accounted for these various responses? Why had seemingly promising initiatives for conversion or adjustment planning withered? To answer these questions seemed like a useful project. Moreover, since military installations and contractors were increasingly located in conservative states such as Virginia, it seemed important to study the Virginia situation carefully.[4]

Although I had not become involved in the task force with the aim of seriously studying defense dependency and conversion policy, I soon began to do so. As it became clear that our group could not, in the short run, influence policy significantly, I began to carefully document community defense dependency and to chronicle the responses of companies, state and local officials, and nongovernmental organizations (e.g., chambers of commerce) to the prospect of defense cutbacks. I thought that a thorough review of public and private responses in Virginia could at least identify problems and suggest better responses. The Town Creek Foundation of Oxford, Maryland, supported some of my research during 1994. Between 1991 and 1995 I conducted quantitative analyses of defense dependency in six Virginia communities.[5] I followed local newspaper accounts, reviewed U.S. Defense Department publications and other pertinent documents, and attended public conferences and meetings on defense cutbacks and public policies sponsored by Virginia business associations as well as by state and local governments. Between 1991 and 1997 I attended national conferences of conversion organizers and researchers, where I compared notes on Virginia with others from across the United States and from Europe; I also conducted formal interviews with conversion organizers in some American communities. I learned that, although some features of Virginia's response to defense downsizing were peculiar, many were common to communities throughout the United States and even, to some extent, in Eastern and Western Europe.

Most importantly, from 1993 to 1995 I conducted face-to-face, private interviews as well as telephone interviews with company presidents, public officials, military-installation representatives, and others throughout Virginia. The 121 persons interviewed comprised the following (nonoverlapping) categories: 53 elected or appointed public officials, 23 business owners, 13 business-organization representatives or business-service providers, 10 defense-adjustment consultants or academics, 9 military-installation representatives, 4 economists, 3 organized-labor representatives, 3 community-organization representatives, and 3 newspaper reporters.

The use of multiple research methods—quantitative analysis of written documents and in-depth interviews—to explore how and why social processes (here, the regional response to defense-spending cutbacks) unfold is not unusual. Through "triangulation," the researcher looks for convergence among the various methods used.[6] Where divergence arises the researcher must try to reconcile it, a process that often enriches the overall analysis. A notable characteristic of triangulation methodology is the absence of established rules for weighting each type of information. The researcher must use considered judgment in evaluating information and organizing it into a plausible framework. This study generally gives more weight to interviews than to written documents.[7]

The research process gathered accounts of varying responses to defense-spending cutbacks in Virginia. A particular response is presented in the text without qualifying statements if at least three unrelated informants reported basically the same situation, or if one informant's statements were corroborated by other types of information (e.g., newspapers or government documents). Occasionally, the discussion presents information provided by only one informant because it is plausible and fits with other information that is widely supported. In such instances, the word *reportedly* is used to alert the reader. Each interviewee was promised complete confidentiality, so the findings are reported in a way that makes it impossible to identify particular informants. All published material is, of course, cited. In many instances, published materials corroborated statements made in personal interviews. However, only that written material is cited, although it is backed up by interview material.

In 1996 I completed a report of the response to defense-spending cutbacks that was distributed throughout Virginia with funding provided by the Town Creek Foundation. Several interview subjects who read the report affirmed its conclusions, and some corrected minor factual inaccuracies. In 1999, while preparing this book, I reinterviewed some subjects from the 1996 Virginia report and compiled pertinent information that had appeared since 1996. Chapters 3 through 6 of this book contain material on the Virginia experience.

I also reinterviewed conversion organizers and public officials from other defense-dependent states and localities in the United States and studied additional documents on these regions. These include some of the most defense-dependent regions in the United States—San Diego, Tucson, St. Louis, Western Washington State, Southeastern Connecticut, and Maine. Their experiences with defense cutbacks, community resistance, and conversion organizing are detailed in chapter 7. These cases highlight both the importance of local political culture in determining responses to defense spending cutbacks, as well as the features common to community responses across the United States.

Chapter 1 is an overview of the concept of defense conversion, the federal defense budget, conversion-assistance policies in the 1990s, and the responses by defense prime contractors.[8] The chapter also explores why defense expenditures were not cut more deeply during the 1990s. Chapter 2 is a primer on urban political economy. It identifies the major economic forces and political interests that influence local development policy—setting the stage for the account of community and statewide responses to defense-spending cutbacks that appears in chapters 3 through 7. Chapter 8 ties together the overview material in chapters 1 and 2 with the cases presented in chapters 3 through 7. This final chapter summarizes the reasons why American communities did so little to reduce their defense dependency through proactive conversion and draws lessons for national, state, and local conversion policy.

As this project has evolved I have benefited from the insights and assistance of many people. I am indebted to the members of the Task Force on Economic Conversion in Virginia, especially John Gallini, who first inspired me to become involved in this issue and who read portions of this manuscript. I am grateful also to activists in the economic-conversion movement, especially Michael Closson of the Center for Economic Conversion and Greg Bischak and Miriam Pemberton of the National Commission on Economic Conversion and Disarmament, whose good work provided a wealth of information and clarity on the issues. Robert Griffis, former chief economist of the Virginia Employment Commission, graciously shared his reports on and insights into the workings of Virginia's defense economy. I am also indebted to the conversion activists who described their experiences to me. I have drawn inspiration and insight from the scholars whose works are cited throughout this volume, especially Sanford Gottlieb and Ann Markusen. And I am grateful to the elected and appointed officials, business owners, and many other persons who shared their time, knowledge, and expertise in hours of interviews.

Several people also helped in the preparation of this manuscript. Karen Becker produced splendid maps of Virginia's defense-dependent communities. The folks at Greenwood Publishing Group and Doric Lay Publishers handled the manuscript capably and expeditiously. And my wife, Anne-Marie McCartan, provided advice and encouragement throughout the entire research and writing process.

NOTES

1. The task force included a Virginia state economic-development staff person, a retired chemical-industrial engineer, a retired military officer, educators, economists, and, for a short while, a state legislator.

2. The "Gunbelt" is a term coined by Markusen, Hall, Campbell, and Deitrich to describe the Cold War–era shift of defense-procurement spending away from the nation's industrial heartland and toward the coasts. The resulting distribution of defense-dependent states resembles a belt around the nation's perimeter: New England, New York, Washington, DC (and Northern Virginia), Florida, Missouri, Colorado, Utah, Texas, Arizona, California, and Washington. If one adds military bases and federal research labs to the mix, the Hampton Roads area of Virginia as well as Nevada and New Mexico would figure prominently, further accentuating the "belt" shape. The southern, southwestern, and mountain regions of the Gunbelt share roughly similar economic histories (marked by plantation-style agriculture, extractive industries, and manufacturing branch plants) and have generally conservative political cultures. See Ann Markusen, Peter Hall, Scott Campbell, and Sabina Deitrick, *The Rise of the Gunbelt: The Military Remapping of Industrial America* (New York: Oxford University Press, 1991).

3. Indeed, Virginia has fewer thriving grass-roots-advocacy groups than many other states do, and even fewer than in other southern states.

4. See note 2 above.

5. I conducted location-quotient analyses for each local economy for the years 1979, 1989 (the two most recent business-cycle peaks), and 1993 by using the *Covered Employment and Wages in Virginia* series, commonly known as ES-202, which includes all public and private employment except for the military. (ES-202 is derived from employers' quarterly unemployment-insurance reports and is available for every state and locality in the United States. It is widely used by regional economists.) Military-employment statistics were derived from U.S. Defense Department data compiled by Robert Griffis of the Virginia Employment Commission in the series, *Department of Defense Employment, Military and Civilian*. I supplemented this information with defense prime-contractor lists provided by the U.S. Defense Department to the Virginia Employment Commission and with various wage and unemployment statistics developed by the Virginia Employment Commission. Spreadsheet tables depicting these data and location-quotient calculations (which provide an estimate of the extent to which a local economy depends for its livelihood upon certain industries) are available through my office at Virginia Commonwealth University in Richmond.

6. See, for example, Todd D. Jick, "Mixing Quantitative and Qualitative Methods: Triangulation in Action," *Administrative Science Quarterly* 24, December 1979.

7. In the Virginia interviews, networking was used to identify relevant actors and informed observers. First, groups were identified that might be concerned with defense downsizing: defense prime contractors and subcontractors, business associations, public economic-development agencies, grass-roots organizations, and elected public officials. These individuals and organizations were contacted and asked to describe the local situation (or their particular situation in the case of defense contractors) and the responses that they or the community as a whole had undertaken. When specific community-wide responses were identified, those involved were contacted. In the course of discussions with the leaders or informed observers of those efforts, names of proponents and opponents surfaced, and those persons were then contacted for their views. In the case of installations slated for closing through the Base Realignment and Closure process, installation

representatives were contacted and asked to describe their efforts at defense and then at adjustment planning. It soon became evident that while networking was very useful for understanding responses to defense-spending cutbacks, it yielded less information about nonresponses—or, more importantly, about how community attention or resources were directed elsewhere, with the effect of precluding effective responses to defense-spending cutbacks. I addressed this shortfall by expanding the network to include more people not associated with defense (mostly public officials) and by probing in all the interviews for the importance of issues other than defense cutbacks.

8. Prime contractors are those who contract directly with the contracting agency (here, the Pentagon) to provide goods or services. In most cases, prime contractors outsource part of the work to subcontractors.

1

The National Context: Defense Spending and Conversion Policy in the 1990s

THE COSTS OF THE COLD WAR

The fall of the Berlin Wall in 1989, symbolizing the end of the Cold War, spurred optimism that the world might now be spared a nuclear winter. It also prompted hopes that the massive sums that had been spent on defense could now be directed toward other pressing needs: Improving the nation's physical infrastructure and public education, cleaning up the environment and developing alternative energy sources, supplying housing, mass transit and health care, and improving industrial productivity. Although the United States could legitimately claim to have won the Cold War, the cost of victory had been staggering. Between 1948 and 1991 the United States had spent $13.1 trillion (1996 dollars) on the military, an average of $298.5 billion per year. Even with the Korean War and Vietnam War years excluded, average annual military spending for the period stood at $285.4 billion (1996 dollars).[1] This sum equals about 60 percent of total annual discretionary spending and about 5 percent of the nation's annual gross domestic product (GDP).[2]

Employment in defense industries and in the U.S. Department of Defense (both military and civilian) occupied 6 million persons in 1991, or 5 percent of the nation's 119 million workers.[3] The total number of jobs that depended on defense spending was even larger, however, because money flowing into a community through a base or a defense contractor is then spent on ancillary services, supplies, retail, and other activities. On average, a multiplier of 2, whereby one military or defense contractor job supports an additional service job in the community, is a reasonable estimate. Thus, 12 million persons, or roughly 10 percent of the U.S. workforce, were directly or indirectly dependent upon defense employment in 1991.

Besides direct costs, defense spending exacts opportunity costs—the value of nonmilitary activities that defense workers could otherwise pursue. One can begin to grasp the significance of these costs by observing that in 1992, 69 percent of the nation's aeronautical and astronautical engineers, 34 percent of the physicists, 50 percent of the oceanographers, 32 percent of the electrical and electronic engineers, 50 percent of the aircraft assemblers, and 20 percent of the machinists depended upon the U.S. Defense Department for their livelihoods.[4] Those percentages reflect the high degree of technical sophistication of American ships, planes, and tanks, but they also represent expertise not available to improve the productivity of civilian industry or to design badly needed public capital goods such as new transportation infrastructure and environmentally friendly vehicles, alternative energy, and pollution-abatement systems. Moreover, because the military generally pays higher salaries and provides better equipment and facilities than do its civilian research and development (R&D) counterparts, it drains the best and the brightest technologists from the civilian sector.[5]

During the 40-year Cold War, the United States plowed vast sums into building military physical capital. According to Lloyd Dumas, by 1990 "the total book value of physical capital directly owned by the Department of Defense (including plant, equipment, structures, weapons, and related equipment and supplies) was more than 80 percent of the total book value of capital equipment and structures in all U.S. manufacturing facilities combined."[6]

As Dumas points out, the nature of military spending is "noncontributive"— that is, unlike civilian production, its function is not to provide material well-being. Like churches, courthouses, and police forces, the military serves other, noneconomic needs. The more resources that a society diverts to noncontributive activities, the fewer it has for consumption and for producing more consumer goods, more efficiently.[7] Of course, some military R&D creates spin-offs used in the civilian sector—for example, jet engines, computers, integrated circuits, lasers, and microwave ovens. Indeed, the birth and development of those industries owes a great deal to Pentagon procurement policies, which financed early R&D and provided a large market where early versions could be perfected before being spun off into the commercial sector. Nevertheless, in most cases the later civilian value of military products does not begin to offset their development costs. For example, a 1989 study found that fewer than 1 percent of 8,000 patents resulting from Navy research and available for licensing were actually licensed, as compared to 13 percent of U.S. Department of Agriculture patents.[8] In short, America's investment in the Cold War diverted resources from productive purposes. By the time the Berlin Wall came down, America had built up a massive "social deficit."[9]

Ironically, 40 years of spending on military preparedness at the expense of the domestic economy actually undermined military security. Two developments brought this about. Over those 40 years, the failure of American industries and of the U.S. government to invest in commercial R&D and in modernizing the manufacturing sector contributed to the loss of American competitiveness (not to mention jobs) in one industry after another (e.g., machine tools and semiconductors).[10] Yet, modern weapons use increasingly sophisticated electronics and other components. Although the Pentagon spent billions on the development of new weapon systems, it did not invest in the basic technologies underlying the development of new components. Thus, by 1980, commercial technology development had outpaced military technology so that commercial spin-ons to defense products had become prevalent, rather than defense spin-offs to commerce. And these commercial components were increasingly purchased, not from American manufacturers, but from Japanese and other foreign companies. In the late 1980s, alarm over the vulnerability of the U.S. defense industrial base to foreign control of vital components led the federal government to provide limited support to the semiconductor and machine-tool industries. That concern also inspired the technology-development policies of the Clinton administration.[11]

THE PROMISE OF CONVERSION

In view of the Cold War's demise, many economists both called for and predicted less defense spending over the decade of the 1990s.[12] Lawrence Korb, Assistant Secretary of Defense under President Reagan, called for a defense budget of $200 billion by 1995. Jerome Wiesner, Philip Morrison, and Kosta Tsipis of MIT suggested that by the year 2000, U.S. military spending should be reduced from its nearly $300 billion annual Cold War average (1996 dollars) to $145 billion. William Kaufman of the Brookings Institution called for a budget of $141 billion. Randall Forsberg of the Institute for Defense and Disarmament Studies suggested an annual defense budget of $70 billion, to fund a defensive U.S. military force and an expanded peacekeeping role for the United Nations.[13]

Seymour Melman, Lloyd Dumas, Ann Markusen, and other economists had long since championed not simply a reduction in military spending, but a planned transition of defense plant, equipment, and personnel to civilian purposes. As Dumas argued:

Shrinking the military sector will do nothing to repair the economic damage of the arms race unless the released resources are reconnected to contributive civilian activity. In economic terms, nothing will have been accomplished if those people and facilities are released from the military sector and become unemployed.[14]

For such a reconnection to succeed, planning is essential at the national, state, and local government levels, as well as at the levels of the defense contractor and subcontractor, the military base, and the individual defense worker or soldier. A planned transition can take three forms: conversion, diversification, or adjustment. Through conversion, a defense firm uses the same workers who previously produced defense products to make civilian products, and sometimes the same machinery may be used as well. Military bases are considered to be converted (and reused) if their existing facilities are shifted to civilian uses. Through diversification, a company adds new, civilian operations to its existing work. Adjustment occurs when a defense worker is laid off but finds a job in the civilian sector.

In the 1960s, conversion proponents began calling for a national conversion policy. On August 2, 1963, Senator George McGovern, impressed by the work of Seymour Melman—an industrial-engineering professor at Columbia University—called for national plans to facilitate conversion. Since then, other congressmen, especially Representative Ted Weiss (D-NY), inspired by Dr. Melman's ideas, have proposed legislation for national conversion planning.[15] According to the Defense Budget Project, some 38 pieces of conversion legislation were introduced in 1992.[16]

The range of recent conversion proposals, many of which were included in proposed national legislation in the late 1980s and early 1990s, included several key elements. The first was a significant reduction in defense expenditures from their Cold War average of almost $300 billion, to be commensurate with our actual security needs. As noted above, the recommended budgets varied from about $70 to $200 billion. Some recommendations relied on alternative, collective security arrangements that would reduce the military's nuclear dependency in favor of multilateral cooperation. A second key element was a set of alternative national-spending priorities: for mass transit, environmental restoration, improved infrastructure, and alternative energy sources. Such a shift in federal expenditures would create a market large and stable enough for defense firms to view conversion as worth the effort, and would help rebuild the nation's productive capacity.[17]

Conversion advocates also urged the federal government to require defense contractors with more than 100 employees to establish "alternative use committees" comprising labor and management representatives to study and recommend commercial products that the company could manufacture if its defense contracts were reduced or lost.[18] A related recommendation was that large defense contractors be given advance notification (up to two years) of contract cancellations.[19]

Worker retraining was also a central tenet of conversion proposals. Advocates view company conversion as a superior path to a peacetime economy because it creates new jobs for specific workers as they are trained for those jobs, which avoids worker dislocation and hardship and is more efficient as well. Government subsidies could be important for bringing this training about. Moreover, because large defense contractors use more managers and engineers than commercial firms do, and because in a market economy nothing is entirely predictable, some layoffs would be unavoidable. To help those persons, as well as those laid off among Defense Department military and civilian personnel, conversion proponents have advocated generous worker-retraining subsidies tied to state and local economic-development programs.[20] The alternative national spending policies outlined here also would be essential to generate good jobs for former defense workers.

Most proponents of national conversion policy have maintained that state- and local-level planning is necessary as well. Their knowledge of local conditions puts state and local governments in the best position to administer aid to defense companies and their workers and to plan new uses for the closed installations. But to perform that role effectively, states and localities also would need federal funds for planning, business assistance, and training.

Many conversion proponents also called for the commercialization of the nation's nuclear-weapons research laboratories. Los Alamos, Sandia, and Lawrence Livermore in New Mexico and California as well as other federal research labs conduct military research. Much of the nation's R&D capacity is bound up in these labs (and in universities conducting research for the Pentagon). Conversion advocates argue that the labs' missions should be redirected to civilian purposes and that their research results should be made available for quick commercialization.[21]

The overall concept of converting defense manufacturing, however, has been far from universally embraced. Joel Johnson, Vice President of the Aerospace Industry Association, spoke for many defense contractors when he said: "I think conversion is bull. Big companies are highly specialized technologies. No one suggests that the automotive industry shift to toasters."[22] Norman Augustine, CEO of Martin Marietta Corporation (now Lockheed Martin), agreed: "The record of conversion is unblemished by success."[23] Yet, according to the U.S. Office of Technology Assessment: "Conversion after World War II was massive, fast, and successful."[24] Indeed, about 30 percent of U.S. total output was converted from military to civilian production in one year without unemployment rising above 3 percent.[25] That transition after World War II, however, is more appropriately called "reconversion," since the companies that produced tanks and fighters had, only a few years earlier, manufactured automobiles and civilian aircraft. They still had the equipment and, more importantly, the corporate cultures needed for civilian production. Furthermore, in the aftermath of war rationing and delayed family formation, they enjoyed a powerful surge of demand for consumer goods.

In contrast, at the end of the Vietnam War, few defense prime contractors had previous experience (or at least none recently) with commercial markets. Many who tried to embark on producing civilian products were not equal to the challenges. For instance, in the 1960s, when the Boeing Company's Vertol division received fewer orders for its Chinook CH-47 military helicopter, it decided to make light-rail vehicles, assuming that it could apply its aerospace expertise and experience in systems integration. Moreover, Boeing expected a large market to emerge shortly after the federal Urban Mass Transit Administration (UMTA) issued national standards for transit cars: municipal governments were expected to demand 2,000 of them during the 1970s. Boeing's first contract—175 vehicles for the City of Boston—was a fiasco, as the cars developed serious problems after delivery. Then too, the expected UMTA standards, which would have effectively lowered per-unit production costs, never materialized. Boeing did much better on its subsequent light-rail vehicle contracts with San Francisco and Chicago. But in the end, Boeing took advantage of the revival of defense budgets in the 1980s to make an escape from its adventure with conversion. Rohr Industries also failed in its 1970s attempts to apply aerospace technology to building mass-transit vehicles, as did Grumman when it tried to build buses for New York City.[26]

But there is more to those conversion "failures" than meets the eye. First, all three companies had assumed that building light-rail vehicles would be easy to do, so they never tested their prototypes in real-world conditions. They also had agreed to overly ambitious production schedules.[27] These puzzlingly inept oversights can be explained in terms of the unique corporate culture of military prime contractors during the 1970s and also the 1990s. The environment they conformed to is virtually free of the price competition and tight delivery dates of the commercial world. The Pentagon requires production quality and durability to exacting tolerances, but is willing to pay almost any price, including massive cost overruns; furthermore, it is not very particular about deadlines. Thus, the management and product-development arms of military contractors operate differently from commercial firms. Clearly, successful conversion requires painful corporate change. In addition, since large defense prime contractors employ more managers (to deal with the Pentagon and manage every production detail) and more engineers (to design highly sophisticated systems) than commercial firms do, conversion generally entails some layoffs among those employees.[28] In light of these realities, the conversion failures of Boeing Vertol, Rohr, and Grumman may more aptly be seen as attempts to switch production, but without first converting the firm.

Smaller companies may make such a transition more easily than larger ones do. Indeed, along with the well-publicized conversion "failures" among major firms, there have occurred well-known successes among small firms. For example, when Frisby Airborne Hydraulics, which had produced advanced hydraulic control systems for the Grumman and Fairchild-Republic Corporations, lost an important Defense Department contract in 1987, its owner turned to diversification. Without laying off any workers, Frisby reduced its defense dependency from 90 to 25 percent through aggressive commercial marketing, a strong aftermarket customer-service program, and worker participation in production decisions. Although Frisby's success is partly due to its small size and the fact that its products were readily adaptable to commercial needs, the firm's owner gave much of the credit to the "unprecedented communication and cooperation between labor and management."[29] Advocates of economic conversion similarly emphasize the role of such cooperation if conversions are to succeed.[30]

Conversion efforts also must be able to rely on support from national policies. In the Boeing Vertol case, the company worked out the design and production bugs, only to be left high-and-dry when the UMTA failed to issue national light-rail vehicle standards. Ultimately, without such standardization, Boeing Vertol was priced out of the market.[31]

A fairly clear record of defense conversion successes and failures had developed by the end of the Cold War. Those who were interested in the possibilities recognized what policies were needed if the nation were to see conversions succeed. The question was whether Congress and the president would enact such policies. Americans were ready for significant defense-spending cutbacks.[32] Although defense-dependent communities looked upon that prospect with trepidation, even there some leaders began considering possible alternative economic enterprises. Some localities began studying the nature and extent of their defense dependency and began planning ways to soften the impact of probable defense cutbacks.

DEFENSE CUTBACKS AND NATIONAL ADJUSTMENT POLICIES

Base Closings

The most prominent form of defense cutback had been put in place even before the Berlin Wall fell. In 1988, the U.S. Congress had passed the Defense Base Closure and Realignment Act (1990 title) to establish an orderly and relatively nonpartisan way of closing military installations.[33] Under the 1988 act and its later reauthorizations, bases were scheduled for closure or realignment in 1988, 1991, 1993, and 1995. In each year, or "round," the process worked roughly as follows: Each of the armed services reviewed its current force through a "data call" in which local base commanders had to provide information about their facilities to armed-services planners. The services used that information to evaluate each facility in terms of its military value, infrastructure capacity, and environmental and economic impacts. Then, after applying the desired ratio of forces to existing infrastructure (bases), the service planners recommended some facilities for closure or realignment. About March 1, the Secretary of Defense submitted a list of proposed closures and realignments to an eight-member Base Realignment and Closure (BRAC) Commission appointed by the president (with Senate approval) a few months earlier. The Commission visited those facilities, held hearings, considered additional facilities, and recommended a set of closings to the president by July 1. By September 1, the president had to have transmitted his approval or rejection of the recommendations to Congress, which then could accept or reject the entire list but not individual facilities. These steps were intended to depoliticize what had become a very political process; so much so that between 1976 and 1988 Congress had not closed a single major base.[34]

The BRAC Commission rounds in 1988, 1991, 1993, and 1995 closed or realigned 222 major bases and 291 minor bases or installations, out of the total of about 3,800 military facilities.[35] The Defense Department estimated the total annual recurring savings from all those closings at approximately $6 billion (1996 dollars).[36] Some analysts, however, charged that the costs of environmental clean-up at the closed bases (e.g., from unexploded ordnance and chemical waste) were much higher than the savings.[37] Nevertheless, aided by the Defense Department's Office of Economic Adjustment, communities began to plan for the reuse of their bases as commercial facilities. The history of earlier base closures suggested that in seven to ten years, such communities might even do better economically than they had with the military bases.[38]

In 1989, Congress took a small step toward conversion of its military research labs as well with passage of the Cooperative Research and Development Act, which authorized the labs to form R&D partnerships with companies and universities for projects of mutual benefit. The partnerships often take the form of Cooperative Research and Development Agreements (CRADAs), which are financed by matching grants.[39] Accompanying all these changes were cutbacks in total defense spending. From the post–Korean War high of $376.2 billion in 1989, U.S. military spending was cut to $328.6 billion by 1992 and to $265.6 billion by 1996.[40] Over the 1989–1997 period, defense-related employment fell by 2.6 million workers.[41]

Conversion versus Deficit Reduction

Yet, despite the euphoric anticipation of a peace dividend after the Berlin Wall fell, and after some steps in that direction, the hope that the nation would now restore its productive capacity and address social needs soon dissipated. The Persian Gulf War of 1990–1991 quashed the assumption that peace had been established. In place of the Soviet Union as America's foe, some military analysts now identified many new ones: "rogue states" led by adversaries such as Saddam Hussein and Moamar Qaddafi, and, later, Slobodan Milosevic. In any case, the administration of President Bush had no interest in the defense conversions on which proponents of a smooth transition to a peacetime economy had pinned their hopes. Indeed, he even refused to spend the retraining funds Congress had authorized for laid-off defense workers.[42] The Bush administration's laissez-faire, free-market philosophy held that after cutting the defense budget, Congress should allow the market's working to decide what became of laid-off workers and other productive resources.[43] Advocates of conversion pointed out in vain that defense companies and workers who saw no alternative economic prospects were more likely to vigorously oppose defense budget cuts.

Hopes that reduced military spending would mean more resources for infrastructure and social needs also suffered from 1980s politics. Facing the $221 billion deficit (1986 dollars) achieved by simultaneous income tax cuts and increases in military spending, President Bush maintained that any savings must go to reduce it. The Budget Enforcement Act of 1990 established both an overall cap on discretionary spending and a "firewall" between domestic and defense spending, so that savings from defense cutbacks could not be used to increase domestic spending. Thus, the sort of program envisioned by defense-conversion advocates was effectively precluded. Any conversion or adjustment programs that might arise were bound to be military-led, designed as part of the defense budget—and thus directed by the military—so as not to take more money from an already-straitened domestic budget. When President Bush left office, defense spending had been reduced from its high-water mark of the Reagan era and some bases had been slated to close, but nothing in the way of a planned transition to a peacetime economic structure was in sight.

The Clinton Conversion Policies

The election of 1992 revived prospects for a purposeful conversion to a peacetime economy. In March 1993, President Clinton announced a $20 billion Defense Reinvestment and Conversion Initiative, stating: "[We will] continue to reduce defense, as we must, but we're trying to plan for the future of those people and those incredible resources [being released from the defense sectors]."[44] Of the almost $16.7 billion actually spent between 1993 and 1997 under this

Initiative, some went for aid to military personnel—about $3.4 billion—but by far the largest amount—$11.5 billion—went to programs aiding defense industries: the Technology Reinvestment Project (TRP), Other Dual-Use Initiatives, programs of the National Institute for Standards and Technology (NIST), and conversion-related high-tech initiatives.[45]

This legislation looked to high-technology development to resolve the defense-spending issue. The TRP and its successor, Other Dual-Use Initiatives, helped firms to spin off defense technologies into commercial fields, apply lower-cost technologies to defense purposes, and develop new technologies that would serve both defense and commercial purposes. In theory, a compromise had been managed between conversion supporters in Congress and those who wanted to keep the defense base "warm" (i.e., prepared for the next escalation). But it also furthered the goal, discussed previously, of strengthening the defense industrial base by "spinning on" new commercial technologies to defense products and production processes.

In actuality, according to analyses of TRP over the 1993–1997 period, only about 20 percent of the funds supported conversion and 80 percent funded military projects.[46] Similarly, only about 10 percent of the Other Dual-Use programs funded such commercial projects as R&D of electric-car technology, advanced electronics, computing systems, and new composite materials.[47] Despite that record, in 1995 the new, Republican-led Congress attacked both programs as being too focused on conversion. The Clinton administration forswore any such focus for its programs; indeed, when labor unions argued that TRP funds should help retain existing jobs and create new ones through technology-development projects, TRP officials "quickly made it clear that 'this isn't about jobs.' The TRP was a defense-technology program, and any employment that resulted was purely incidental to the main objective of creating better, less-expensive merchandise for the Pentagon."[48] By 1997, TRP had been cut to 18 percent of its original funding.

Although some large defense contractors did use the dual-use initiatives, most of their energies went to downsizing, acquisitions, mergers, and exports. The Clinton administration supported the mergers by reimbursing defense firms for merger costs. The merger of Lockheed and Martin Marietta created the world's largest defense firm, with 9 percent of all FY95 U.S. Defense Department contract awards. In the process, the two firms laid off a total of 47,000 workers.[49] Boeing acquired McDonnell Douglas aircraft and Rockwell International's defense aerospace division, raising the company's defense dependency to 50 percent. Raytheon laid off 17,000 workers in the early 1990s and then acquired Hughes' and Texas Instruments' defense divisions, making it the third-largest company in defense sales and the dominant defense-electronics firm in the industry. Northrup and Grumman merged, laying off a total of 36,000 workers in the process, and then acquired Westinghouse Electric's defense division. General Dynamics cut its workforce by 35,000, stripping down to tank and nuclear-submarine production, and then acquired Bath Iron Works of Maine. By the end of the 1990s eight prime contractors accounted for two-thirds of Pentagon contracts, and most were concentrated in four large, so-called systems houses: Lockheed Martin, Raytheon, Boeing, and Northrop Grumman. At least one effect of the mergers was a dramatic rise in those companies' stock prices.[50]

Other prime contractors such as TRW (aerospace, ground transportation), Texas Instruments, Textron, and Allied Signal diversified into commercial markets while being still involved in defense business. A few prime contractors did exit the defense industry: Hughes Electronics Corporation laid off 14,000 workers and then sold its defense division. Westinghouse sold its defense division to Northrup Grumman; Tenneco spun off its Newport News Shipbuilding and Drydock Company; and General Electric sold its defense division to Martin Marietta.

Because the Clinton administration had, early on, promised federal reinvestment in alternative transportation, environmental remediation, telecommunications, and modernization of the air-traffic-control system, some defense companies had planned commercialization in those fields. But federal funding in those areas was scaled back during 1995 and 1996 and the companies promptly refocused on traditional defense work.[51] This again underscores a previous point: The federal government has the power to stimulate conversion by creating alternative markets. The Clinton administration's program, however, produced mostly "a more highly concentrated, more defense-dedicated industry structure among the top-tier firms"—and tens of thousands of displaced workers.[52]

The 1990s produced somewhat different results for small- and medium-sized defense contractors and subcontractors. Many were squeezed out of the market as larger contractors narrowed their use of subcontractors, bringing work in-house and negotiating tougher deals. In response, some smaller firms aggressively pursued commercialization. They expanded commercial sales, developed commercial applications for defense technologies, or pursued joint commercial ventures with other companies. Some former defense company managers and engineers created new, commercial spin-offs. For example, Lau Technologies, a small Massachusetts electronics firm that had done work for the Bradley fighting vehicle, reduced its defense dependency from 98 to 50 percent and created 100 new jobs by developing digital-imaging systems that make drivers' licenses for state motor-vehicle departments.[53]

Successful small-business conversion requires "an early and sustained research and development effort, an adoption of commercial best practices in quality and cost controls, a reduction in defense-related overhead costs for accounting and quality control, and production process improvements."[54] Financing for product development and worker retraining is clearly one of the first hurdles. Unfortunately, however, banks usually do not want to finance conversion by small defense firms. Two sources of public aid were available: The U.S. Small Business Administration's Defense Loan and Technical Assistance program provided some firms with equipment and debt financing. The National Institute of Standards and Technology's (NIST's) Manufacturing Extension Partnership program not only helped companies improve technology and productivity, but also, in some cases, helped them convert to civilian production.

Nevertheless, many small firms that were squeezed by the reshaping of the defense industry struggled and went under, taking employees with them.

Small defense-oriented firms tried innovative worker-training programs in connection with company-conversion initiatives. Most of the Department of Labor's displaced-worker-retraining programs, however, were not helpful to those firms looking to convert to new markets. They need to train workers *before* they lose their jobs (so-called "incumbent workers"). With the exception of some demonstration projects, Department of Labor programs assisted only workers who had already lost their jobs.[55]

The Defense Department provided $3.4 billion of retraining assistance to departing military personnel from 1993 to 1996, the years of the heaviest personnel reductions. (Active duty troops were cut from 2.2 million down to 1.5 million.[56]) The U.S. Department of Energy provided separation benefits and other assistance to laid-off research-lab workers, whose numbers fell from 149,000 to 110,000 during that period.[57] And the Department of Labor spent $159 million from 1993 through 1997 to train displaced defense workers. Although those programs all were considered helpful, critics charged that the Department of Labor's retraining for displaced defense workers did little to link them with good job opportunities.

The gap between retraining and access to new jobs is a critical drawback. It can be explained, in part, by the lack of funding for effective career counseling or for long-enough retraining programs. It can also be traced to the absence of institutional linkages between state and local economic-development offices and worker-retraining programs. Then, too, local agencies often do not follow up on worker outcomes.[58] These obstacles have been surmounted by some state and local programs. But the point frequently made by conversion advocates remains important: Reducing the defense establishment without planning for shifting workers to commercial production *at their existing workplaces* does not make optimum use of human resources.

The Clinton administration's Defense Reinvestment and Conversion Initiative also provided about $1.3 billion to support conversion and adjustment-planning assistance in communities where bases had closed or defense contractors were laying off employees. The Defense Department's Office of Economic Adjustment (OEA) provided technical assistance and planning grants (mostly where bases were closing). The Commerce Department's Economic Development Administration made grants to communities dealing with plant shutdowns for economic-development planning, business loans, and infrastructure development. The Department of Energy made planning and improvement grants to communities where a nuclear weapons facility was closing. Although these programs received high marks for responsiveness, critics noted that their funding fell short of significant planning assistance.[59]

Thus, by 1997, the hopes of conversion advocates had once more evaporated. Instead of a bold move toward a peace economy and a "new world order," as President Bush had pledged after the Cold War vanished, the United States had taken only modest steps toward a smaller military budget. President Clinton had cut the budget by 19 percent between 1992 and 1996, but this reduced it no further than 80 percent of its Cold War average. And after 1996, Congress and the president would slowly increase military spending until, by FY2000, it neared the $290 billion mark (current dollars). In 1999, the United States still would spend more than the combined expenditures of its allies (NATO plus Japan and South Korea) and its possible adversaries (Russia, China, Cuba, Iran, Iraq, Libya, North Korea, Sudan, and Syria).[60] Although some bases had closed, some companies had converted to civilian production and others had diversified operations; most large prime contractors had simply downsized, leaving their employees to fend for themselves, and many smaller companies had gone out of business.

The lack of policy attention to converting defense industries is demonstrated by the fact that the federal government had spent far more on export subsidies to help American arms manufacturers sell to foreign buyers than it had spent to encourage conversion. In 1996 and 1997, for example, the federal government spent $7.8 billion promoting foreign arms sales, through grants and loans to buyer countries, gifts of excess military equipment, money for international air shows and expositions, and for the salaries of the 6,300 federal employees who facilitate such exports. Although the exports brought the U.S. share of the shrinking global arms market to 50 percent in 1995, they saved fewer jobs than might be expected. The so-called offset agreements to produce the weapons in the buyer countries claimed 35 to 80 percent of the value of the contracts.[61] Meanwhile, as noted, the federal government was encouraging and subsidizing the merger, consolidation, and downsizing of the nation's largest defense contractors.

After some bases had been slated for closure or realignment and over a million Defense Department employees had been laid off, the Base Realignment and Closure process ended, for political reasons. Fearful of losing the support of California voters in the 1996 election, President Clinton did not ask Congress to authorize a 1997 round. Congress reciprocated in 1999 by refusing to authorize BRAC rounds for 2001 and 2005.[62]

Why did the nation not make more of its opportunity to shift to a peacetime economy? Part of the answer lies in Congress's and President Bush's 1990 decision to support deficit reduction rather than conversion. And a rationale for those who wanted military spending kept at high levels was soon found in the Persian Gulf War, and then in regional conflicts in Central Africa, the Balkans, the Korean Peninsula, and the former Soviet republics. Also, the election of several defense hawks to Congress in 1994 undermined the Clinton administration's few conversion programs.

But the Clinton conversion program had begun to weaken even before the 1994 election. During the 1992 presidential campaign and shortly thereafter, Bill Clinton had advocated significant military-spending cutbacks, increased federal spending for infrastructure and environmental improvements, and an aircraft industrial policy to reemploy laid-off aerospace workers. But within six months after assuming office, he had succumbed to the pressure of Pentagon officials, defense contractors, and industry spokespersons as well as some labor unions and members of Congress, who lobbied against deep cuts.[63] The result was reflected in the Pentagon's Bottom-Up Review, conducted by Defense Secretary Les Aspin in 1993. Although it called for modest spending reductions, the review essentially continued the Bush Administration's policies based on the Cold War doctrine of massive offensive-force projection and the perception that U.S. interests were at stake in virtually every part of the noncommunist world. The defense program it recommended would enable the United States to simultaneously fight two regional wars the size of the one in the Persian Gulf on short notice, without allies, and obtain decisive victory (conditions that had not obtained in previous wars). In defining military preparedness, the review ignored multilateral, collective-security arrangements that would allow for a smaller budget and a different type of fighting force. The administration and Congress held to that definition throughout the 1990s. The two-war, offensive military doctrine established a floor under which defense spending could not fall.

The Pentagon announced that it would meet the spending reductions envisioned in the Bottom-Up Review through increases in procurement efficiency. To this end, it encouraged defense contractors to strip down to their core, defense specialties. That process resulted in thousands of layoffs and effectively precluded company diversification into civilian markets. In general, during the 1990s the Clinton administration's driving preoccupations—with deficit reduction as represented by the 1990 bill's "firewall," with fending-off charges of undermining military preparedness, and with supporting U.S. defense manufacturers' global competitiveness—left its campaign promises of defense conversion in the dust.

DEEPER CAUSES: DEFENSE ADDICTION

The reasons for America's failure to take more decisive steps toward a peacetime economy go deeper than a conservative Congress and a failure of presidential leadership. America suffers from what Sanford Gottlieb has aptly called a "defense addiction."[64] The addiction is the result of "the Iron Triangle": the Pentagon, the defense prime contractors, and Congress, all pursuing their own narrow interests. Two additional factors, the United States's tradition of laissez-faire, anti-industrial policy and American military ideology as it has evolved since World War II, deepen the problem.

The Iron Triangle

Ultimate control of America's military budget rests not with a single agency or organ of government but with a complex of entities—principally the Pentagon, military–industrial firms, and Congress—each pursuing its own interests and containing within it contending parties that pursue their own, narrower interests. As early as 1961, President Eisenhower perceived the dangers of that recently emerged system:

This conjunction of an immense military establishment and a large arms industry is new in the American experience. The total influence—economic, political, even spiritual—is felt in every city, every statehouse, every office of the Federal Government. . . . In the councils of government, we must guard against the acquisition of unwarranted influence, whether sought or unsought, by the military–industrial complex. The potential for the disastrous rise of misplaced power exists and will persist.[65]

By the "military–industrial complex," Eisenhower referred to two angles of the triangle—the Pentagon and the defense contractors. As a decorated and popular war hero, he was the last president able to issue such a warning without the Iron Triangle accusing him of undermining the nation's defense.

The Pentagon, the central component of the Iron Triangle, is itself not a monolith. Rather, three individual services—army, air force, and navy—compete fiercely for resources to develop and maintain their own weapon systems, personnel and installations. Modern weapons are so complex and the interservice competition is so intense that it takes 10 to 15 years to move a large weapon system through the maze of approvals and funding decisions from concept to production.[66] In short, although national security is cited as justification, it is primarily interservice competition and technology breakthroughs that drive the weapons-procurement process. Each service maintains its own laboratories for basic research in weapons development; the Navy, for instance, runs 21 labs in New England and California, which employ 40,000 people.[67] Through this work and that of defense contractors, each service continually tries to develop new, follow-on versions of its existing weapon systems. One consequence of this interservice rivalry is that the Defense Department acquires more different systems than it otherwise would. Another is that the production schedule spreads over longer periods of time, which increases costs.[68]

Military–industrial firms constitute the second angle of the triangle. The interests and activities of defense prime contractors, or military–industrial firms (MIFs), also drive the weapons-acquisition process. The MIF is unique. It operates in a monopsonistic market (one characterized by a single buyer—the government). Thus, its planning and marketing functions do not resemble those of the typical commercial market-oriented firm. Rather, they are focused solely on influencing the purchasing behavior of the single, military customer. Influence is exerted through prolific cross-fertilization and close personal relationships between military planners and procurement officers in the Pentagon, and marketing and product-development managers in MIFs. The MIF managers, to a large extent, are retired Pentagon officials.[69] Contractors' influence on Pentagon planners arises in other ways as well. Contractors often serve as experts on Pentagon planning committees.[70] They also conduct basic research on weapon systems, which positions them to receive the contracts to build the systems once those are approved for production.[71] In short, in many ways MIFs have more technical knowledge of the weapon systems than Pentagon planners do. They inevitably influence Pentagon planning and decisions.

The MIFs have other peculiar features as well. Because of the great technical sophistication of modern weapon systems and the high level of secrecy required, the MIFs are subjected to intense regulation and oversight by the armed services. They must build each unit of each weapon system to exacting military specifications, or "mil-spec," and carefully document their work. As a result, the average MIF comprises about one-third skilled production workers, one-third scientists and technical workers, and one-third managers.[72] Few, if any, commercial firms could afford to operate with such a structure. Military firms, however, can support an expensive workforce for one important reason—cost-plus contracting. The MIFs are compensated for their costs of production plus a negotiated allowance for profit. Cost overruns, which occur routinely, are then absorbed by the Pentagon. A predictable consequence of this arrangement is that MIFs underbid on procurement competitions or they underestimate costs that the Pentagon must report to Congress when seeking initial approval for a weapon system, and then submit higher costs later.[73] During the 1980s the Pentagon began to require fixed-price contracts, to contain costs. But this goal was undermined by the problem of "requirements creep": the contracting agency repeatedly requires design modifications that add extra costs and production delays.[74]

Congress is the third player in the Iron Triangle. Although it has constitutional authority over the military, it is in a weak position to second-guess the Pentagon and has its own reasons for not doing so. The Pentagon gives Congress such voluminous technical data (thus distracting it from important issues) that it has neither the time nor the expertise to digest them. Congress established the Congressional Budget Office and the Office of Technology Assessment to get a handle on the problem, but it still persists. As a result, Congress focuses its attention only on specific line items in the Defense Department's budget, not on the budget as a whole or on military policy or strategy.[75] Throughout the Cold War, and even when its members criticized President Reagan's military build-up, Congress usually approved the administration's military budget.[76]

Nevertheless, controversy over the Vietnam War, opposition to President Reagan's military build-up, and procurement scandals in the 1980s did bring about more Congressional scrutiny of the defense-budgeting process. By 1985, Defense Department officials were testifying before 100 House and Senate committees, subcommittees, and task forces each year.[77] In response, the Pentagon has perfected strategies in addition to information overload that appeal to Congress's interests. Chief among them are demonstrations of how congresspersons' communities will gain jobs from defense contracts and military bases.

The Pentagon encourages defense contractors to lobby Congress with the message about community jobs. The contractors do more than lobby—they deliberately spread subcontracts (which account for up to 50 percent of a contract's value) throughout the country, to give many congressional districts a stake in a particular weapon system. Although congresspersons generally have little influence over which MIFs get particular contracts, they claim credit when local firms get the contracts and cry foul when they don't. Moreover, pork-barrel politics prompts the continuation of contracts. For its part, the Pentagon plays along by announcing many contract awards in the months immediately before elections.[78]

Congress's role in the procurement process is generally passive; however, it can influence the location of military installations. Members who understand the

Defense Department, who build relationships with Pentagon planners, and who seek to influence the House and Senate Armed Services Committees and budget subcommittees will often be able to bring home the bacon for their constituents.[79] As members generally try to serve on committees that deal with issues of particular concern to their constituents, a strong, self-reinforcing pattern is created: Once a community has a military installation, it is likely to keep it and see it enhanced. That is why a special Base Realignment and Closure Commission had to be created to close bases, and why even that eventually fell victim to politics.

Taken together, the Pentagon, the defense prime contractors, and Congress constitute a formidable force—an Iron Triangle—that holds defense spending at high levels. In their 1993 book, Cassidy and Bischak add scientists and organized labor to the diagram, making an iron pentagon, since a high percentage of the nation's research scientists depend on the Defense Department for their livelihoods.[80] Moreover, a large percentage of the skilled, highly paid craftsmen in MIFs belong to labor unions, so, predictably, few labor unions have called for the establishment of a peacetime economy.[81] (Nevertheless, during the 1980s the Pentagon sought to weaken the role of organized labor in the heavily unionized aerospace industry by promoting two-tier wage systems and by subsidizing contractor relocations to nonunion areas. Pentagon procurement policies in the 1990s continued to support such relocations of defense production work to anti-union areas, where workers were paid less.[82])

The military–industrial complex draws much of its power in Congress from its ability to represent itself as the source of community jobs, and from community fears of the consequences of job loss. Defense contractors often provide the highest-paying jobs in town. Military bases may or may not pay high wages, but often they are so woven into the culture of their communities that for many people, life without them seems unthinkable. Both contractors and bases create employment multipliers, so that the number of jobs that depend on a particular facility is at least double the number it employs. It is easy for MIFs and military bases to muster their host communities and subcontractors to put pressure on Congress. Indeed, in many cases, no overt request is necessary. Congressional representatives of districts with military installations seek appointments to the committees that oversee military spending so as to direct more of it to the local installations.[83] And communities with defense contractors are more likely to elect defense hawks, who are then likely to serve on defense committees and promote defense expenditures.[84]

Defense as Industrial Policy in a Laissez-Faire Society

Other than military arrangements, the federal government has little to offer a community in the way of job creation. The United States has always, apart from broad monetary and fiscal policies, espoused a laissez-faire economic philosophy—allowing markets to make major investment and distribution decisions. Unlike Western Europe and Japan, America has eschewed industrial policies such as stimulating and nurturing nascent industries through government markets and strategic subsidies, or helping mature industries restructure and salvage the competitive segments. With the exception of isolated programs such as the Tennessee Valley Authority and the Appalachian Regional Commission, the United States has had no major policies (beyond pilots or demonstration programs) to aid economically depressed regions or inner cities.

Over the past 20 years, however, many economists have urged the need for an explicit, democratically accountable industrial policy to help the United States regain the competitive edge in manufacturing that it once enjoyed. The 1984 reelection of Ronald Reagan—whose administration staunchly opposed industrial policy—effectively ended that debate. Congress did, later, adopt policies to aid both the semiconductor and the machine-tool industries because they were perceived as vital to the defense industrial base.[85] Shortly after Bill Clinton's election in 1992, he floated the ideas of an aircraft industrial policy, and of federal R&D funds to stimulate alternative transportation, environmental remediation, telecommunications, and modernization of the air-traffic-control system. But the aircraft industrial-policy idea was quickly dropped, and only modest R&D funding went to alternative industries.[86]

Ironically, it is U.S. military policy that has amounted to a de facto industrial policy, one that is completely unacknowledged and therefore unaccountable. As Chapman and Yudken explain:

As part of military policy, the federal government has targeted a relatively small number of industries and firms, granting them advantages enjoyed by few other sectors in a free-market economy. These have included guaranteed markets, subsidies for research and development, and capital for facilities and modernization. The government has bailed out troubled firms through loans and subsidies, limited competition through preferential procurement practices, and promoted foreign arms sales to bolster exports.[87]

The Pentagon's military–industrial policy did stimulate the development of the semiconductor, computer, and satellite industries. But because of its lack of accountability as an industrial policy and lack of market discipline, the U.S. military–industrial policy does not resemble a modern industrial policy so much as it does state capitalism or centralized socialism.[88] Moreover, because it lacks market discipline and democratic accountability, U.S. military–industrial policy has actually weakened the defense industrial base.

Nevertheless, U.S. military–industrial policy serves a clear economic purpose: It constitutes a form of countercyclical, macroeconomic demand-management policy.[89] The Reagan administration's military build-up furnished an excellent example of this as it pulled the country out of the 1980–1982 recession. Conversely, the 1990–1992 recession undermined public support for defense cutbacks in the early post–Cold War period. In the absence of a labor movement strong enough to press the national government to maintain aggregate demand through domestic spending when recession looms, the military provides a rationale for doing so that conservative policy-makers can accede to. But the costs of such an industrial policy are very high. Rather than creating jobs by spending to alleviate the nation's pressing domestic problems and improving overall productivity, the United States spends vast sums on "noncontributive" weapons and military personnel that it does not need.

Military Ideology

The United States emerged from World War II with the single most powerful economy and military establishment in the world, a giant towering over the rubble of war-torn Europe and Asia. Its dominant role in the post–World War II economic and military order was perhaps inevitable. To maintain it, however, the nation's leaders had to overcome strong strains of isolationism and even some pacifist sentiments in the population. This they did by convincing Americans that a strong U.S. role was needed to protect Americans and other nations from the Soviet Union and from communism generally. By early in the Cold War, an indelible image of the danger of communism dominated American politics, reinforced by the actuality of Stalin's ruthless repression of his own people and then by episodes such as the Berlin Blockade. Throughout the Cold War period, American military-intelligence agencies furnished frequent reports alleging Soviet military superiority as a prod to U.S. military spending. During the 1950s the nation was said to face a "bomber gap." During the 1960s it was a "missile gap." During the 1970s U.S. silo-based missiles faced an alleged "window of vulnerability" and President Reagan's 1980s Strategic Defense Initiative was developed to close it. As Chapman and Yudken point out, "nearly all of [the supposed gaps] turned out to have been concocted."[90]

Since the demise of the Soviet Union, military-spending advocates have turned their attention to so-called "rogue states"—for example, Libya, Iraq, and Serbia to justify military spending at near Cold War levels. In the mid- and late-1990s defense hawks in Congress alleged sagging U.S. "preparedness" for military confrontations and called for higher defense budgets.

U.S. military ideology crowds out serious consideration of alternative approaches to national security. With few exceptions and belying rhetoric to the contrary, the United States has not been diligent in creating new collective-security arrangements. The share of its GDP allocated to foreign aid is smaller than that from other industrialized countries. And far from trying to halt the spread of weapons of mass destruction, through subsidies of foreign arms sales, which accelerated under the Clinton administration, the United States has promoted the proliferation of weapons to lesser-developed countries. (Ironically, in military actions in Panama, Iraq, Somalia, Haiti, and Bosnia, U.S. soldiers have faced forces armed with American weapons sold to them in prior years.[91])

Despite the prominence of the U.S. military in the world during the past half century, the average American remains largely ignorant of the nature and magnitude of U.S. defense spending and is even more unaware of the possibilities for alternative national-spending priorities.[92] Polls conducted during the 1990s showed that Americans favored military-spending cutbacks, but were nervous that they might result in the loss of jobs. Polls also show that although Americans are reluctant to risk the lives of American soldiers in combat, they are cautious about changing the U.S. role in global security and are almost totally uninformed about alternative collective-security arrangements that would permit the United States to have a less-expensive system of defensive security.[93]

U.S. military policy formed during the Cold War is an example of what Pages calls a "policy monopoly"—a set of concepts, axioms, and deductive inferences directed toward the analysis of a public issue and bolstered by an established institutional arrangement—in this case, the Iron Triangle.[94] Even the end of the Cold War itself would prove not to be enough to end that policy monopoly in the absence of a strong challenge from other interests with compelling alternative policies.

But the Iron Triangle and U.S. military policy have not gone completely unchallenged. Throughout the Cold War and especially during the 1970s and 1980s, advocates of peace and defense conversion waged highly visible campaigns to reduce military spending and abolish nuclear weapons. Many of these initiatives, such as the well-known nuclear-freeze campaign of the 1980s, were waged at the local level; for example, they succeeded in passing local-government resolutions calling for a freeze on nuclear-weapons development. Although such campaigns obviously did not change national military policy, they constituted an important counterforce that, together with other voices urging curbs on military spending, emboldened members of Congress to oppose excessive military spending. Without the work of peace and conversion activists and like-minded groups, even the modest conversion programs of the Clinton administration might not have been enacted.

MIXED NATIONAL SIGNALS AND LOCAL RESPONSES

During the 1990s the federal government sent mixed signals to defense companies and communities. On the one hand, the end of the Cold War meant that the defense budget would be cut significantly, and base closures and defense-company layoffs demonstrated that. The federal government provided modest aid for community and worker adjustment and defense companies could avail themselves of federal grants to help them move into commercial markets. On the other hand, it was not clear by just how far the defense budget would be reduced or whether it might even be increased again, because no new policy on national security was articulated. The only military policy that was announced— the Bottom-Up Review—called for a military force that seemed to many to be under-funded. Thus, the entire process—both base closings and procurement policies—appeared to be driven not by a clear and rational plan, but by shifting political considerations.

This ambiguity and abdication of policy leadership at the national level left the response to the end of the Cold War to be shaped, in part, by companies and communities themselves. Their perceptions of their own economic strengths and vulnerabilities, their reading of possible future Pentagon plans, and their capacities for dealing with the consequences of defense cutbacks were to decide what responses ultimately emerged. The nature and organizational capacities of local interest groups also would determine how communities perceived federal policies—whether as a continuation of military spending or as defense downsizing with conversion assistance. And through their congressional representatives, communities and companies would in turn affect the development of national policies on those issues.

The remainder of this book explains those state and local responses. It describes the political–economic structure of local decision-making and identifies the political–economic interests operating at state and local levels. It shows how such interests interacted with national policies to produce a variety of responses: resistance to cutbacks and attempts to increase defense spending, acceptance of cutbacks and adjustment planning, and proactive conversion planning. The ways in which preexisting public capacities influenced the choices made by states and localities are traced. The upshot is that, while federal policy set the parameters, states, localities, and companies shaped the outcomes.

NOTES

1. Martin Calhoun, *U.S. Military Spending, 1945–1996*. Washington, DC: Center for Defense Information, July 9, 1996.

2. Discretionary spending includes items over which Congress has direct control and that it can change annually. In contrast, entitlement spending such as Medicaid is controlled by the number of people who are eligible to receive assistance.

3. U.S. Congress, Office of Technology Assessment, *After the Cold War: Living with Lower Defense Spending*, OTA-ITE-524. Washington, DC: U.S. Government Printing Office, February 1992, pp. 3–5.

4. Gary Chapman and Joel Yudken, *Briefing Book on the Military–Industrial Complex* (Washington, DC: Council for a Livable World, December 1992), p. 25; Ann Markusen, "How We Lost the Peace Dividend." *American Prospect*, no. 33 (July–August 1997), pp. 86–94.

5. Lloyd J. Dumas, "Finding the Future: The Role of Economic Conversion in Shaping the Twenty-first Century," in ed. Lloyd J. Dumas, *The Socio-Economics of Conversion from War to Peace*. Armonk, NY: M.E. Sharpe, 1995, pp. 3–20.

6. Dumas, "Finding the Future," p. 9.

7. Ibid., pp. 8–9.

8. Chapman and Yudken, *Briefing Book on the Military–Industrial Complex*, p. 23.

9. Jonathan Feldman, "Constituencies and New Markets for Economic Conversion: Reconstructing the United States' Physical, Environmental and Social Infrastructure," in ed. Gregory Bischak, *Towards a Peace Economy for the United States*. New York: St. Martin's Press, 1991; Pat Choate and Susan Walter, *America in Ruins: Beyond the Public Works Pork Barrel*. Washington, DC: Council of Planning Agencies, 1981.

10. Michael L. Dertouzos, Richard Lester, Robert Solow, and the MIT Commission on Industrial Productivity, *Made in America: Regaining the Productive Edge*. Cambridge: MIT Press, 1989.

11. Erik R. Pages, *Responding to Defense Dependence: Policy Ideas and the Defense Industrial Base*. Westport, CT: Praeger, 1996.

12. U.S. Congress, Office of Technology Assessment, *After the Cold War*; Marion

Anderson, Greg Bischak, and Michael Oden, *Converting the American Economy: The Economic Effects of an Alternative Security Policy.* Lansing, MI: Employment Research Associates, 1991.

13. Randall Forsberg, "Wasting Billions," in Randall Forsberg and Alexei Arbatov, "Cooperative Security: The Military Problem." *Boston Review* 19, no. 2 (April/May 1994). See also "Introduction" in Chapman and Yudken, *Briefing Book on the Military–Industrial Complex.*

14. Dumas, "Finding the Future," p. 10.

15. Sanford Gottlieb, *Defense Addiction: Can America Kick the Habit?* Boulder, CO: Westview Press, 1997, pp. 137–38; James Raffel, "Economic Conversion Legislation: Past Approaches and the Search for a New Framework," in *The Socio-Economics of Conversion from War to Peace.*

16. Chapman and Yudken, *Briefing Book on the Military–Industrial Complex*, p. 30.

17. Ibid., p. 28.

18. Domenick Bertelli, "Military Contractor Conversion in the United States," in *The Socio-Economics of Conversion from War to Peace.*

19. Raffel, "Economic Conversion Legislation."

20. Raffel, "Economic Conversion Legislation"; Elizabeth Mueller, "Retraining for What? Displaced Defense Workers and Federal Programs in Two Regions," in *The Socio-Economics of Conversion from War to Peace.*

21. Gottlieb, *Defense Addiction*, pp. 137–38; Gregory A. Bischak, *Towards a Peace Economy in the United States.* New York: St. Martin's Press, 1991.

22. "High Stakes Gambling." *Boston Sunday Globe*, February 11, 1996, p. B10.

23. Bertelli, "Military Contractor Conversion in the United States," p. 67.

24. U.S. Congress, Office of Technology Assessment, *After the Cold War*, p. 206.

25. Dumas, "Finding the Future," p. 11.

26. U.S. Congress, Office of Technology Assessment, *After the Cold War*, p. 208.

27. Bertelli, "Military Contractor Conversion in the United States," p. 71.

28. Dumas, "Finding the Future," p. 15.

29. U.S. Congress, Office of Technology Assessment, *After the Cold War*, pp. 225–26.

30. A well-known conversion "failure" that underscores this point is that of Lucas Aerospace Industries, a British company that dissolved after military contracts were cancelled and management refused to consider various commercial product designs that the company's engineers and skilled workers had developed. See Dumas, "Finding the Future"; also Gottlieb, *Defense Addiction*, chap. 5.

31. Chapman and Yudken, *Briefing Book on the Military–Industrial Complex*, p. 28.

32. Markusen, "How We Lost the Peace Dividend."

33. U.S. Public Law 101-510, Defense Base Closure and Realignment Act of 1990.

34. Patrick Lloyd Hatcher, *Economic Earthquakes: Converting Defense Cuts to Economic Opportunities.* Berkeley, CA: Institute of Governmental Studies Press, 1994, p. 173.

35. Calhoun, *U.S. Military Spending, 1945–1996*; cf. Greg Bischak, *Brief 9: U.S. Conversion after the Cold War, 1990–1997: Lessons for Forging a New Conversion Policy.* Bonn: Bonn International Center for Conversion, July 1997. Bischak counted 146 major bases as closed or realigned.

36. Center for Defense Information, "Base Realignment and Closure Statistics." bracstat.html at <www.cdi.org>, April 1999.

37. Bischak, *Brief 9*, p. 5.

38. Andy Isserman and Peter Stenberg, "The Recovery of Rural Economies from Military Base Closures: Control Group Analysis of Two Decades of Experience." Paper presented at the Southern Regional Science Association Meeting, Orlando, Florida, April 1994, in Michael Brzoska and Ann Markusen, "The Regional Role in Post–Cold War Military–Industrial Conversion," *International Regional Science Review* (January 2000).

39. Although many CRADAs have been formed, the results, says Gottlieb, are mixed. Companies want the labs' expertise and financial help, but the labs are "oblivious to cost and lack experience with 'how to make it happen.'" Gottlieb, *Defense Addiction*, p. 80.

40. Calhoun, *U.S. Military Spending, 1945–1996*.

41. Bischak, *Brief 9*, p. 5.

42. Raffel, "Economic Conversion Legislation."

43. The Bush Administration also adhered to a view expressed by economists such as Murray Weidenbaum, who argued that defense workers had been very well paid and did not deserve more taxpayer dollars just to keep their incomes at that level. See Gregory N. Stone, "In Seattle, Boeing Doesn't Like to Discuss Conversion." *Day* 112, no. 130 (November 8, 1992), pp. A-1–6.

44. White House, 1993, in Bischak, *Brief 9*, p. 6.

45. Bischak, *Brief 9*, p. 6.

46. Ibid., p. 8.

47. Ibid.

48. Jeff Crosby, President, International Union of Electrical Workers Local 201, telephone interview, in Laura Powers and Ann Markusen, *A Just Transition? Lessons from Defense Worker Adjustment in the 1990s*. Washington, DC: Economic Policy Institute Technical Paper No. 237, April 1999.

49. Bischak, *Brief 9*, p. 10.

50. Powers and Markusen, *A Just Transition?*, pp. 12–13.

51. Bischak, *Brief 9*, pp. 12–13.

52. Ibid., p. 13.

53. Ibid., pp. 13–14.

54. Ibid., p. 14.

55. Powers and Markusen, *A Just Transition?*

56. Bischak, *Brief 9*, p. 8.

57. Ibid., p. 9.

58. Mueller, "Retraining for What?"; see also Powers and Markusen, *A Just Transition?*; and chapters 3–7 of this book.

59. Dumas, "Finding the Future."

60. Chapman and Yudken, *Briefing Book on the Military–Industrial Complex*; Jim Bridgman, *Foul Play*. Washington, DC: Peace Action, n.d. <http://www.webcom.com/peacact/foulplay.html>.

61. Powers and Markusen, *A Just Transition?*, p. 15.

62. *Richmond Times-Dispatch*, "Senate Shuts Door on Base Closings" (May 27, 1999), p. A9.

63. Powers and Markusen, *A Just Transition?*, pp. 10–11.

64. Gottlieb, *Defense Addiction*.

65. Ibid., p. 5.

66. By the time they reach the field, some weapon systems are already obsolete. To speed the process, the Pentagon initiated the practice of "concurrent development," whereby weapon systems are not tested before production begins, but concurrently with

production. This, however, has led to performance failures in the field. Nevertheless, as the process evolves, the service's sunk costs increase to the point where it is better to have a flawed weapon system than to have to start the process over. See Chapman and Yudken, *Briefing Book on the Military–Industrial Complex*, p. 9; see also Kenneth R. Mayer, *The Political Economy of Defense Contracting*. New Haven, CT: Yale University Press, 1991, chap. 3.

67. Mayer, *The Political Economy of Defense Contracting*, p. 44.

68. Ibid., chap. 3.

69. Gottlieb, *Defense Addiction*, p. 27.

70. Markusen, "How We Lost the Peace Dividend," pp. 86–94.

71. Mayer, *The Political Economy of Defense Contracting*, chap. 3.

72. As discussed earlier, the "mil-spec" culture has contributed to a weakening of the U.S. defense industrial base. See Dumas, "Finding the Future."

73. Mayer, *The Political Economy of Defense Contracting*, chap. 3.

74. Chapman and Yudken, *Briefing Book on the Military–Industrial Complex*, p. 8.

75. According to Gregory Hooks (*Forging the Military–Industrial Complex: World War II's Battle of the Potomac*. Urbana: University of Illinois Press, 1991, cited in Markusen, "How We Lost the Peace Dividend"), Pentagon planners and defense contractors did not always command such high respect in the councils of government or in American public opinion. World War II changed that. Having established in the 1930s, but never fully used, a centralized planning apparatus for social-welfare purposes, President Roosevelt did use it during the war. Pentagon planners became the heroes of a legitimate war effort. As the Cold War followed immediately upon the heels of World War II, the planning apparatus was not questioned, let alone dismantled. It took on a life of its own. Perhaps more importantly, as Chapman and Yudken point out, the creation of a civilian-led Defense Department under executive control in 1947 politicized the defense-acquisition function, making it possible for the president to use pork-barrel politics to get Congress to approve his defense budget. See Chapman and Yudken, *Briefing Book on the Military–Industrial Complex*, p. 3.

76. Chapman and Yudken, *Briefing Book on the Military–Industrial Complex*, p. 17.

77. Mayer, *The Political Economy of Defense Contracting*, p. 17.

78. Ibid., chap. 2.

79. Ibid.; see also Gottlieb, *Defense Addiction*, chaps. 1 and 11.

80. Kevin Cassidy and Gregory Bischak, ed., *Real Security: Converting the Defense Economy and Building Peace* (Albany: SUNY Press, 1993), cited in Markusen, "How We Lost the Peace Dividend."

81. There are important exceptions to this rule, however. For example, many locals of the International Association of Machinists have consistently championed conversion to a peacetime economy.

82. Chapman and Yudken, *Briefing Book on the Military–Industrial Complex*, p. 26.

83. Peter Hall and Ann R. Markusen, "The Pentagon and the Gunbelt," in ed. Andrew Kirby, *The Pentagon and the Cities*. Newbury Park, CA: Sage Publications, 1992.

84. Ibid.; see also Mayer, *The Political Economy of Defense Contracting*, chap. 2.

85. Pages, *Responding to Defense Dependence*.

86. Powers and Markusen, *A Just Transition?*, p. 41.

87. Chapman and Yudken, *Briefing Book on the Military–Industrial Complex*, p. 11.

88. Seymour Melman, "From Private to State Capitalism: How the Permanent War Economy Transformed the Institutions of American Capitalism." *Journal of Economic Issues* 31, no. 2 (June 1997), p. 311; see also Dumas, "Finding the Future."

89. Thomas Cusack, "On the Domestic Political–Economic Sources of American Military Spending," in ed. Alex Mintz, *The Political Economy of Military Spending in the United States.* London: Routledge, 1992.

90. Chapman and Yudken, *Briefing Book on the Military–Industrial Complex*, p. 3.

91. Women's Action for New Directions Education Fund, *Women Take Action: Control U.S. Arms Trade.* Arlington, MA: WAND, March 1999.

92. Randall Forsberg, "Force Without Reason." *Boston Review* 20, no. 3 (summer 1995).

93. See, for example, Forsberg, "Force Without Reason."

94. Pages, *Responding to Defense Dependence*, pp. 36–38.

2

The Community Context: Development Interests and Economic Dependency

How did communities respond to the mixed signals they received from a federal administration ambivalent about defense-spending cutbacks and conversion? As it happens, proactive conversion planning does not come any more naturally to American communities than, as the previous chapter described, it does to federal politics. The institutional constraints on local governments and the economic interests that dominate local policy-making discourage community-wide planning for alternative futures—until a calamity strikes. Rather, those forces encourage dependency on existing industries. Nevertheless, change is possible, especially during economic crises. This chapter is an overview of how institutional, economic, and political forces shape local-development policies in the typical American community. It is intended as background for the subsequent discussion of how in particular those forces operate in defense-dependent communities. This chapter focuses on the actors that most influence local-development policy, namely, local government and businesses.

LOCAL GOVERNMENT RESPONSIBILITIES AND POWERS

Local government officials are elected and statutorily empowered to promote the public welfare. Over our history, as communities expanded in size and complexity, that responsibility came to encompass more government activities. By the twentieth century, local governments provided not only police- and fire-protection services, but also health and sanitation facilities and schools as well as parks and other amenities. Local officials regulated physical development and buildings in addition to business practices and residential behavior that could impinge on neighboring residents. As the century has progressed, localities and states have increasingly taken on responsibility for promoting a healthy local economy as well, with particular attention to policies that promote job creation.

The inherent instabilities of the market economy coupled with the expansion of local democracy forced state and local politicians to take constituents' employment needs into account. Since 1930, virtually all states and cities and even many counties and towns have created agencies and policies to foster employment. Just as the president's approval rating rests in large measure on the state of the national economy, so too do state and local politicians know that they must be perceived to be working hard to ensure jobs.

Although local governments today are complex organizations, their powers are narrowly circumscribed by the legal framework of the U.S. Constitution. Under the Constitution, all powers not reserved for the federal government reside in the states; localities, in turn, are subdivisions of states. They can exercise only those powers expressly given them by their states. For example, localities may not raise revenue from any source without state permission, nor may they regulate private property except as provided for in state enabling laws.[1]

The limitations on local autonomy have led to political fragmentation within areas that are linked economically. Annexation, by which cities acquired the outlying areas where their populations had spread, gradually ceased as more and more states permitted the middle- and upper-income exurbanites in outlying areas to incorporate instead as independent municipalities. The larger cities now are surrounded by incorporated municipalities. As a result, local political boundaries are much smaller than the boundaries of local economies and local problems. A local economy—that is, the area in which people live and work—thus comprises an entire metropolitan area with many, sometimes a dozen or more, independent political jurisdictions.[2]

Local political weakness and fragmentation have gone hand in hand with suburban sprawl, creating a cycle that has proven impossible to contain. Local governments must raise tax revenues to finance public services. State laws limit these revenues to a few key sources, the largest of which is the tax on real property (land and buildings). Since commercial and industrial properties are far more lucrative than housing as sources of tax revenue, local jurisdictions compete for those so-called ratables. Land-use, zoning, and transportation policies aim to attract commercial and industrial properties and upper-income housing, and exclude low- and moderate-income housing, which is a net revenue loser.[3] Central cities and older suburbs are generally at a disadvantage in this competition, because their infrastructure is older and they lack the large "greenfield" sites that attract present-day manufacturing facilities, office parks, and super stores. Upper-income persons also often prefer the newer housing found in automobile-dependent suburbs. As ratables and population grow in the suburbs, central cities lose both their tax bases and their political power in the statehouses and thus have few options for improving their conditions.[4]

Political fragmentation makes community-wide (i.e., metropolitan-wide) planning almost impossible to carry out during stable economic times and even difficult when given impetus by a crisis. Each local jurisdiction has its own planning-and-development apparatus and views its material interest only in fiscally lucrative development, hoping that nearby localities will house the persons who work in its low-wage retail and service businesses. Only a few communities have overcome the resistance to metropolitan-wide planning by establishing regional-government structures.[5] Although many communities have developed interjuris-dictional, cooperative arrangements to manage particular issues, these do not begin to overcome the structural conflict that keeps local governments at logger-heads. Thus, in providing public services and safeguarding the general welfare, most American local governments compete with nearby localities for capital and tax base.

BUSINESS INTERESTS

The market economy places the most significant constraints on the power of government—local, state, and national. For in a market economy,

> it is business that decides what goods and services are to be produced, in what quantities, and how that production will be allocated. Because of the central role business plays in determining the standard of living, governments feel compelled to defer to the conditions business deems necessary in order to ensure that such vital functions are performed. Consequently, business assumes public functions and business people frequently act as unelected public officials. . . . At the national, state, and local levels this unequal rela-tionship between public and private sectors has traditionally relegated to the public sector those tasks deemed necessary to stimulate private growth.[6]

To put that relationship another way, a community's economic and financial health depends upon its ability to attract and retain investment capital. This is a struggle for most communities, because capital is not stagnant. It flows to indus-tries and areas where expected profit rates are high and leaves areas where expected profits are low.[7] Capital movement continually challenges communi-ties. When capital flows in, it creates jobs, attracting new workers and their fam-ilies. They need housing and will require schools, police protection, roadways, and other public services. If local tax revenues and outlays for services do not rise as rapidly as the population does, such problems as overcrowded schools and congested roads result. Rapid growth also may exact a toll in other ways on the social fabric and perceived quality of life. Capital loss, however, creates far greater challenges. When jobs are lost, people usually do not leave the commu-nity; their life savings may be bound up in their home equity and they are reluc-tant to leave social attachments such as kinship networks. So unemployment in the locality rises, rippling to retail and service industries, and local government's tax revenues decline. But public-service demands do not decline; indeed, because of added social needs, they increase.[8]

In this century, capital has become increasingly mobile. Our communication and transportation systems have made it possible to locate production or even office facilities in many places and still have quick access to markets. Although locally owned businesses and financial institutions tend to leave their capital in place, with long-term commitment to their communities, the last several decades have witnessed the increasing concentration of capital. Companies in one industry after another have merged or been acquired by holding companies. Such megacorporations significantly affect the markets where they function, and the entry or departure of their facilities affects the economic health of entire regions.[9]

Thus, business is the principal actor in local development and a key determinant of community welfare. But businesses also have constraints: taxes, government regulations, and their need for community resources, which government can help mobilize. Different types of businesses have different needs and interests within the community.

In distinguishing among businesses, the dimension most relevant to the present discussion is the market environment. Businesses that depend primarily upon local or regional markets have different interests from those that mostly export out of the local economy to national or global markets. Although both types need local resources and seek them partly through government, the resources that they need differ, so their effects on local development policy differ as well. Local growth-oriented businesses seek local policies that promote real estate development and population growth, since that is how they increase profits. Export-oriented industries seek local policies that help them compete in national and global markets. To the extent that either interest draws on community resources, it replaces the influence of other economic and social interests that might create different economic-development patterns. A brief look at each type of interest and its consequences for local development will elucidate these points.

Local Growth Interests

In their treatise on local development and urban policy, Logan and Molotch set up a model of how growth-oriented industries may organize to secure public resources that advance their interests. Their "growth machine" model is more of an ideal type than a universal outcome, but variants of it do appear in most cities. It provides a useful analysis of local growth-oriented industries. Logan and Molotch distinguish two fundamental types of interest in real property (land and buildings): *use value* and *exchange value*. Those whose primary interest is the property's *use value* include local residents and most industries, including manufacturing. The interest of "place entrepreneurs," on the other hand, is in its *exchange value*—the possibility for profit from the property. Place entrepreneurs seek to "create differential rents [returns on investment] by influencing the larger arena of decision-making that will determine locational advantages."[10] For example, they may seek to influence the location of a defense plant or installation or a freeway route; or they may encourage government subsidy of a business that will move to their property; or they may lobby for changes in the municipality's land-use plan or zoning designations to permit more intensive development. They may encourage ambitious downtown-revitalization projects through public–private partnerships that require substantial government investment.

To succeed in their efforts, place entrepreneurs must organize and work with allies who share an interest in local growth. There are three sets of such allies: The first and strongest set of allies comprises those who profit directly from development projects—developers, financial institutions, construction firms and construction unions, and development professionals such as architects, planners, and real estate brokerages. The second set of allies benefits indirectly from development projects as they boost total population and demand for its products and services. This set includes utilities, local media, and retail chains such as grocery stores. The third set of allies comprises those that benefit from some types of growth and would in any case be harmed by population decline. These include universities, cultural institutions, professional sports teams, and small retailers. The resulting "apparatus of interlocking pro-growth associations and governmental units [makes up the] growth machine."[11]

The growth machine, or growth coalition, is not concerned about particular products or production processes, or the effects of products or production processes on others. As Logan and Molotch put it: "[T]hey invite capital to make anything—whether buttons or bombs, toasters or tanks—in their own back yards. Aggressive growth is portrayed as a public good. [It is] believed to help the whole community."[12] Nor do growth coalitions usually consider the quality of jobs or the wages that new employers will pay. Indeed, to attract businesses, many growth coalitions advertise their union-free environments or low prevailing-wage rates. The growth coalition advocates developing real estate by attracting investment, either from outside the region or from elsewhere within it. Little account is taken of any costs the investment may incur for the local government or the community as a whole. The development projects are funded by public–private partnerships, with the public sector providing a substantial share.[13]

Local chambers of commerce often are led by growth interests, so they often organize and articulate a pro-growth community agenda. Not that growth advocates wear their interests on their sleeves. Rather, through business networks and participation on local planning commissions, in civic organizations, and in special public projects, they pursue a (perhaps only tacit) vision of the good community that is built around growth, albeit perhaps with broader interests as well.

Politicians often ally themselves with local growth interests, or are even drawn from them. In rapidly developing counties, for example, it is not unusual for a majority of the board of supervisors to comprise real estate brokers, developers, or land owners, whose interest in public policy derives from their business interests. In addition, growth-oriented industries tend to actively support candidates for local office. Even politicians whose primary support does not come from the growth coalition can ill afford to ignore it. Without business investment, local governments cannot raise enough tax revenues to provide public services. Then, too, since real property taxes account for about one-third of local revenues, localities often find themselves forced to pursue policies that increase land values at the expense of neighboring localities.[14] Moreover, since politicians must always be on the side of job creation, they usually support growth on the grounds that it will increase local jobs.

Growth does not benefit everyone, however. Neighborhood residents may find their quality of life diminished if it brings congestion and loss of a "home town feel." People who rent their homes or live on fixed incomes generally suffer as growth inflates costs, especially in the short run.[15] Some growth, such as new freeways and downtown-revitalization projects, may directly threaten the homes of neighborhood residents. Postwar urban revitalization, in particular, was scarred by battles between development interests and urban neighborhoods. In recent years, advocates for environmental conservation also have clashed with pro-growth interests, in both urban and suburban settings. However, a growth coalition often can marginalize such opposition by arguing that the entire community will benefit from the jobs and tax revenues that growth will bring.

Manufacturing firms, which, with the exception of local newspapers, usually sell in national or global markets, may derive no benefits from local growth and may even suffer losses through traffic congestion and rising land and labor costs.[16] Indeed, despite their economic importance to their host communities and despite the fact that originally the growth coalition may have recruited them to the community, the coalition may take them for granted. For if they are not expanding their facilities or workforces, manufacturing businesses do not contribute to new profit opportunities for local growth interests. Small manufacturers may even find themselves threatened by encroaching residential and retail growth if it brings neighbors who object to the trucks, noise, and other pollutants that manufacturing may generate.[17] Large manufacturers, on the other hand, are generally able to exert more influence over their local environment.

To forestall possible opposition from neighborhood or environmental groups and prevail over indifference from others, the growth coalition relates its goals to civic pride, which is a sentiment arising naturally from social bonds and people's appreciation of their community's positive characteristics vis-à-vis others that are less attractive. Civic pride does not necessarily attach itself to the interregional competition for new businesses, but it is easy to see how it may do so, especially in communities that have lost jobs or fear their economic futures. Growth interests may actively enlist civic pride to support new projects. Local newspapers, for instance, which generally enjoy widespread respect and also stand to gain from a larger market, usually give front-page coverage to a locality's efforts to attract new investment or develop new real estate but little serious analysis of the possible costs. Their coverage stresses how many persons the new project will employ (usually overlooking whether they will be previously unemployed local residents or simply new residents), and the prestige the project will bring to the community.

The stultifying effects of growth-oriented development policy reach beyond simply other interest groups. A policy mix devoted to serving current market forces by recruiting new businesses and developing real estate and infrastructure may also eclipse alternative policies that might use labor and capital resources more efficiently, or which would produce a stronger economy in the long term. Such policies might seek to retain existing businesses by helping them restructure production, upgrade technology, retrain their workforces, or improve their access to markets.[18] Other policies scanted by growth-oriented development policy are those that stimulate entrepreneurship or small-business development; locally owned businesses lacking direct ties to global capital are ignored completely. Nor is community-based development that attacks structural poverty or that promotes environmentally responsible development usually high on the agenda of the growth coalition; such efforts do not boost total population or jobs and may even conflict directly with the growth-interest aims.[19] Also, the question about the skill levels and wages of the jobs its recruitment efforts yield often gets short shrift. (Although most communities now pay at least symbolic heed to these issues, few resources are allocated to deal with them.)

Export-Oriented Businesses

To prosper, an urban economy needs more than local growth-oriented industries. It must specialize, at least to some extent, in producing some goods or services for export out of the community, whether to a neighboring community or overseas. The money thus brought into the community (in company revenues and workers' pay) then supports retail stores, local services, and local government (as well as imports). If a community's export base has only a couple of industries, a downturn in one or more of those industries will undermine the entire local economy, including local retail and services, because less money will be available for local spending. Conversely, in a community with a diversified base, declines in specific industries cause less overall dislocation.[20]

The goal of developing a diversified economic base is easily understood but it is not easily achieved. History casts a long shadow. Many communities owe their origins to a single industry, having attracted an entrepreneur or branch plant (or been built around a plant) because that industry needed some local feature such as a raw material, an appropriate labor force, or a location near a market or transportation network.[21] Then, over time, a community molds itself to the needs of its dominant industries, which improves their competitive advantage in national and global markets, to the community's ultimate benefit. Public and private institutions alike focus on meeting the needs of the dominant export industries. But if the base is narrow, with only one or a couple of key industries, community features that might suit a wider range of industries will not be fostered. That leaves the community highly vulnerable to declines in its key basic industries. The more vulnerable it becomes, the more it may resist planning for change.[22]

Pittsburgh as a Paradigm Case

An excellent, if extreme, illustration of such economic dependency is writ large in Pittsburgh's dependence upon the steel industry—United States Steel Corporation in particular. Pittsburgh arose at the confluence of the Allegheny, Monongahela, and Ohio Rivers in the eighteenth century. But only in the mid-nineteenth century, with the production of coke, steel, and glass, did the community begin to grow. From the 1870s on, Andrew Carnegie developed what became a completely vertically integrated steel-manufacturing complex along 37 miles of the Monongahela River. Mill towns and Pittsburgh itself grew around the industry and the company. A town developed around each of the company's mills, separated by the river valley's topography from neighboring steel towns. Incorporated as separate municipalities, they never came together to work as a region. Indeed, the company promoted their division, often pitting them against each other in competition to keep or add facilities, since the municipalities knew that they depended on the employee and property taxes that the mills paid. Municipalities offered the mills free land, public services (roads, water, and transport) and special tax treatment.[23] Municipal tax structures came to favor heavy-manufacturing industries; by default, they also discouraged small, entrepreneurial businesses.

Local governments were reluctant to impose regulations on U.S. Steel or other manufacturers. Local officials were so intimidated by the company that the question of air pollution, for example, was simply never raised. Matthew Crenson, in a 1971 study of 48 cities, discovered that where suspended particulate levels were high—especially in Pittsburgh—and therefore clean-up costs would be high, steel company influence kept the issue off the policy agenda for many years.[24]

The Pittsburgh-area labor force also developed to suit U.S. Steel's interests. Early in the century, thousands of Hungarians, Poles, Russians, Serbs, Croatians, Greeks, and Italians were recruited to work in the mills. They settled in the geographically segregated communities along the Monongahela River and maintained social segregation, even in the mills. Language and cultural barriers reinforced the geographic barriers and kept the workers from unionizing until the 1940s.[25] Over the years, the mill towns adopted high school and vocational technical-school curricula that prepared young men for jobs in the mills rather than for college. In most of the mill towns, no other jobs offered wages as high as those in the mills, especially after the union began to negotiate contracts. U.S. Steel also sought other ways to ensure that other employers did not compete for the local labor force.[26]

The needs of local steel companies shaped other aspects of the local economic infrastructure as well. Carnegie Mellon University was modeled on the Massachusetts Institute of Technology (MIT), which conducts basic and applied research useful to business development. But unlike MIT, which by World War II had begun to focus on electronics and other emerging industries, Carnegie Mellon's research focused on the basic-metals industries until the 1980s.

Pittsburgh's lack of an appropriate research base or training ground for engineers in new fields precluded the development of some industries there. For example, between 1920 and 1950, Westinghouse Electric Corporation, a Pittsburgh-based company, conducted research in radio, television, radar, and nuclear physics. But with no university research base in electrical and electronic engineering and no local pool of engineers trained in those fields, Westinghouse found it hard to land U.S. Defense Department contracts, the major source of development financing for the electronics industry. The lack of an electronics-engineering milieu in Pittsburgh also undermined Westinghouse's efforts in 1960 to attract Robert Noyce, who later invented the silicon chip, to Pittsburgh.[27]

· Similarly, Pittsburgh's financial infrastructure served the metal-fabrication industries, but not others. Indeed, Pittsburgh's Mellon Bank was founded to handle capital for the Mellon family's manufacturing empire. As late as the 1980s, the bank evinced little understanding of, or willingness to finance entrepreneurs in, emerging technologies.[28]

Carnegie and Mellon also left lasting marks on the region's cultural institutions. Carnegie built the city of Pittsburgh's public-library system (but gave no money to operate it), as well as the city's museum. A town is named after Carnegie and parks are named after Mellon. Art galleries and cultural institutions bear the names of Carnegie, Mellon, or their relatives. Perhaps most notably, the city's professional football franchise not only is named after the steel industry, but the players' helmets to this day bear the corporate logo of U.S. Steel Corporation, years after the corporate name has ceased to exist.

Thus over the course of a century the Pittsburgh area evolved with the steel industry and U.S. Steel Corporation in particular. Steelworkers and the entire region became accustomed to the ups and downs of employment that are typical of durable-goods industries and that occur with the national business cycle. Workers came to believe that if they just did their jobs, the company would keep the work coming and their union would make sure that they received a fair wage. They were wrong. Although the American steel industry (much of which was in Pittsburgh) accounted for 54 percent of the world's raw steel production in 1946 and employed over 80,000 people in the Monongahela Valley, by 1990 it retained only 12 percent of the global steel market. During the decade of the 1980s Pittsburgh lost over 100,000 manufacturing jobs—over 70,000 in the Monongahela Valley alone.

The decline had begun as early as the 1950s, as Germany, Japan, and later South Korea invested in new, more efficient basic oxygen furnace and continuous-casting technologies. The American steel industry refused to modernize, continuing to rely on large, open-hearth furnaces and traditional rolling mills until long after it had lost the battle for global market share. At the same time, global steel-production capacity, but not demand, increased. Indeed, the development of plastics and lighter-weight metals over the past 50 years has reduced the demand for steel in many products.[29]

By the late 1960s the American steel industry had begun to modernize a few plants, but not in time to stave off a rise in steel imports. Therefore throughout the 1970s and into the '80s it sought import protections from the federal government. The industry channeled the frustration of steelworkers toward foreign producers, accusing them of dumping their steel on the American market (i.e., selling below production cost). The United Steelworkers union and many others in the Pittsburgh region supported those claims, as well as the industry's call for federal tax credits to modernize the plants. So also did the area's local, state, and congressional politicians, who felt compelled to show their concern for local jobs. (Nevertheless, when some restrictions on plant closings were, later, proposed to protect jobs, the area's politicians joined business interests in opposing them.) Thus, at a time when impending crisis should have inspired community-wide planning for alternative futures, local political fragmentation and especially the long economic dependency provoked a defensive response and appeal to the federal government for help.[30] Protections and tax credits were granted, but to no avail. U.S. Steel closed most of its steel operations, purchased Marathon Oil Company and even some nonmanufacturing companies, and renamed itself USX.

The Pittsburgh steel case is not only a story of economic dependency. It is a story of the failure to manage economic conversion, not from defense to civilian production, but from an outmoded product and production process to new ones. In a more perfect world, conversion planning would have begun at U.S. Steel by 1950 at the latest, first at the corporate level, where global market trends and new technologies were apparent. Planning would then have been introduced at the plant level, to incorporate workers' suggestions about production-process changes and improvements that could help implement corporate-led and union-approved conversion. But U.S. Steel's myopia precluded such planning, and generations of top-down bureaucratic management, both at the plants and in the union, left no way for workers to contribute their first-hand knowledge in improving production.

The mill towns and city and county governments could have seen by the 1960s that the steel industry and overall manufacturing in the region were declining, and that community-wide alternative-futures planning was called for. But the mill towns trusted the corporation to do the planning. Moreover, the fragmented structure of local government blocked community-wide planning until long after the damage was done. It was not until 1986 that a Steel Valley Authority, organized by labor unions and supported by the City of Pittsburgh and eight mill towns, was incorporated and empowered to use *eminent domain* to reopen closed plants and issue tax-exempt bonds to finance alternative manufacturing uses.[31]

The Pittsburgh case is extreme but not unique. Many towns and even some cities bear the imprint of a single corporation or industry. During the 1970s and '80s, Youngstown, East St. Louis, Detroit, and Flint made headlines as global restructuring changed the steel and automotive industries upon which they had built their economies. The manufacturing-based cities that have declined in recent decades had shaped their physical infrastructures, their labor forces and financial institutions to serve the needs of their dominant industries. Moreover, those cities are not the only ones vulnerable to economic catastrophe. Between 1986 and 1993, IBM—a symbol of the modern, high-technology economy if ever there was one—laid off 41 percent of its workers in the Binghamton/Endicott, New York area (140,000 worldwide). That community also had come to take for granted a paternalistic corporation, trusting its continuous optimistic pronouncements and believing that employment stability would last forever, despite signs to the contrary.[32]

Local Growth and Export Businesses in Accord

Both local growth interests and export-oriented businesses are usually present in urban areas. The two may peacefully coexist by respecting each other's turf and accommodating each other's needs, though not without some conflict when interests collide. Pittsburgh's redevelopment provides an example. In 1943, Richard King Mellon of Mellon Bank organized a group of growth-oriented businesses called the Allegheny Conference on Community Development with the enthusiastic support of the city's mayor to rid the city of its grimy, steel-town image. The Allegheny Conference drew up the redevelopment plans for review by the city, which then used its redevelopment authority to assemble and clear land for corporate development.[33] Some manufacturing was moved outside the city and low- and moderate-income neighborhoods and warehouse districts were replaced by office towers and a sports arena. Over the ensuing decades, the "Pittsburgh Renaissance" came to include the construction of a new 60-story corporate-headquarters building for U.S. Steel as well as office towers for Westinghouse, Rockwell International, Pittsburgh Paint and Glass, and other corporations. Room was made for the expanding financial-services industry and, in the adjacent university quarter, for the health-services industry. Thus the Allegheny Conference acted as a typical growth coalition, developing real estate to house the activities that would pay the most for the site (but using public subsidies to acquire land and stimulate the market). The Pittsburgh growth coalition had few areas of conflict with the export-oriented steel industry, which had what it needed in the mill towns. Where necessary, the steel industry was accommodated. For example, until the late 1970s, Jones and Laughlin Steel Company continued to operate a large blast furnace within one mile of the central business district, along a major access road by the Monongahela River.

Should either the growth coalition or an export-oriented corporation falter, observations suggest that the other will step into the breach. For example, an account by Todd Swanstrom (1985) shows that when Cleveland's populist Mayor Dennis Kucinich undermined the growth coalition in the late 1970s, Cleveland's export-oriented corporations stepped in. They rejuvenated the coalition and deposed Kucinich.[34] The downtown-based corporate headquarters of the export-oriented corporations had concluded that a physically rejuvenated central business district was needed in order to project a desirable image and to attract a suitable labor force. A healthy growth coalition was their chosen means to that end.

The direction of assistance reverses when a key export-oriented corporation falters or disappears. The local growth-oriented business interests are directly affected by the consequent loss of employment and population and decline in real estate values. They are likely to apply traditional tools—new business recruitment and new real estate development—to the task of reviving the community; often they rely on public–private partnerships (i.e., public subsidies). Here again, Pittsburgh provides instructive examples. During the 1980s the Allegheny Conference embarked on a revitalization plan for the mill towns along the Monongahela River. The Conference's well-funded Mon Valley Initiative challenged the

Steel Valley Authority and other labor-based efforts that were developing new manufacturing jobs. Instead, the Conference advocated recreational and residential uses that are easier to develop, but which pay lower wages.[35] And in 1982, when only a few large manufacturing plants remained in the city, a Save Nabisco Action Coalition pushed a bill through City Council that required a company to give its employees and the city notice when it planned to close a plant. The Allegheny Conference obliged manufacturing firms by convincing the mayor to veto the bill.

Challengers of Traditional Business Interests

In an economic crisis, new groups may bring other interests and alternative economic-development approaches to the fore. (The Steel Valley Authority mentioned above is an example.) Their influence depends on several factors: The perceived shortcomings of the existing development policies, their own organizational power and perceived legitimacy, the extent to which their alternative proposals are believed to address local problems, and the local, state, and national resources they can attract. New initiatives also have to survive any backlash from existing interests—for example, the Cleveland corporate elite's attack on the Kucinich administration. An example of a new activist group that did not surmount such hurdles is Youngstown's Ecumenical Coalition, made up of local religious leaders with liberal labor backing, which emerged in the aftermath of the Youngstown Sheet and Tube mill closing in 1977. The group quickly gathered local momentum and some outside support. But its plan for community ownership of the mill was very expensive, and the community thought its professed agenda for a "new American socialism" was more important to it than solving the community's problems. The group was perceived as being both too radical and too impractical to benefit the community, and it did not obtain federal support for the mill buy out.[36]

During the 1970s and '80s, alternatives to the growth machine emerged in many American cities. Coalitions of low- and moderate-income neighborhoods that had been directly harmed or whose needs had been ignored through growth-machine policies, together with middle-class intellectuals, succeeded in electing "progressive" local governments in Hartford, Berkeley, Santa Monica, Cleveland, and Burlington. Opposition to growth-machine policies also arose in Boston, Chicago, Louisville, Milwaukee, Pittsburgh, Sacramento, and many other cities, as neighborhood groups organized and pressed their demands in the political arena.[37] Such groups shifted the focus of local government spending from downtown development to neighborhood revitalization. In some cases, they induced local government to change the very nature of public–private partnerships, requiring contractors to hire minority workers and securing a better rate of return for the city from the deals.

Labor- and community-based coalitions in some states and cities have also taken steps to retain export-oriented industries and enhance their competitiveness as a way of preserving jobs. An example is the Springfield, Massachusetts,

Machine Action Project (MAP).[38] Frustrated by their inability to stop the closing of several large metalworking plants in the early 1980s, several union locals joined with community organizations, training providers, high schools, and community colleges to study the possibility of keeping the remaining metalworking firms in the area. They discovered that 350 small to mid-size shops, unlike the large branch plants, were thriving by producing for various high-tech markets. However, the small firms faced a growing shortage of skilled labor, and the workers laid off by the huge automated plants had neither the skills to serve the small firms' wide variety of customers nor the knowledge to keep up with technological changes. Furthermore, the closings of the large plants had discouraged young people from choosing careers in metalworking and machining. If the small shops' labor shortage was not addressed, they would begin to lose business and eventually close. Having analyzed the problem, MAP secured state funds and contributions from the small firms for coordinated education and training in the machining trades through local vocational high schools.

MAP then turned its attention towards diversifying the local economy. Unlike the traditional growth machine (which asks, "What's growing and how can we get it?"), MAP asked, "How can we build on what we have to get where we want to be?"[39] MAP identified printing, graphic arts, and auto mechanics as local industries with growth potential, but ones that faced technological change and needed to upgrade workers' skills. It developed training programs, as it had done for the metalworking and machining industries. As Joan Fitzgerald (1993) points out, this strategy "builds upon the strengths of the local labor force and uses available training resources as part of a broader strategy of maintaining living-wage employment, particularly in manufacturing."[40]

The MAP approach is unconventional in other ways as well. It involves workers in studying industry problems and in designing and overseeing the training programs. This motivates workers to take the training and also improves labor–management communication on ways to increase the use of new technology on the shop floor. And because MAP is a coalition based on members of the community and the labor force, it has brought new people, specifically ethnic minorities and women, into the skilled trades. MAP is an example of how community-based alternative-futures planning can produce a distinctive local-development policy, serving different aims from those of a traditional growth coalition or a dominant export-oriented corporation. It also suggests how proactive defense conversion might work at the community level.

Although traditional growth interests tend to dominate in most communities, economic crisis and the policy changes that organized opposition groups can accomplish promote community-wide learning. When such learning becomes embodied in public agencies and programs and in community beliefs about appropriate economic policies, the community can effectively address future economic crises early on. It is not surprising, perhaps, that some states and localities in the Northeast and Midwest that had been forced to deal with industrial decline in the 1970s and '80s were better prepared to handle defense downsizing in the 1990s than were regions that had not previously suffered economic restructuring.[41]

LOCAL INTERESTS AND MILITARY DEPENDENCY

The foregoing analysis of local economic-development interests and policies suggests hypotheses about the community roles of large defense employers and their relationships with other community interests. One might expect a military base or large defense contractor to play much the same role in the local economy as any export-oriented firm. The base or military–industrial firm may create significant employment-multiplier effects through local businesses that supply it directly and through the local retail and personal-service businesses that sell to base personnel or to the contractor's workers. One would therefore expect it to enjoy strong support in the community, especially from growth interests. Or do growth interests neglect it as they pursue new growth opportunities? It also seems possible that, like IBM in Binghamton/Endicott, the base or defense contractor may be paternalistically benevolent, contributing in many ways to the community culture and endearing itself to residents in the process.[42] On the other hand, federal military installations do not pay local real property taxes nor do their military commissaries and exchanges pay sales taxes, so their presence does not contribute to the municipal treasury as much as do private defense or commercial firms. Do local elected officials therefore appreciate them less, or does the large number of workers employed at such facilities counterbalance tax-revenue considerations? Are local officials as intimidated by large defense contractors and bases as they are by large commercial firms, or do they attempt to work political connections in Washington to achieve leverage over local facilities?

A community that relies primarily upon a military base or a single defense contractor for its economic livelihood would seem to be as vulnerable to economic dislocation as a mill town in western Pennsylvania was in the 1980s or as Binghamton/Endicott was in the early 1990s. But there are important differences between the military town and the company town. As described in chapter 1, decisions about military employment and defense-procurement spending are made by the Iron Triangle; through their congressional representatives, local interests potentially participate in the process. Do these relationships affect the community's vulnerability to defense-spending cutbacks and its responses when cutbacks occur?

How do local interests respond when federal priorities are shifting and ambiguous? Where, if at all, in defense-dependent communities do pressures for defense conversion or alternative-futures planning arise? How do federal and state conversion policies affect local economic-interest groups and their fortunes? These questions will be explored in the next several chapters.

NOTES

1. In the late-nineteenth century, Justice John F. Dillon summarized this legal fact of life, which has since been known as Dillon's Rule: "It is a general and undisputed proposition of law that a municipal corporation possesses and can exercise the following powers and no others: First, those granted in express words [by the state]; second, those nec-

essarily or fairly implied in or incident to the powers expressly granted; third, those essential to the accomplishment of the declared objects and purposes of the corporation—not simply convenient, but indispensable. Any fair, reasonable, substantive doubt concerning the existence of power is resolved by the courts against the corporation, and the power denied." J. Richard Aronson and Eli Schwartz, *Management Policies in Local Government Finance.* Washington, DC: International City Management Association, 1987, p. 12. Localities governed by "home-rule" charters have more autonomy than others, but the state determines the content of the charter.

2. John P. Blair, *Local Economic Development: Analysis and Practice.* Thousand Oaks, CA: Sage Publications, 1995, chap. 1.

3. Municipalities usually lose money on lower-income housing and on most family housing, since it costs more to provide public services to the residents than they pay in real property taxes.

4. John M. Levy, *Contemporary Urban Planning.* Englewood Cliffs, NJ: Prentice-Hall, 1991, chaps. 8 and 9.

5. Myron Orfield, *Metropolitics: A Regional Agenda for Community and Stability.* Washington, DC: Brookings Institution Press, and Cambridge, MA: Lincoln Institute of Land Policy, 1997; David Rusk, *Cities without Suburbs.* Washington, DC: Woodrow Wilson Center Press, 1993.

6. Gregory D. Squires, ed., *Unequal Partnerships: The Political Economy of Urban Redevelopment in Postwar America.* New Brunswick, NJ: Rutgers University Press, 1989, p. 4.

7. Edward J. Blakely, *Planning Local Economic Development: Theory and Practice.* Thousand Oaks, CA: Sage Publications, 1994, chaps. 1 and 3.

8. John M. Levy, *Economic Development Programs for Cities, Counties, and Towns.* New York: Praeger, 1990, chap. 12.

9. Bennett Harrison, "The Return of the Big Firms." *Social Policy* 21, no. 1 (summer 1990), pp. 7–19; see also Michael J. Kinsley, *Economic Renewal Guide: A Collaborative Process for Sustainable Community Development.* Snowmass, CO: Rocky Mountain Institute, 1997.

10. John R. Logan and Harvey L. Molotch, *Urban Fortunes: The Political Economy of Place.* Berkeley: University of California Press, 1987, p. 30.

11. Ibid., p. 32.

12. Ibid., p. 33.

13. Gregory D. Squires, "Public–Private Partnerships: Who Gets What and Why," in *Unequal Partnerships.*

14. Logan and Molotch, *Urban Fortunes*, p. 66; see also Aronson and Schwartz, *Management Policies in Local Government Finance*, chap. 9.

15. Timothy Bartik, *Who Benefits from State and Local Economic-Development Policies?* Kalamazoo, MI: W.E. Upjohn Institute for Employment Research, 1991.

16. Ibid.

17. Wim Wiewel, David Ranney, and George W. Putnam, "Technological Change in the Graphic Communications Industry: Implications for Economic-Development Planning." *Economic Development Quarterly* 4, no. 4 (November 1990), pp. 371–82; see also the film by Isabel Hill and Betsy Newman, *Made in Brooklyn.* Hohokus, NJ: New Day Films, 1993.

18. John J. Accordino, *The United States in the Global Economy: Challenges and Policy Choices.* Chicago: American Library Association, 1992, chap. 6.

19. An exception that proves the rule is the June 1999 subsidy of Intel Corporation

by a Portland, Oregon, area community. The deal extended an existing tax break for Intel to keep its existing plant operating, but removed a portion of the tax break for each additional job Intel created at the plant. The purpose of the unorthodox deal was to retain existing jobs but discourage new growth. Although the local chamber of commerce supported the deal, some growth advocates voiced concerns. From the standpoint of local fiscal health, the deal appeared to be quite sound—Intel would remain in Portland rather than relocate to another state, and tax revenues from Intel would increase somewhat over previous years. At the same time, population (from the plant, at least) would not increase, so local public-service costs would not increase. Apparently, the strong environmental movement in the Pacific Northwest has made inroads on the terrain of the growth coalition. An accommodation between the two seems to be taking place. See Sam Howe Verhovek, "Intel's Oregon Deal Includes Limit on Jobs." *New York Times* (June 9, 1999).

20. Blair, *Local Economic Development*, chap. 6.

21. Constance McLaughlin Green, *American Cities in the Growth of the Nation*. New York: Harper & Row, 1957; Blair, *Local Economic Development*, chap. 3.

22. Jeffrey S. Luke, Curtis Ventriss, B. J. Reed, and Christine M. Reed, *Managing Economic Development: A Guide to State and Local Leadership Strategies*. San Francisco: Jossey-Bass, 1988.

23. Ross J. Gittell, *Renewing Cities*. Princeton, NJ: Princeton University Press, 1992, pp. 136–37, cited in Karen L. Becker, "Community Economic Disaster Planning: Dynamics of Perception and Response to Economic Threat." Virginia Commonwealth University, Department of Urban Studies and Planning, Master's thesis, 1994, pp. 41–42.

24. Matthew A. Crenson, *The Un-Politics of Air Pollution: A Study of Non-Decision-making in the Cities*. Baltimore: Johns Hopkins University Press, 1971.

25. John Hoerr, *And the Wolf Finally Came: The Decline of the American Steel Industry*. Pittsburgh: University of Pittsburgh Press, 1988, cited in Becker, "Community Economic Disaster Planning," p. 38.

26. Hoerr described his discussion with a U.S. Steel executive who claimed that steel firms had dissuaded an aircraft manufacturer from locating in the Pittsburgh area during World War II. He also reported a warning that U.S. Steel gave to public officials that the local labor force "belonged to U.S. Steel." Cited in Becker, "Community Economic Disaster Planning," p. 41.

27. See Aydan Kutay, "Prospects for High-Technology-Based Economic Development in Mature Industrial Regions: Pittsburgh as a Case Study." Unpublished paper, Carnegie Mellon University, Department of Engineering and Public Policy, November 1988, pp. 14–18.

28. Ironically, a century of corporate capital accumulation has generated substantial wealth in Pittsburgh—enough to capitalize large venture-capital funds that could finance new industries. But the culture of corporate bureaucracy has left a lasting residue in the city. During the 1980s, Pittsburgh's largest venture-capital fund (and one of the few that exist in the area) shifted its primary focus to Boston and California. See Kutay, "Prospects for High-Technology-Based Economic Development in Mature Industrial Regions," pp. 22–24.

29. Kutay, "Prospects for High-Technology-Based Economic Development in Mature Industrial Regions"; see also Seymour Melman, "Profits without Production: Deterioration in the Industrial System," in ed. Suzanne Gordon and Dave McFadden, *Economic Conversion: Revitalizing America's Economy*. Cambridge, MA: Ballinger Publishing, 1984, pp. 19–32.

30. As late as 1993, local observers contended that some public officials still had not

grasped what had happened to the steel industry and that some still expected it to rebound. See Becker, "Community Economic Disaster Planning," p. 45.

31. Alberta Sbragia, "The Pittsburgh Model of Economic Development: Partnership, Responsiveness, and Indifference," in *Unequal Partnerships*, p. 117; Becker, "Community Economic Disaster Planning," p. 50; Gordon L. Clark, "Pittsburgh in Transition: Consolidation of Prosperity in an era of Economic Restructuring," in ed. Robert A. Beauregard, *Economic Restructuring and Political Response*. Newbury Park, CA: Sage Publications, 1989.

32. Becker, "Community Economic Disaster Planning," pp. 1–2.

33. Redevelopment authorities were authorized in the U.S. Housing Act of 1949 for the express purpose of revitalizing central cities by acquiring older areas, razing them, and then redeveloping them.

34. Todd Swanstrom, *The Crisis of Growth Politics: Cleveland, Kucinich, and the Challenge of Urban Populism*. Philadelphia: Temple University Press, 1985, cited in Alan Harding, "Elite Theory and Growth Machines," in ed. David Judge, Gerry Stoker, and Harold Wolman, *Theories of Urban Politics*. London: Sage Publications, 1995.

35. Joan Fitzgerald and Louise Simmons, "From Consumption to Production: Labor Participation in Grass-Roots Movements." *Urban Affairs Quarterly* 26, no. 4 (June 1991), 512–31, cited in Becker, "Community Economic Disaster Planning," p. 50.

36. Becker, "Community Economic Disaster Planning," p. 69.

37. Pierre Clavel, *The Progressive City: Planning and Participation, 1969–1984.* New Brunswick, NJ: Rutgers University Press, 1986; *Unequal Partnerships*; John J. Accordino, *Community-Based Development: An Idea Whose Time has Come.* Richmond: Federal Reserve Bank of Richmond, 1997.

38. Joan Fitzgerald, "Labor Force, Education, and Work," in ed. Richard D. Bingham and Robert Mier, *Theories of Local Economic Development: Perspectives Across the Disciplines.* Newbury Park, CA: Sage, 1993.

39. Ibid., p. 137.

40. Ibid.

41. David Osborne and Ted Gaebler make the related point that government responses to change depend in part upon the inertia of existing public policies and bureaucratic routines, as well as the state of knowledge as to how tasks can be achieved. See *Reinventing Government: How the Entrepreneurial Spirit Is Transforming the Public Sector* (New York: Penguin Group, 1993), cited in "Community Economic Disaster Planning." See also S. Elkin, *City and Regime in the American Republic.* Chicago: University of Chicago Press, 1987, cited in Gerry Stoker, "Regime Theory and Urban Politics," in *Theories of Urban Politics.*

42. Becker, "Community Economic Disaster Planning," pp. 88–90.

1. JAMES CITY:
- Naval Supply Center, Cheatham Annex, N

2. NEWPORT NEWS:
- Fort Eustis, A

3. YORKTOWN:
- Naval Weapons Station, N
- Coast Guard Reserve Training, CG

4. HAMPTON:
- Langley, AF
- Fort Monroe, A

5. PORTSMOUTH:
- Fifth Coast Guard District, CG
- Norfolk Naval Shipyard, N
- Naval Hospital, N
- Naval Electronics Systems, N

6. NORFOLK:
- Armed Forces Staff College, JS
- Camp Elmore, M
- Little Creek Naval Amphibious Base, N
- Norfolk Naval Air Station, N
- Norfolk Naval Station, N
- Naval Aviation Depot, N
- NAVCOMM Area Master Station, N

7. VIRGINIA BEACH:
- Dam Neck Fleet Combat Training Center, N
- Naval Surface Warfare Center, N
- Oceana Naval Air Station, N
- Camp Pendleton, NG
- Fort Story, A

8. CHESAPEAKE:
- Fentress Naval Auxiliary Landing Field, N
- NW Naval Security Group Activity, N
- Fleet NUSW Training Center, N

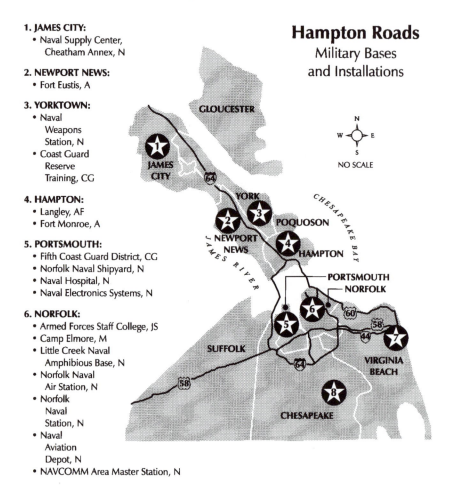

Hampton Roads
Military Bases and Installations

NO SCALE

HAMPTON ROADS LOCATION

A=Army, AF=Air Force, CG=Coast Guard, JS=Joint Services, M=Marines, N=Navy, NG=National Guard. Map adapted from: "Major Military Bases and Installations," *Governor's Commission: Base Retention and Defense Adjustment*, 1994.

3

The Military Metropolis: Boosters, Bases, and Shipbuilding in Hampton Roads

BUILDING THE MILITARY METROPOLIS

The Norfolk–Virginia Beach–Newport News metropolitan statistical area, which, thanks to the efforts of local growth boosters, increasingly goes by the name of Hampton Roads, comprises two geographically distinct portions of Southeastern Virginia: the Virginia Peninsula and Tidewater. The Peninsula, which lies north of the James River, includes the cities of Hampton, Newport News, Poquoson, and Williamsburg, and the counties of Gloucester, James City, Matthews, and York. Tidewater, which lies south of the river, includes the cities of Norfolk, Portsmouth, Virginia Beach, Chesapeake, and Suffolk[1] (see facing map, "Hampton Roads").

From its earliest days as an English colony, the area's deep-water harbors on the James and Elizabeth Rivers, protected from the Atlantic Ocean by Virginia's Eastern Shore and the Chesapeake Bay, made it attractive for military fortifications and shipbuilding. Almost immediately upon landing in 1607, Captain Christopher Newport established Point Comfort—the present site of Fort Monroe in Hampton—as a defensive works against possible Spanish attack.[2] Shipbuilding along the banks of the Elizabeth River, which separates Norfolk from Portsmouth, began as early as 1620. In 1798 the just-established U.S. Navy purchased the Gosport Shipyard in Portsmouth (now called the Norfolk Naval Shipyard). As the shipyard grew during the nineteenth century, so did supporting industries as well as a Navy hospital and other Navy facilities.[3] The Civil War, besides accelerating the yard's growth, brought a Union Army camp to Newport News, which became a staging area for the Virginia campaign.

It was in the twentieth century that the area rose to prominence as a center of shipbuilding and military operations. From the turn of the century onwards, aggressive and continuous recruitment by Norfolk's growth interests brought into the area one of the largest concentrations of military activity in the world. And through the investments of railroad magnate Collis P. Huntington, it became home to one of the world's largest shipbuilding companies. These and other undertakings put the community in an excellent position to exploit the development opportunities presented by two world wars. To understand the political economy of development in Hampton Roads today, especially the community's responses to defense-spending cutbacks in the 1990s, one must appreciate the development patterns established earlier in the twentieth century.

Norfolk and Portsmouth

In 1900 Norfolk was still a relatively sleepy southern town of 47,000 inhabitants in the midst of an agricultural hinterland and with the much smaller towns of Portsmouth and Hampton nearby. But its merchant shippers, financiers, and other commercial interests "brimmed with the entrepreneurial spirit that inspired urban boosters throughout the South . . . [and] unflagging optimism that the city could overcome nearly a century of inertia through aggressive promotion of its links to the sea."[4] To advertise their community to would-be investors, the boosters raised $1 million to host the 1907 Jamestown Exposition. In honor of the occasion, President Theodore Roosevelt assembled a navy fleet at Norfolk for an around-the-world cruise. The idea was thereby planted in the minds of local developers that the navy might provide the growth engine they sought.

After the Exposition, a real estate developer, T. J. Wool, proposed to sell its 340-acre site to the U.S. Navy for $1 million. Congress demurred, but Wool persisted. By 1913, the Norfolk Chamber of Commerce had formed a Naval Affairs Committee to organize a city-wide promotional campaign. With the help of Virginia's U.S. Senator Claude Swanson, the Norfolk committee kept continuous pressure on Washington to establish a naval base on the Exposition site.[5] When President Wilson appointed the North Carolinian Josephus Daniels as Navy Secretary, the campaign finally succeeded. He commissioned studies that showed the strategic advantages of the site's deep harbor and channel for homeporting, refueling and supply, training, and as a submarine base. In 1917 President Wilson signed Senator Swanson's bill to purchase the site. By 1921 the navy had invested $37 million for landfills, acreage expansion, temporary buildings, and docking facilities at the operating base.[6] Meanwhile, World War I had transformed Portsmouth into an instant boomtown: The navy yard added three new drydocks and built four destroyers, a battleship, and the navy's first carrier, and was employing over 11,000 workers by 1918.[7]

The armistice brought about a sharp decline in work at the navy yard, reducing the workforce to 2,538 by 1923, and it also reduced activity at the new operating base. That pattern of drastic shrinkage would recur throughout the century, each time bringing economic dislocation to the entire community. The 1920s also saw a loss of friends in Washington, as Navy Secretary Daniels left office and two senators who had advocated naval development in southern ports died. A congressional committee even recommended transferring a naval training facility from Norfolk to another city, citing the poor condition of Norfolk's buildings and the high cost of modernizing them. But Norfolk's Chamber of Commerce quickly sprang into action, establishing another enduring pattern. Its Naval Affairs Committee met with the Navy Secretary Edwin Denby to elicit assurance that Norfolk would remain "the one great battleship base on the Atlantic Coast." Back in Norfolk, the chamber wined and dined officers and men of the Atlantic fleet and urged Norfolk's supporters in Congress to block the proposed transfer.[8]

Throughout the 1920s the Norfolk Chamber continued to be the liaison between the military and the city, thus presenting a united front to the federal government, for example, by sending resolutions to Washington favoring pay increases for local officers or protesting the transfer of officers who had demonstrated loyalty to the city. Indeed, the chamber's Naval Affairs Committee was made up not only of bankers and other growth interests, but of naval officers. Over the years, that committee worked closely with Virginia's congressional delegation to resist even minor budget cuts at the Norfolk base and to press for continued expansion and improvements, as well as for ship-repair contracts at the naval shipyard in Portsmouth. The effectiveness of that lobbying improved after Senator Swanson was appointed Navy Secretary in 1930; millions of federal dollars flowed in during the 1930s in preparation for the next war.[9] By June 1941, several months before the attack on Pearl Harbor, the war effort had already pumped up employment and population to unmanageable numbers:

[T]here were 15,559 officers and enlisted men at the naval base and 14,426 more on the ships based there; while at the navy yard civilian workers numbered 20,893 [there would be 43,000 by 1943] and navy personnel 3,716. Altogether sailors and naval employees in the Norfolk area numbered 71,669 and their wives and children 37,916.[10]

Growth stimulated by the navy's investments brought the opportunities for land and commercial development that the Norfolk Chamber had sought, but they came at a price. Employment in the city's commercial manufacturing industries remained stagnant between 1914 and 1945, while military employment increased sevenfold. The naval base alone occupied 3,400 acres—one-fifth the total land area of the city—some of which had been designated for civilian industry. When the navy expanded its facilities, the local government had to supply the water, sewerage, roadways, and other services. When the city was slow in doing so, the navy threatened to pull out. Yet, as a government entity, the navy paid no real estate taxes, which at that time produced most local government revenues. Furthermore, the community quickly learned that life as a military town meant huge employment increases and tremendous housing shortages during build ups and wars, followed by double-digit unemployment rates and housing market gluts when peace came.

Newport News

The operating base and navy yard were not to be the only defense employers in Hampton Roads. After the Civil War, western railroad developer Collis P. Huntington determined to link the Atlantic and Pacific coasts by rail. He chose

Newport News, a mostly rural area on the Virginia Peninsula, with its natural deep-water harbor, as his Atlantic terminus. By 1881 Huntington had finished the Chesapeake and Ohio line, and soon afterwards the Newport News rail terminal became a bustling shipping center. Meanwhile, Huntington had already launched new projects. For one thing, through his Old Dominion Land Company he had purchased, planned, and developed land for the entire town of Newport News, including parks and schools. As Rouse says: "[E]arly Newport News was a Huntington enterprise."[11] And in 1886 Huntington formed what would soon be known as the Newport News Shipbuilding and Drydock Company. Using a large available labor pool that included recently emancipated blacks, the shipyard began by repairing the vessels that hauled goods the railroad brought to the port. But by 1889 its drydock was serving navy ships. The railroad terminal, port, and shipyard attracted skilled engineers, designers, and unskilled workers, so that by the eve of World War I the combined population of Newport News and adjacent Warwick County had reached 35,000.[12]

Like Norfolk across the James River, Newport News soon discovered the cyclical employment patterns of war and peacetime in a military town. During World War I, as Newport News Shipbuilding and Drydock Company built battleships and destroyers and repaired 1,000 ships, its employment doubled from 7,000 to 14,000 workers. The port also became a major military-embarkation point, serving 583 convoy ships during the war. The army established camps Eustis, Hill, Alexander, Morrison, and Stuart as training and staging areas and built warehouses and other facilities throughout the Newport News area.[13] By 1918 the combined population of Newport News and Warwick County had swelled to 100,000 and a severe housing crisis had set in.

Just as quickly, however, the bubble burst at war's end. By 1922 the navy had cancelled $70 million in contracts at the shipyard, causing employment there to plummet to 2,200 workers. The company began making locomotives, heavy machinery, and water turbines to keep its small workforce busy. Nevertheless, the 1920s proved to be hard years for this one-company town.

In 1933, during the Great Depression, employment at the Newport News Shipyard actually picked up, with navy contracts to build its two new aircraft carriers. In 1936, when the U.S. Maritime Administration began building 50 merchant ships a year for possible conversion to military use, the first contract went to Newport News. More navy contracts followed. By 1943, two years into World War II, the shipyard had sprawled along two miles of riverfront, its employment had soared to 31,016, and the population of the surrounding area had reached 189,000. Again, the port served as a major point of embarkation to the European theater, this time for over 730,000 soldiers.[14]

Thus by the end of World War II strong patterns had been established that would mark the Hampton Roads area for the rest of the century. Local growth interests had spawned a military-based economy and had developed close ties to the military establishment in Washington to keep it growing. Added to the operating base and navy yard were facilities established throughout the community by the army, navy, the newly formed air force, and even NASA. Those facilities continued to expand during the Cold War years. Newport News Shipyard continued to nurture its own connections in the Navy Department in order to secure contracts. Other shipbuilders and repair companies along the Elizabeth River had developed as well, most with large military workloads. And the workers and community as a whole had begun to accept the growth and decline cycles of defense spending.

Yet Peninsula growth interests were not entirely satisfied with the fruits of their labors. They regretted the cyclicality of defense spending and wished for a more diverse economy. They sought diversity—not by helping Peninsula businesses expand into new markets, not by replacing imports with local firms that could form a competitive complex, and not by stimulating entrepreneurship—but by traditional business recruitment and downtown office development. The Peninsula Chamber of Commerce successfully urged the formation of a Newport News–Hampton Regional Redevelopment Authority to build, and recruit new firms to, an industrial park.[15] And when the Rockefeller family invested in the restoration of Colonial Williamsburg in the 1960s, the area began to exploit its historic resources as tourist attractions. The development of a NASA research lab, originally established as an air force lab in 1916 on what would become the Langley Air Force Base in Hampton, stimulated enthusiasm for advanced technology in Hampton and at local colleges and universities. During the 1980s the efforts of Hampton, Newport News and others brought the U.S. Department of Energy's Jefferson National Accelerator Laboratory to Newport News. However, until the 1990s, no steps were taken to create advanced technology-based manufacturing in the area.

Meanwhile, Newport News and Hampton watched in dismay as the development of surrounding counties bolstered competing governments and sapped the vitality of their central cities. Indeed, the fragmentation of local government would prove to be the bane of the community's existence for the remainder of the century.[16] The merger of Newport News with Warwick County and of Hampton with Elizabeth City and Phoebus staved off financial crisis, but only for a time. The fiscal problems were exacerbated by the presence of military facilities on much of the community's developable land, because the federal government does not pay local real property taxes. By the 1980s Norfolk, Portsmouth, Newport News, and Hampton consistently ranked among the state's most fiscally stressed jurisdictions.[17]

Norfolk's growth boosters had similar aims: Diversification beyond a military economy and downtown revitalization to stem migration to the suburbs. In 1948 they established the Norfolk Port Authority to promote civilian use of the port and later to develop an industrial park for commercial businesses. In 1954 they established the Tidewater's first regional economic-development agency to promote the area to outside investors. Beginning in the 1950s, the Norfolk Redevelopment and Housing Authority demolished hundreds of acres of low-income housing, as well as the honky-tonks, flophouses, and tattoo parlors that had established themselves near the naval operating base, to make way for downtown offices and civic centers.[18] Old Dominion University, Norfolk State

University, and Tidewater Community College in Norfolk were established during that period, and tourism along the sandy beaches of Virginia Beach grew dramatically. All those changes began to diversify the local economy.

Norfolk's boosters were looking beyond the city limits as well to fulfill their growth visions. In 1953 the banker John S. Alfriend proposed a metropolitan government that would encompass all the Tidewater jurisdictions under the leadership of Norfolk.[19] By that time, however, the suburban communities had already grown too powerful for this to be politically feasible. Norfolk settled for annexing additional territory in the adjacent county. Meanwhile, several competing jurisdictions were merging into the geographically huge cities of Virginia Beach, Chesapeake, and Suffolk. With metropolitan government thus precluded, regional efforts to promote growth took the form of cooperative infrastructure projects such as bridge-tunnels across the James and Elizabeth rivers and across the Chesapeake Bay.

During the 1980s regional initiatives began to cross the James River more frequently.[20] Throughout the 1990s, local growth interests, especially in the chamber of commerce in Tidewater (called the Hampton Roads Chamber of Commerce), continued to push for regional cooperation to attract business investment. Still, the Chamber did not concern itself with the structural causes of local fragmentation—the heavy reliance on the real property tax to finance local government and the lack of region-wide revenue sharing. As a result, interjurisdictional competition for capital and tax base continued to undermine the regional aspirations of metropolitan growth interests. Not only was cooperation between the Peninsula and Tidewater slow to materialize (Peninsula communities feared the economic and political might of their neighbors across the water), cooperation also was difficult to engineer even among jurisdictions on the same side of the water. For example, throughout the 1980s the Tidewater Chamber of Commerce and the local governments in Tidewater funded a business-recruitment organization, but its effectiveness was undermined by conflict among the jurisdictions. By the end of the decade, the Chamber had grown frustrated with these and other difficulties and had created its own regional business-recruitment organization—called Forward Hampton Roads—without local government involvement. This constituted a rift in the local growth coalition that would affect the region's response to defense-spending cutbacks.

Defense Dependence

By 1969 overall growth of the area's economy had brought the share of military employment down to 45 percent of all jobs, and by 1993 it had fallen to 28 percent. Nevertheless, with the exception of tourism, higher education, port activity, and a small amount of civilian manufacturing, the region's export base continued to rest upon defense-related jobs.[21] Assuming an employment multiplier of 2, whereby each job in the economic base supports an additional job in the nonbase of local services, in 1969 upwards of 60 percent of all community jobs remained dependent upon the Department of Defense.[22]

By 1994 the number of persons employed directly by the Defense Department in Hampton Roads and present there year-round had reached 86,000. Of that number, 49,000 were military personnel and 37,000 were civilians. However, the total number of military and civilian personnel employed through Hampton Roads facilities, including those working on ships and whose families lived in Hampton Roads, was about 180,000.[23] The navy employed over two-thirds of these workers, mostly at the Norfolk Naval Operating Base (by this time the largest base in the world and home to the U.S. Atlantic fleet and the NATO Atlantic Command), at the Little Creek Amphibious Base, at the Norfolk Naval Shipyard in Portsmouth, and at Oceana Naval Air Station in Virginia Beach. Other large military-employment centers included the army's Fort Eustis, a transportation and logistics center in Newport News; and the navy's Yorktown Naval Weapons Station and Suffolk Undersea War Center. The air force maintained the Training and Doctrine Command at Fort Monroe, the Air Combat Command at Langley Air Force Base, and the NASA/Langley Research Lab, which specializes in aeronautics and aerospace research[24] (see map at beginning of chapter).

In addition to direct military employment, the region's economy included roughly 75,000 workers in defense prime and subcontractor firms that engaged in shipbuilding, ship maintenance and repair, business services, engineering and management services, construction, and, to a small extent, other manufacturing (e.g., nonelectrical machinery, electric and electronic equipment, and instruments). The largest of these firms was (and still is) the Newport News Shipbuilding and Drydock Company, which employed about 29,000 workers in 1989, and just under 18,000 in 1999. The huge shipyard specializes in the construction of nuclear carriers and submarines. Large private employers in the ship-repair industry included Norfolk Shipbuilding and Drydock Company, Metro Machine Corporation, Marine Hydraulics International, Jonathan Corporation, Moon Engineering Company, and Colonna's Shipyard. The largest facility dedicated to repair and maintenance, however, is still the navy's Norfolk Naval Shipyard, with about 8,000 employees.

Hampton Roads's defense dependency is reflected in more than its workforce and military installations, however. The bases and shipbuilders dominate much of the local skyline. The Norfolk Naval Base alone now uses over 4,000 acres, and the remaining installations in the area easily occupy an estimated 20,000 acres. Two miles of Newport News's waterfront are occupied by the shipyard; the Elizabeth River is dominated by shipbuilders and repairers. Fifteen percent of the community's working-age population are military retirees—mostly from the officer ranks—who take jobs in government and the private sector. (Enlisted men, on the other hand, especially those with technical skills, often leave the area upon discharge. Local growth interests and economic-development agencies have not fostered civilian jobs that use skilled workers.[25]) Spouses of military personnel work in the community as nurses, teachers, catalog fulfillment-center staff and retail clerks. The armed services participate in the cultural life of the community through organizations such as the U.S. Atlantic Fleet Band and the Armed Forces School of Music Facility. And the community shows its appreciation for the military in many ways, including the chamber of commerce's annual Military Appreciation Week. As Parramore notes: "Norfolk and the navy are one community."[26]

Thus over the course of the twentieth century the Hampton Roads community has developed around two basic industries—shipbuilding and the military. Although the military presence owes much to local growth interests, their modus operandi differs from their counterparts in nonmilitary cities such as Pittsburgh: In the military metropolis, growth interests operate through the community's congressional representatives and contacts with local "management" at the bases to pressure the "CEO" in Washington to retain and expand the employer's local facilities. Local growth interests do not conduct such relations with private firms, even military–industrial ones like the Newport News Shipyard. Nevertheless, in its promotion of overall local growth, the growth coalition's role does resemble that found in nonmilitary communities.

Given the strength of these growth interests—a relationship with the military that is as old as Pittsburgh's relationship with steel and, as it happens, the absence of organizations such as peace or conversion advocates that articulate alternative visions—it would be surprising if Hampton Roads had enthusiastically accepted defense cuts or developed conversion initiatives. Indeed, the actions of the largest defense firms and organized interests in the 1990s illustrated the depth of the community's defense dependency and its belief that defense spending would rebound, as it had in the past. Nevertheless, some firms did shift at least part of their work into commercial markets, and some purchased commercial operations. And even as the community fought to keep its military installations, growth advocates identified some alternative development opportunities they could pursue if the community lost the fight and that might, in the long run, considerably improve the local economy. For a time, there emerged an interest in high-technology development in which company conversion featured as part of a broad business-development strategy that differed from the traditional growth model. These efforts and their fates are described in the remainder of the chapter.

DEFENSE-SPENDING CUTBACKS AND PRIVATE-SECTOR RESPONSES

During the 1988–1995 period the region suffered economic dislocation due to defense-procurement cutbacks and military-installation downsizing. The downsizing of the navy's fleet from a projected goal of 600 ships to 346 and the deferred maintenance on existing ships cut directly into the workloads of Hampton Roads employers. Between 1989 and 1994 the region lost an estimated 15,000 jobs, mostly through reductions at Newport News Shipbuilding and Drydock Company but, to a lesser extent, through downsizing as well at the Norfolk Naval Shipyard, Fort Eustis, Langley Air Force Base, NASA/Langley Research Lab, and various ship-repair contractors. Yet, throughout the period, there was uncertainty and ambiguity about the nature and magnitude of the cutbacks and the extent to which Hampton Roads might be able to avoid them. This ambiguity influenced both private and public responses to the cutbacks. Most defense contractors retained their core operations and laid-off workers in the belief that this downturn, like others before it, would be followed by an upswing. Some purchased nondefense businesses or sought foreign markets. A few took on commercial work as well, thus converting their existing defense workforces.

Newport News Shipbuilding and Drydock Company Responds

By the 1980s Newport News Shipbuilding and Drydock Company had become totally dependent upon military work—specifically, the construction of nuclear carriers, submarines, battleships, and a variety of smaller military vessels. Although defense had constituted the bulk of its work since World War I, the shipyard had supplemented that with commercial work, especially during defense-spending downturns such as that experienced after the Vietnam War. In 1981, however, the Reagan administration ended domestic subsidies for commercial ship construction, although other countries were increasing such subsidies to their domestic firms. Having thus undermined the international competitiveness of the American commercial shipbuilding industry, President Reagan declared his intention to build a 600-ship navy, which induced shipyards such as Newport News to focus all their energies on military contracts. By mid-decade, employment at the shipyard had climbed to 31,000 workers.

The next turn of events, from the Pentagon's 1993 Bottom-Up Review, brought the recommendation to reduce the navy to 325–350 ships; the slowdown and then ending of the Seawolf submarine program; the slower pace of spending for the nuclear-powered carrier then under construction (the *Harry S. Truman*); and the possibility that the next carrier (the *Ronald Reagan*) might not be funded at all. In response to the deep cuts in its workload, the shipyard reduced its permanent workforce from 29,000 in 1989 to 18,000 in 1997, cut wages for the remaining workers, and hired back some laid-off workers as project-specific, temporary workers with lower pay and no benefits.[27]

Conversion to commercial shipbuilding was also placed on the agenda. In 1994 the shipyard's vice president, Greg Cridlin, announced: "Newport News intends to be a competitor in the international commercial ship market." He stated that the shipyard would raise its percentage of commercial work from 0 to 35 percent by the year 2000. The shipyard contracted with Eletson Corporation of Greece to build four tankers, using Newport News's double-eagle design that allows double-hull ships to be modified to include special features. The shipyard's ability to win the contract was secured by the U.S. Maritime Administration's Title XI loan-guarantee program, which Congress expanded in 1994 to extend loan guarantees to foreign firms that buy ships from U.S. yards.[28]

The commercial work could not support the large numbers of workers that the shipyard had employed during the 1980s, since even the most sophisticated commercial ship requires far less electronic equipment and other hardware than do military ships. In fact, knowledgeable observers did not expect the shipyard to pursue commercial work for long, for two reasons: First, when the shipyard abandoned commercial shipbuilding in the early 1980s, it fell many years behind the global competition in product design and production technology, as did many other defense contractors producing to military specifications. Secondly, because the shipyard continued to use military specifications when estimating for construction jobs, it could not compete on price for commercial work.[29] For example, critics noted that on the above-mentioned Eletson project, a $4 million job, the shipyard lost about $1 million and that much of the work was subcontracted out to smaller contractors who used the shipyard's drydocks.[30] To become competitive in the commercial construction business, observers claimed that the shipyard would have to have embarked on an ambitious, ten-year program of investment in capital equipment and technology.

Instead of doing that, the shipyard was seen to be biding its time until the mood in Congress once again favored aggressive construction of navy ships and submarines. With the help of the Virginia congressional delegation (and, no doubt, the navy), the shipyard worked hard to alter the congressional mood. In 1994 it won approval for the carrier *Ronald Reagan* (CVN-76, to be commissioned in 2002) and in 1997 received the contract for the next and last carrier in the series, CVN-77. To make way for the new carriers, 6 old ones were to be retired 9 to 19 years short of their anticipated lifespans. As Sanford Gottlieb (1997) noted wryly: "American central cities, bridges, and sewer systems may decay, but up-to-date nuclear-powered aircraft carriers will continue to serve as the navy's 'forward presence' around the world."[31] But the CVN series will not be the end of carrier work for Newport News Shipyard. In 1998 it began work on a Carrier Innovation Center, subsidized with $98 million in Virginia state funds, to develop concepts for the next series of carriers, the CVX.[32]

In addition, the shipyard has marketed its new fast-frigates to foreign countries, among them the United Arab Emirates, Kuwait, Turkey, and Saudi Arabia.[33] In 1995 and 1996 the shipyard waged a campaign to become the nation's sole nuclear shipyard, by trying to wrest the contract to build the next generation of nuclear submarines away from General Dynamics's Electric Boat Corporation in Connecticut, where the navy had been planning to award it.[34] Although the navy chose to maintain two nuclear yards, Newport News managed to negotiate a teaming agreement with Electric Boat to coproduce the navy's new attack submarine (NSSN). Also, in April 1997, the shipyard won a navy contract for Los Angeles-class submarine-planning work and design and planning-yard work for the third Seawolf-class submarine.[35]

Responses in the Ship-Repair Industry

As of 1994 there were approximately 50 private companies doing ship and boat repair in Hampton Roads, and they employed roughly 7,000 workers. In addition, the Norfolk Naval Shipyard, which services nuclear-powered navy vessels and other ships, employed about 8,000. Employment in the industry is volatile, even during times of peak demand, since work is project-based and all but the largest projects last less than three months. Between 1990 and 1995, workforce fluctuations of 60 to 70 percent in some ship-repair companies were common, but the overall employment trend during those years was downward.

The major repair companies and subcontractors in Hampton Roads all rely upon military work, and almost all of that is with navy ships. Navy repair and maintenance cutbacks began before the 1993 Bottom-Up Review, creating turmoil in the local ship-maintenance and -repair markets throughout 1990–1995, but especially from 1992 to 1994. Overall, within the industry four different strategies were pursued: layoffs, purchase of commercial operations (often non-marine), entry into other markets for military repair (usually smaller craft), and entry into commercial maintenance and repair markets. Virtually every company laid off up to two-thirds of its permanent workforce and turned instead to temporary labor, sometimes hiring back laid-off workers but for less pay and benefits. Some of the smaller, specialty companies, such as two diesel-repair and -maintenance operations, had already used temporary labor for many years as a way of keeping costs down.

The larger companies pursued diversification strategies, sometimes as early as the 1980s, before the military ship-repair market began to decline. For example, Metro Machine Corporation, which employed 725 workers, established a small ammunition ship-repair facility in New Jersey. In 1989 the company began working with commercial tanker operators to perfect a new double-hulled ship technology. When it came time to build a $100 million plant to construct the new tankers, however, Metro Machine found the Commonwealth of Virginia unwilling to help with financing or subsidies. The company turned to Pennsylvania, which offered to fund part of the cost and provide loan guarantees for the remainder.

Likewise, the Jonathan Corporation, which employed 900 workers and owned two drydocks until it filed for bankruptcy in 1994, pursued several diversification initiatives in the late 1980s. It purchased a local steel company and attempted, unsuccessfully, to enter the bridge-repair business; it invested in Hampton Roads real estate during the 1980s boom; and it purchased an electronic equipment company and ship-repair company in Pennsylvania. It developed and marketed a computerized management system that tracked project equipment, materials, and employees, and it developed several environmental-engineering projects. Marine Hydraulics International, a full-service repairer of military vessels with 400 workers in 1994, developed a temporary-employment service. It also acquired an environmental-restoration company and a small ship surface-preparation and -coating company, which it hoped to expand to work on bridges and other steel structures. Neither company, however, attempted to help their ship-repair workers convert to these other operations.

A few large companies and several small ones did diversify their existing maintenance and repair workforces by moving into the commercial ship-maintenance market. Norfolk Shipbuilding and Drydock Company (Norshipco), the largest repair company, with two drydocks and 2,500 workers in 1994, established a partnership with Diesel Marine International to recondition marine and industrial cast-iron components. Colonna's Shipyard, with one drydock and 400 workers in 1994, diversified into repair of commercial tugboats, barges, and ferries. Another small yard that employed 60 persons in 1994 reduced its dependence on navy work from 70 to 50 percent by working on more commercial tugboats, trawlers, and barges as well as on army craft. As in other defense markets, when these larger contractors moved into the small-craft-repair markets, they undercut smaller, general service and repair companies, a number of which subsequently failed.

Some small specialty subcontractors, such as diesel-engine maintenance and repair shops, managed to reduce their military dependence from 100 to under 50 percent by marketing aggressively in Hampton Roads and overseas and by providing services such as "riding crews" who travel with a ship around the world. But many other subcontractors who specialized in plastics and hull coatings, deck work, motors, valve repair, and riggings struggled throughout the period. By the mid-1990s, many had gone out of business.

Responses in the Service Industries

In 1993, the business services and engineering and management services employed a total of 48,533 persons, an estimated 33,000 of them through defense prime contracting or subcontracting.[36] The prime contractors included some of the nation's largest defense firms.[37] However, fewer than 25 percent of the region's prime contractors were headquartered in Hampton Roads, and of the few that were, only one or two had more than 200 employees. In short, defense services in Hampton Roads comprised 50–75 prime contractors that were subsidiaries of large corporations headquartered elsewhere. They worked alone or with over 1,800 subcontractors, the vast majority of which were small and locally owned.

Like the ship-repair companies, business services and engineering and management services rely on the presence of military bases and ships for work. In contrast to ship-repair contracts, however, the Pentagon's demand for engineering and management services did not decline significantly overall, so many of the contractors did well throughout the period. Some had less military work, but many experienced growth. Among those who had fewer orders, the larger ones pursued the diversification and adjustment strategies typical of large defense contractors elsewhere.

The Vitro Corporation chose to diversify into other military work. With headquarters in Rockville, Maryland, Vitro employs over 5,000 persons nationwide, about 80 of whom work in Hampton Roads. Vitro has traditionally focused on software development for systems-engineering projects. In the early 1990s Vitro evaluated a number of options for reducing its dependence on navy work. It found that it could not compete well with smaller companies on fixed-price, commercial projects or on state and local government jobs. However, Vitro found that it could expand to army, air force, and NASA work. It discovered markets for its new geographic information system (GIS) as well as for its new automated data-processing services, because all the armed services had begun to address environmental issues at their facilities and needed the automated systems to effectively do so. Vitro also started to provide various technical assistance services to foreign governments.

One of the few Hampton Roads service companies that diversified some existing operations and workers into commercial markets is Computer Dynamics, Inc. (CDI). The company has headquarters in Hampton Roads and had 450 employees in 1994. CDI has a federal division that develops local-area computer networks for navy offices, and a training division that develops various career training programs, from computer programming to radio and sonar technology to health care. Over two-thirds of the corporation's business was in defense work, mostly for the navy. CDI expected its work to decrease as the navy cut back to a 325–350 ship force, since, with fewer ships, fewer sonar operators and other technicians would be trained and less equipment (e.g., radios) would have to be serviced. To respond to the expected fall-off in navy work, CDI developed a career school for commercial systems integration. Overall, the company saw little difficulty in diversifying into commercial work. As one official put it: "A network is a network." Workers within the company were not designated for *only* defense or *only* commercial work, so the company expected few problems in expanding into more commercial work.

Other large technical-service companies with Hampton Roads facilities enjoyed growing military demand for their services. For example, in 1994 the American Systems Engineering Corporation (AMSEC) had a Hampton Roads office with about 500 workers.[38] Almost all of AMSEC's work is with the Defense Department, mostly with the navy. It plans detailed maintenance procedures for navy ships and carriers, weapons and propulsion systems, carrier elevators, and other systems. AMSEC had robust annual revenue growth in the 1990s, because the reduction in numbers of navy ships meant that existing ships had to work longer and be maintained more often. Moreover, navy ships are becoming more complex, and that will increase the work opportunities for companies such as AMSEC for the foreseeable future. Thus AMSEC found it unnecessary to convert its military business to civilian work.

The same mixed picture obtained among the smaller companies, most of which are locally based. For example, one developer of warfare-simulation software stated that he could not possibly find a commercial use for his particular products. On the other hand, industry observers pointed out that while smaller companies might go out of business or cut back their workforces when they failed to win contracts, their workforces were readily hired by others, so that total employment in the industry would not decline as long as military demand continued at high levels.

With few exceptions, Hampton Roads defense contractors, individually or collectively, did not appeal to the public sector for help in dealing with defense cutbacks. In a few cases, the larger ship repairers appealed to the navy to stop contracting practices that they believed benefited smaller companies. They also complained about a requirement that a certain percentage of repair contracts be filled at the publicly owned Norfolk navy yard. Asked by the author how the government might best help them, the defense contractors' most prevalent responses were "increase defense spending" or "cut taxes." Owners of several smaller ship-repair companies mentioned that they would appreciate low-cost assistance in finding new, commercial markets, but had no idea where to find it. Local industry associations neither offered nor pushed for public assistance in dealing with defense downsizing. The Tidewater Association of Service Contractors pressed for recognition of its role in the local economy, and some members advocated tax cuts, but conversion assistance was not on its agenda. The South Tidewater Association of Ship Repairers confined its efforts to its traditional role of improving training and certification for skilled workers, and it later joined with Old Dominion University to develop improved cleaning and blasting techniques, but it did not address defense-spending cuts or diversification initiatives. According to organization members, the ship-repair companies generally do not cooperate well, so more ambitious initiatives are unlikely to be undertaken.

COMMUNITY-WIDE RESPONSES

Few public or community-wide efforts sought to promote or even to support defense-company conversion or diversification in Hampton Roads. The two most widely publicized and widely supported responses to defense cutbacks were a region-wide economic-visioning exercise called Plan 2007, and a successful effort to defend the community against military cutbacks during the 1995 round of the Base Realignment and Closure (BRAC) process. The Hampton Roads Small Business Development Center (a joint, federal–state–local program) provided some assistance to small defense businesses, and a "technology development" project that initially sought to promote defense conversion through business assistance was also launched. The fate of these initiatives explains a great deal about the nature of dominant interests in this community.

Renewing the Growth Vision: The Plan 2007 Process

In 1991 the director of Forward Hampton Roads, the Tidewater Chamber of Commerce's regional economic-development arm, raised concerns with chamber officers about the local effects of projected defense-spending cutbacks. He advocated a region-wide economic-visioning process to identify new directions for the economy. Other concerns included the effects of the 1990–1992 recession (exacerbated by the departure of the military during the Persian Gulf War) and fears that Newport News Shipyard might not be awarded the contract to build the CVN76 carrier. By the spring of 1992 the leaders of the Tidewater Chamber of Commerce, including a bank president, a railroad CEO, a real-estate-development corporation president, and a health corporation CEO, had decided to initiate the region-wide visioning process. They dubbed it "Plan 2007" to associate it with the upcoming 400-year anniversary of the founding of Jamestown. In keeping with their goal of fostering regional cooperation for economic development, they invited business participants from both the Peninsula and their own Tidewater area. However, local government officials played almost no role in Plan 2007. As one organizer put it: "They were not invited. They don't create jobs, businesses do."[39] The organizers' intent was, first, to develop a business vision for the Hampton Roads area that somehow rose above the rivalries that had prevented the area's local governments from engaging in region-wide development planning, and then to seek the endorsement of the vision by local elected officials.[40]

During the summer of 1993, 163 participants, mostly from the business community, met four times to develop visions for six industry-cluster groups: shipbuilding, ship repair, and the defense industry; tourism, conventions, entertainment, and recreation; technology; other manufacturing (nondefense related); transportation and distribution; and health and biomedical. In the shipbuilding, ship repair, and defense contracting cluster, for example, significant job loss was predicted for the 1993–1998 period due to defense-spending cutbacks. Suggested initiatives for this cluster included demonstrating the strategic significance and competitiveness of Norfolk Naval Shipyard over other shipyards in the United States, reusing closed Department of Defense facilities and equipment, increasing the number of ship arrivals involved in trade or tourism, and collaborating with the Defense Department to make Hampton Roads the primary East Coast port, base, and defense support system.

Thus the plan called for both conversion of shipyards to civilian production and for strengthening their traditional military role. It said nothing about the workers who would be displaced from their jobs, much less how they should be assisted in their efforts to find new ones. Its most glaring omission, perhaps, was an implementation strategy. Indeed, the plan was not actually a plan but rather a collection of visions, a "gadget to create consensus" as one of its organizers called it.

Initially, the Plan 2007 process and the resultant collection of vision statements appeared to enjoy considerable success. The federal Economic Development Administration funded the process retroactively. In October 1993 the nine mayors of Hampton Roads cities officially endorsed the plan. In February 1994 the Hampton Roads Planning District Commission (which includes representatives of each jurisdiction) endorsed the plan's proposal for $200,000 in local funding to study the possibility of greater interjurisdictional cooperation in local economic development policy and to develop a strategy to provide greater access to equity capital for small businesses.

Yet strong support for Plan 2007 was not widespread. Public officials evinced no interest in implementing the plan, because they had not been asked to play a role in its creation. Privately, even business participants distanced themselves from the process itself or from its results. Some complained that the process was controlled by a few of the area's most powerful businesses, who had ensured that the plan would focus mostly on maintaining the status quo rather than on creating a new vision of the area. Others argued that by focusing on visioning and brainstorming, the planning process overlooked the details of actual problems and opportunities in the cluster groups. As a result, maintained the critics, the plan was vague and many of its action steps were ill conceived.

Defense contractors complained that the plan did not address their situations, despite devoting a cluster group to defense shipbuilding and repair. Some said that Plan 2007's origins within, and leadership by, nondefense businesses rather than defense contractors were responsible for its failure to grasp the problems of small defense contractors in ship repair, as well as those of small and large contractors in business and engineering services. In conversations with the author, Plan 2007 organizers stated that they had neither services nor ideas about how to help defense contractors. By 1996 Plan 2007 had for all intents and purposes died, although some of its ideas were taken up by other initiatives; however, its leaders continued to promote a regional cooperation agenda. As noted above, this agenda generally has championed cooperative efforts to recruit business, not changes in the structure of local government financing that drives inter-local competition.

The failure of proactive region-wide defense-conversion planning in Hampton Roads can be traced to a number of factors. These include local political fragmentation, the narrow focus of traditional growth interests, and planning errors. Most important were the absence of understanding of the conversion process and lack of desire to move the community away from defense dependency.

Assisting Existing Businesses:
The Peninsula Advanced Technology Center

The traditional growth interests led by the Chamber of Commerce were not the only ones in Hampton Roads. During the 1980s and '90s another interest began to emerge. This "high-technology" interest offered a different vision of how the region could diversify away from complete defense dependency and improve its economic vitality. The vehicle that focused these interests on a concrete strategy was PATC—the Peninsula Advanced Technology Center. PATC arose from the fortuitous meeting of three persons who had an interest in promoting high-technology-based economic development: Dr. Robert Templin, General John Loh, and Steven Cooper. Dr. Templin, President of Thomas Nelson Community College in Hampton in the early 1990s, believed that high-technology manufacturing held the key to economic competitiveness. He had studied successful high-tech development in five American cities and identified five essential elements, which later became the five services offered by PATC. He also believed that Thomas Nelson Community College could train workers for high-technology manufacturing jobs, especially in the commercial sector.

Early in 1991 General Loh assumed command of the air force's Tactical Air Command at Langley Air Force Base in Hampton. Like others in the Pentagon and armed services, Loh was concerned about the decline of the American defense industrial base (see the discussion in chapter 1). Thus he favored efforts to strengthen the technological sophistication of defense manufacturers. He and others believed that this could come about, in part, through better linkages between commercial and defense applications. As commander of Wright-Patterson Air Force Base and research labs in Ohio, Loh had sought to develop these defense–commercial linkages. Soon after he assumed command at Langley Air Force Base, Loh invited the members of the Virginia Peninsula Economic Development Council to use the resources of the lab by taking advantage of the 1989 federal law that authorized federal labs to form technological partnerships with companies and universities through so-called CRADAs—Cooperative Research and Development Agreements. Although most members of the Peninsula business community reportedly did not appreciate the value of General Loh's offer, Steven Cooper did. Cooper was a technology-transfer agent at the Virginia Center for Innovative Technology, through Thomas Nelson Community College. Technology-transfer agents conduct outreach to businesses and help them access services in high technology and management from the state's colleges and universities. Cooper brought Loh and Templin together. By August 1991 a core group of founders had formed.

From the beginning, the three founders recognized the need to link their effort with traditional growth interests in the area. They approached Joe Cantrell, President of the Peninsula Economic Development Council and publisher of the *Newport News Daily Press* newspaper. At about that time, Cantrell's paper published a year-long series of reports that highlighted the Peninsula's economic problems and suggested diversification as a solution. (Ten percent of the Peninsula's workers were employed at Newport News Shipyard.) The PATC founders also secured the support of John Lawson, Executive Director of the Peninsula Economic Development Council, the Peninsula's business-recruitment organization. Hampton's Mayor Eason, who had long been a proponent of high-technology development, pledged both the support of his economic development staff and official sponsorship of the project.

After a year of planning, the PATC concept was launched. Its mission would be to enable advanced technology-based manufacturing and services employment on the Peninsula, via the following services: (1) *technology transfer*, whereby federal research labs and universities would make new product and process technology accessible to specific businesses; (2) *applied research*, whereby federal research labs and universities would provide services ranging from engineering to marketing to help businesses solve specific problems; (3) *graduate and undergraduate engineering and applied-science education*; (4) *workforce training and retraining*, to create a workforce with the skills requisite to advanced manufacturing and services; and (5) *business-development finance*, to make investment capital available to high-tech businesses. In addition to the federal research labs and Thomas Nelson Community College, other local entities that would play key roles included Old Dominion University, whose engineering school had long been oriented to applied engineering work with Hampton Roads area businesses.

The ensuing year was a productive one for PATC, partly because of the climate of concern created by defense cuts: Newport News Shipyard announced the layoff of 5,000 workers and predicted that more would follow. The recession of 1990–1992 and the aforementioned newspaper series created a platform for PATC to advocate a new direction for business. PATC organizers made many public presentations in which they promoted their concept as a way for defense subcontractors on the Peninsula to diversify into commercial product lines. Through the city of Hampton, the center received a planning grant from the Defense Department's Office of Economic Adjustment to conduct a survey of over 700 Peninsula manufacturing firms. The survey results produced an inventory of product lines, equipment, and excess capacity of manufacturing firms for PATC to use in stimulating business partnerships and networks and in recruiting new high-tech companies to the Peninsula. By 1994 PATC had signed agreements with research labs at NASA/Langley (Hampton), Wright-Patterson (Dayton), Fort Eustis (Newport News), and the Thomas Jefferson National Accelerator Facility (Newport News), providing businesses with access to lab scientists.

PATC also began to broker services that helped a few businesses convert some operations from defense to commercial production. An example is its assistance to a small Peninsula firm that makes air-filtration equipment to defend against biological warfare. Until 1990, almost 100 percent of this firm's work had been on military projects as a subcontractor to Newport News Shipyard. But its president believed that the end of the Cold War was a good time to begin to diversify into commercial work, and he sought opportunities to develop commercial filters. A maker of diesel trucks in Ohio asked the company to design and produce a diesel particulate-filtration system to comply with a new federal regulation. When the company was unable to produce a workable system, it went to PATC, who asked researchers at Old Dominion University to find a technology that would solve the problem. Old Dominion identified a German company with the requisite technology, and then PATC crafted a design and production agreement between the Peninsula company, the Ohio company, Old Dominion University, and the German company. PATC also worked with the Hampton Roads Small Business Development Center on a financing package to help the Peninsula company expand operations to produce the new filters.

Despite these achievements, PATC soon ran into difficulties. A $2.5 million federal Technology Reinvestment Project application filed in 1993, which was to sustain it during its first five years of operation, was not funded. Despite the recommendations of a Virginia Governor's Commission on Defense Conversion in 1992, the state General Assembly declined to support the organization.[41] These setbacks forced PATC to seek substantial funding support from Peninsula businesses and local governments, but certain factors made that difficult. Newport News Shipbuilding and Drydock Company was a key barrier. In 1992 and 1993 company officials stated publicly that any moves to diversify the Peninsula economy away from defense dependency would undermine its efforts to secure more defense contracts, and particularly Congressional approval of the CVN76 carrier, which faced stiff opposition. Shipyard officials asserted that their efforts rested, in part, on claims that the community would be crippled if the shipyard were forced to significantly reduce its employment.[42] Indeed, at the same time that PATC was gearing up, the shipyard was organizing a massive letter-writing campaign by its subcontractors and local officials to convince Congress to support construction of the carrier. PATC advocates acknowledged privately that the funding of CVN76, which would keep employment at the shipyard well above

15,000 through the rest of the 1990s, could reinforce the belief that technology development and diversification were unnecessary. Most of the Peninsula businesses that supply the shipyard are reluctant to make the investments in time and money to move into civilian markets. They also know that they must be ready to respond promptly to shipyard orders if they want to maintain that relationship. Thus, in the final analysis, they simply accept the cyclical nature of shipyard contracts, believing that downturns will inevitably be followed by upswings.

Moreover, even some members of the business community who were worried about cuts in defense spending reportedly did not find the PATC strategies promising. Some said that PATC's approach was too focused on high technology and not enough on medium technology, so its services were not relevant to their needs.[43] Another problem was that many businesses and economic-development officials on the Peninsula hold a traditional view of local economic development that confines its aims to recruiting new businesses into the area, not establishing networks with existing firms. The lack of strong support by the business community, especially the opposition of Newport News Shipbuilding and Drydock Company, and the lack of federal or state government support cost PATC credibility in the eyes of local governments through 1994. Although strong support came from the city of Hampton, support from the city of Newport News was weak and other Peninsula localities failed to support PATC at all.

By July 1995 conditions had improved, but at a price. PATC had dropped all statements about defense conversion from its literature and public remarks. Instead, it focused solely on "growing the technological base," as one staff person put it. Most importantly, PATC founder Robert Templin had become director of the Virginia Center for Innovative Technology and, soon after, that state agency had promised $200,000 to PATC. The cities of Hampton and Newport News had pledged a total of $250,000 over three years, the Virginia Peninsula Economic Development Council had promised $100,000, and other Peninsula businesses had contributed a total of $50,000. PATC began to co-sponsor, with the NASA/Langley Research Lab and others, an annual "Expo Tech" fair where local companies exhibited their products and services and, in some cases, developed new business opportunities. The Expo Tech fairs proved to be the advertising PATC needed to convince skeptical Peninsula businesses of the organization's value. As a result of this positive publicity, PATC was able to increase the volume of its activity, serving about 30 companies during the first half of 1995. Thus, although PATC was no longer promoting defense conversion, it was helping companies to solve problems and take advantage of new opportunities and business relationships, which made it possible for some to diversify away from total defense dependency.[44]

Nevertheless, PATC could not sustain the financial support it needed to continue as an independent organization. By 1998 it had been absorbed by the Peninsula's regional business-recruitment organization. Its original founders, Templin and Loh, had long since left the community, and Cooper had died. Although its staff person continued to broker technology-development services to businesses, the organization lost visibility in the business community. Several factors account for PATC's failure to thrive: the power of the key export employer, Newport News Shipyard, which perceived its interests to be threatened by PATC; the imperfect fit between the espoused high-technology mission of PATC and the needs of some local businesses; and local government fragmentation. Local fragmentation accounts, in part, for the city of Newport News's failure to offer strong support to PATC, since PATC was housed in Hampton. More importantly, PATC never tried to secure support from or to work in the Tidewater, which is a much larger community, with a business base three times the size of the Peninsula's. The PATC founders believed that if it were perceived by Peninsula development officials and businesses as a Tidewater operation, they would not support it.

Defending Hampton Roads against BRAC'95

The defense against the 1995 Base Realignment and Closure (BRAC) process stands in sharp contrast to the halting efforts of Plan 2007and PATC. It illustrates a practice established in the post–World War I years, when local growth interests battled to retain and enhance activities at the Norfolk Naval Base. The effort to fend off BRAC'95 was, if anything, more aggressive than those earlier efforts. Until the 1993 round of the BRAC process, few believed that Hampton Roads would suffer significant losses from military downsizing, partly because the state had lost little in the 1988 and 1991 rounds. Even Virginia's U.S. Senator John Warner voiced confidence, less than two days before the Pentagon released its base-closure list in March 1993. The BRAC Commission's 1993 decision to close both the Naval Aviation Depot (NADEP) on the Norfolk Naval Base and the small Naval Undersea Warfare Center in Suffolk, standing pat against a furious letter-writing campaign by NADEP workers and denunciatory statements by public officials, was a "wake-up call," as local officials put it. (In actuality, the Hampton Roads area had a net gain of 3,503 jobs as a result of the 1993 BRAC decisions.[45])

Public officials determined that they would mount a successful defense effort against the BRAC'95 process. Under the leadership of U.S. Congressman Owen Pickett, two committees—a policy committee and a working committee— were established to defend Oceana Naval Air Station and other local installations, building them up by taking over functions from bases in other states. The policy committee was comprised of members of Virginia's congressional delegation (including Senator Warner, at that time the ranking Republican on the Senate Armed Services Committee and former Secretary of the Navy), mayors and other local officials from the entire Hampton Roads area, a state representative, and a number of retired flag officers. The working committee was comprised of members appointed by the Hampton Roads and Peninsula chambers of commerce as well as staff from the economic-development departments of individual local governments. Staff support for the entire effort was provided by the Hampton Roads Planning District Commission. Two attorneys (one of whom was a former BRAC Commission attorney) were retained to keep the committees informed about Pentagon decisions so that information could reach decision-makers in time for them to act effectively. Hampton Roads localities and the Commonwealth of Virginia provided $500,000 to support the effort.

The working committee provided data on the bases and their local economic impacts, which were then worked into policy papers by the Planning District Commission staff, for signature by the policy committee. To collect data, the working committee visited every military installation in the area, as well as some competing bases in other states. Using detailed data on each facility's functions and capacities, the committee made the case that the Hampton Roads facilities have superior military value. Its reports argued that the military infrastructure that had been developed over many decades and the presence of all three armed services in Hampton Roads facilitate interservice cooperation and constitute "a defense megabase that could not be duplicated elsewhere."[46]

According to persons associated with the effort, these policy reports, which base commanders then sent to the Pentagon planners to describe their facilities as well as other committee actions, had a significant impact on BRAC'95 decisions for Hampton Roads. For example, when, in preparation for the BRAC'93 process, Pentagon planners had asked Oceana Naval Air Station how much air space it controlled over a certain range, Oceana reportedly responded "zero percent." This and similar answers on other questions led Pentagon planners to assign Oceana a military-value rating of thirteenth out of 15 naval air stations. In preparation for the BRAC'95 process, however, Planning District Commission staff reports enabled Oceana to claim that it controlled 100 percent of the required air space, resulting in a military-value rating of first out of the 15 air stations. Similarly, in the 1993 process, Pentagon planners reportedly estimated that it would cost $164 million to prepare a Cherry Point, North Carolina, facility to receive F/A-18 fighter planes from Cecil Field in Florida (which was closing), but failed to take into account factors that would raise the actual cost to $450 million, such as the fact that Cherry Point is surrounded by wetlands. The Hampton Roads committees used this analysis to argue that the new-generation F/A-18s should not be based at Cherry Point, but at Oceana, since Oceana is already constructed, has an additional 2,100 acres available with no adverse environmental implications, and could be prepared for only $60 million. They also argued that since all training and doctrine facilities are located in Norfolk, moving the F/A-18s to Cherry Point would split pilots' time between the two locations and wreak havoc with family lives. For its part, the city of Virginia Beach undertook to improve Oceana's military viability by relocating two schools that the navy had long complained were dangerously close to the base.

Although the community as a whole was behind these mighty efforts, some observers noted that defense downsizing might be handled in a more proactive way. For example, Everett Pyatt, a former Defense Department official, advised the Hampton Roads community in a public speech in April 1994 that it should assess its military facilities in light of a local strategic economic-development plan, identifying those facilities that could be put to better economic use and recommending that the Pentagon close them rather than others.[47] Unfortunately, for such an exercise to succeed, it would have to have been completed well before the BRAC process began (i.e., by the spring of 1994). Ideally, the Plan 2007 process would have constituted such a plan, but as a collection of broad growth visions it had not come close to specific planning. Nor were local leaders interested in the type of planning that Pyatt recommended. At the conference where he spoke, area mayors stated that they had no intention of considering alternative uses for the community's military facilities. Rather, they were intent on demonstrating the community's loyalty to the military.

In private conversations, however, some chamber of commerce officers, defense-company presidents, and local government officials admitted that, for some of the area's military facilities, there might be better uses. For instance, a chamber official stated that Oceana would meet the region's need for an international airport that could handle large cargo planes in order to attract larger companies that might bring better jobs. A local government official noted that Fort Eustis is the last piece of prime, undeveloped land in Newport News and that its development might help relieve the city's fiscal stress. Still, all these persons agreed with the state and local officials' determined public stance not to relinquish any land or military jobs without a fight. To do otherwise, they insisted, would be political suicide.

By October 1995 events appeared to have vindicated this aggressive stance. Defense Secretary William Perry's proposed base closures and realignments, which had been endorsed by the BRAC'95 commission and signed by President Clinton, produced a net gain of at least 3,843 jobs for Virginia. Oceana Naval Air Station, for example, gained over 5,000 jobs and became the largest naval air base on the East Coast, as the home for all the navy's F-14 fighters and the East Coast hub for its F/A-18 Hornets.[48]

The BRAC'95 defense had far-reaching implications. It reinvigorated the military-community alliance that the Norfolk Chamber of Commerce's Naval Affairs Committee had established early in the century, but which had grown moribund in recent years. Ironically, although the laudable purpose of the BRAC process was to downsize the military in a rational and equitable way, it had the effect of reinforcing the community's ties to the military. In the wake of this success, several local officials and observers mused that it would be wise to keep the two-committee structure intact in order to maintain effective relations with the Pentagon and, if possible, position the area to exploit business opportunities as the Pentagon privatizes functions such as food service on the bases. Moreover, unlike the Plan 2007 process, this effort galvanized the entire community in a regional cooperative effort. The local media noted that the usually contentious Hampton Roads local governments had seldom, if ever, cooperated so well to accomplish a task.[49] As one participant explained: "By the end of the [Pentagon planning] process [in December 1994] we could get policy papers signed by all of the policy committee representatives in 48 hours—we were working that well together."

Converting Defense Workers: A Fragmented Approach

In addition to its high-profile visioning program and its efforts to defend the bases, Hampton Roads also took steps to help dislocated defense workers. Two state/local offices—the Job Transition Resource Center in Norfolk and the Worker Retraining and Support Program in Hampton—were established to administer the federal Economic Dislocation and Worker Adjustment Assistance (EDWAA) program, which funds short-term training for dislocated workers. Each office also offered a standard array of services, including labor-market information, access to college catalogs, job leads, resume-writing assistance, photocopying and telephone services, and stress-reduction workshops.

Only about 10 percent of the thousands of workers laid off at Newport News Shipyard and other companies reportedly sought retraining through the EDWAA program, however. Many reportedly took jobs as temporary workers, expecting to be called back by their former employers before long, in the century-old pattern of downswings and upturns in Hampton Roads. Others found new jobs without any retraining, perhaps because EDWAA provides no living stipend during retraining. Those who did retrain found new jobs mostly as truck drivers, HVAC service and repair technicians, computer technicians, and auto mechanics. Some became nurses or business administrators.

Neither the Hampton nor the Norfolk program found it possible to link up its career counseling and retraining referral services to local economic-development efforts. In 1994 the Norfolk office asked the Hampton Roads Chamber of Commerce's business-recruitment organization, Forward Hampton Roads, to create such a link, and they agreed to do so. Within a year, however, the idea had been dropped, reportedly because the companies that the chamber recruited had no need for workers with specialized skills. Both programs also found that, because of the secretive nature of business recruiting, business recruiters could give them only 30 to 60 days' notice of a new business opening—a period apparently too short to organize retraining to the particular labor need.

Local economic-development officials also failed to utilize the 17,500 highly skilled military enlisted personnel who are discharged each year from bases in Virginia, mostly in Hampton Roads. (At their request, the Commonwealth of Virginia tried to get a skills list of departing personnel from local installations, but this effort did not succeed.) Thus, unlike the retiring military officers who often settle in Hampton Roads, skilled technical workers generally are recruited to work elsewhere in the United States by one of a number of private recruitment firms that do business in Hampton Roads.[50] The lackadaisical attitude on this point caused some resentment among navy personnel after BRAC'93 decided to close the Norfolk Naval Aviation Depot (NADEP) on the Norfolk Naval Base. NADEP had 4,000 skilled technicians who maintained the navy's F-14 Tomcat fighters and the A-6 aircraft; many of them wanted to stay in Hampton Roads. Yet neither the Forward Hampton Roads recruitment organization nor the city of Norfolk's economic-development department moved to find companies that might employ these skilled workers. NADEP's personnel-transition officers complained to the author that they made repeated requests to those agencies to accept NADEP's lists of employee skills for use in business recruitment.

Although the Tidewater economic-development organizations failed to link dislocated skilled workers with new job opportunities, the Peninsula Advanced Technology Center (PATC) tried to do so. The aforementioned survey of Peninsula businesses asked them to identify unmet skill needs over the next couple of years. This information was passed along to the Hampton Worker Retraining and Support Program, which used it to help counsel dislocated defense workers.

CONCLUSION

The responses of the Hampton Roads community to defense-spending cutbacks illustrate the power of traditional growth interests and key export employers to protect and advance their own interests, through both public as well as private actions. Like Pittsburgh and its mill towns, the Hampton Roads community is highly dependent upon its relatively narrow base of military and shipbuilding employment, so it is not surprising that it would launch aggressive efforts to retain these activities, despite the fact that more diversity would probably improve the economy in the long run. To be sure, the uncertainty introduced by defense downsizing *did* prompt some defense contractors to attempt conversion and diversification initiatives, and it also created some space in which other interests could articulate alternative community-wide visions: The high-technology interest established and supported PATC, and certain growth interests identified alternative-growth opportunities that the community could pursue if it lost some of its defense facilities. But those new approaches never got anywhere. Established interests, especially Newport News Shipyard, undercut the PATC initiative. Intergovernmental fragmentation and conflict undermined both PATC and the Plan 2007 process. Only the BRAC'95 effort to defend the existing military structure was popular enough to overcome local political fragmentation. Clearly, some measure of local political cohesion is necessary to carry out new initiatives that go against the grain.

Other than the growth and high-technology interests, there were no viable sources of conversion or diversification advocacy in Hampton Roads. Local unions, which represent workers at Newport News Shipyard, Norshipco, the Norfolk Naval Yard, and the Norfolk Naval Aviation Depot, did not consider conversion. Rather, they joined with their employers and others in the community to oppose the cutbacks and hoped for the best. The Virginia AFL-CIO headquarters in Richmond opined that nothing could be done about the situation; there would simply have to be layoffs.[51] Nor does the community have strong peace-advocacy organizations that might have publicly articulated the value of building a peace economy to serve human needs.[52] And as noted above, neither the South Tidewater Association of Ship Repairers nor the Tidewater Association of Service Contractors advocated public-sector conversion or diversification assistance for their members, much less a peacetime economy.

Thus, despite the conversion and diversification efforts of a number of defense businesses, Hampton Roads at the end of the 1990s looks as it had at the beginning of the decade, or perhaps, as it had at the beginning of the 1980s, before the Reagan administration's defense build-up began in earnest. It is heavily dependent upon defense and has an even larger portion of the nation's defense employment than it had a decade ago.

Hampton Roads's growth interests continue to promote more of everything—more military activity and also more downtown retail development, tourism, and even high-technology-based manufacturing. But it is not clear that they can have everything. As noted previously, military installations occupy considerable land already, and Oceana is expanding as its employment increases by 60 percent. NASA/Langley's research is highly touted, but after a century of Pentagon-led development that has stunted the development of a competitive manufacturing complex, the area lacks the entrepreneurial, financial, and manufacturing infrastructure needed to commercially exploit these inventions. Although the city of Hampton has established a number of small-business incubators, including a technology incubator that it hopes will commercialize NASA inventions, to date almost all new patents have gone to out-of-state firms. Even Newport News Shipyard has failed to create a competitive cluster of shipbuilding firms or to spin off new firms in the area. It purchases only modest amounts locally; more importantly, it requires its subcontractors to focus solely on supplying its needs, which precludes their developing new products for other markets.

The public sector has not made the investments that would give commercial shipbuilding—a logical extension from military work—a foothold. As noted above, Virginia refused to subsidize a double-hulled tanker facility for the Metro Machine Corporation. When ship-repair companies asked the city of Norfolk to help dredge the Elizabeth River to allow the entry of larger ships (both military and commercial), the city refused. As discussed above, the region's economic-development agencies do not focus on placing skilled former defense workers in positions that use their skills.

Rather, in the mode of traditional growth promotion, both the chamber-led regional-development agencies and the development departments of each jurisdiction focus on downtown commercial real-estate development and attracting corporate branch plants, not labor-based development. To be sure, that is the path of least resistance, since creating a high-tech, entrepreneurial economy would require region-wide efforts as well as substantial new resources, sustained over many years. Given the poor fiscal condition of many jurisdictions in Hampton Roads, the effort would entail a substantial sacrifice. Community opinion-makers are not particularly satisfied with the status quo, however. Growth advocates decry the region's lower-than-national-average wages[53] and continue to promote regional cooperation for business recruitment as the way to raise them.[54] If defense employment continues to be its mainstay, however, the community may be incapable of adopting policies that could achieve the vibrant, high-wage economy it seeks.[55]

NOTES

1. The MSA also includes Currituck County in North Carolina, which generally does not participate in community initiatives and therefore is not included in this analysis.

2. Robert Arthur, *History of Fort Monroe.* 1930, pp. 1–27. Reprint, Ann Arbor, MI: University Microfilms International, 1979.

3. Marshall W. Butt, *Portsmouth Under Four Flags, 1752–1961.* Portsmouth, VA: Portsmouth Historical Association, 1961, pp. 14–27.

4. Christopher Silver, "Norfolk and the Navy: The Evolution of City–Federal Relations, 1917–46," in ed. Roger W. Lotchin, *The Martial Metropolis: U.S. Cities in War and Peace.* New York: Praeger, 1984, p. 109.

5. As Lotchin points out, many Sunbelt cities established military-affairs committees during the twentieth century to attract military installations. See *The Martial Metropolis.*

6. Silver, "Norfolk and the Navy."

7. Butt, *Portsmouth Under Four Flags, 1752–1961*, pp. 28–29.

8. Silver, "Norfolk and the Navy," p. 114.

9. Ibid., p. 116.

10. Thomas J. Wertenbaker, *Norfolk: Historic Southern Port.* Durham, NC: Duke University Press, 1962, pp. 347, 359.

11. Parke Rouse, Jr., *Endless Harbor: The Story of Newport News.* Newport News, VA: Newport News Historical Committee, 1969, p. 33.

12. Ibid., pp. 34–48.

13. Ibid., p. 51.

14. Ibid., pp. 57–68.

15. Ibid., pp. 77–80.

16. David G. Temple, *Merger Politics: Local Government Consolidation in Tidewater Virginia.* Charlottesville: University Press of Virginia, 1972.

17. Commonwealth of Virginia, Commission on Local Government, *Report on the Comparative Revenue Capacity, Revenue Effort, and Fiscal Stress of Virginia's Counties and Cities 1988/89*, September 1991, and *1995/96*, July 1998.

18. Wertenbaker, *Norfolk*, p. 368.

19. Ibid., p. 365.

20. The region's port facilities were merged into one local authority. New regional-development organizations were formed: the Cultural Alliance of Greater Hampton Roads, the Tourism Coalition of Hampton Roads, and Future Hampton Roads (a chamber-led regional-development think tank and growth advocate). The Hampton Roads Small Business Development Center was formed in 1990 with sponsorship by both the Peninsula and Tidewater.

21. As a local economy expands, nonbasic (i.e., nonexport, local-service) jobs generally grow faster than basic jobs, as basic industries attract local suppliers and the expanding population attracts retail outlets. Thus, even if Hampton Roads's economic base had not diversified at all between 1945 and 1993, one would expect that the proportion of military jobs would have declined simply due to growth of the nonbase.

22. Virginia Employment Commission, *Covered Employment and Wages (ES-202 series) by 2-digit SIC Industry, 1979, 1989, 1993*; Robert J. Griffis, Ann D. Lang, and Timothy O. Kestner, *Department of Defense Employment Military and Civilian, 1993–94*, Virginia Employment Commission, July 1995. See also Robert J. Griffis and Timothy O. Kestner, *Department of Defense Employment Military and Civilian 1989–92*, September 1993. Calculations performed by the author. Regional economists calculated a multiplier

of about 1.5 for Hampton Roads military bases. However, the total multiplier for defense contractors is undoubtedly much higher, so an average regional multiplier of 2 is not unreasonable.

23. Mylene Mangalindan, "Hampton Roads, Hoping for Best, Braces for Worst." *Virginian-Pilot* (February 14, 1995). See also Griffis, Lang, and Kestner, *Department of Defense Employment Military and Civilian, 1993–94*; and Griffis and Kestner, *Department of Defense Employment Military and Civilian 1989–92*.

24. Griffis, Lang, and Kestner, *Department of Defense Employment Military and Civilian, 1993–94*.

25. Courtney Anderson, "Capturing a Labor Force for Virginia's Growth Industries." *Virginia News Letter* (Charlottesville: University of Virginia, Weldon Cooper Center for Public Service) 75, no. 5 (May 1999).

26. Thomas C. Parramore, *Norfolk: The First Four Centuries.* Charlottesville: University Press of Virginia, 1994.

27. Knowledgeable observers believe that part of the shipyard's initial downsizing, from 29,000 to 20,000, was not so much a response to defense-spending cutbacks as it was an internal restructuring to clean out a bloated administrative structure that had grown during the 1980s. On this view, some of the workforce reductions would have occurred without defense cutbacks. Observers also have pointed out that cutbacks and expansions are part of the shipyard's history, as they are of the shipbuilding and repair business generally. After the Vietnam War, for example, shipyard employment reportedly dropped to about 10,000 workers.

28. Under the Newport News Shipyard–Eletson deal, the Maritime Administration guaranteed $133 million of the $150 million financing for the vessels, which resulted in a much more favorable interest rate on the loan to Eletson. Other factors that favor commercial sales for the Newport News yard include growing world demand for double-hulled petroleum tankers, passenger ships, and container ships, as well as the cheaper U.S. dollar, improved American technology, and, reportedly, rising labor productivity. See James R. Herndon, "Local Shipyards Should Survive." *Virginian-Pilot* (March 13, 1995).

29. Indeed, the navy's insistence on its own military specifications required Newport News to use technology and equipment that were 20–30 years older than global standards according to some engineers. However, this is changing with the advent of the Department of Defense's new "open systems" specifications, which are to be compatible with commercial standards.

30. Because financially the shipyard performed well during the 1980s, the company and its parent until December 1996, Tenneco, had the "deep pockets" to enable it to absorb losses on commercial work, and some observers stated that this approach would ultimately interest other buyers in the shipyard's new double-hull tanker design. Still, without the necessary capital investments, critics doubted that the shipyard would be able to make commercial ships profitably and would soon revert back to 100 percent military contracting.

31. Sanford Gottlieb, *Defense Addiction: Can America Kick the Habit?* Boulder, CO: Westview Press, 1997, pp. 126–27. See also Laura L. Clauser and John L. Knapp, *Virginia's Local Economies 1998 Edition: Hampton Roads Planning District Number 23.* Charlottesville: University of Virginia, Weldon Cooper Center for Public Service, 1998.

32. Clauser and Knapp, *Virginia's Local Economies 1998 Edition*, p. 51.

33. "Newport News Shipbuilding Bids on Kuwait Frigate." *Virginian-Pilot* (May 3, 1995); and Christopher Dinsmore, "Shipyard Takes First Steps into Global Market—Frigates." *Virginian-Pilot* (March 19, 1995).

34. The navy has traditionally divided work between General Dynamics's Electric Boat facilities in New England and Newport News Shipyard, under the philosophy that having two yards provides sufficient capacity to meet a crisis requiring large-scale production, and to continue building if one yard suffers an accident. Since Electric Boat has only submarine-building capacity, it has received most submarine contracts in recent years. Newport News Shipyard builds and maintains nuclear carriers and has the capacity to build and maintain submarines as well, so it argued to Congress—against the navy's wishes—that it could build the new submarines more cheaply than Electric Boat, in part because it could spread overhead costs over its commercial and other military contracts. This position seemed to confirm the views of critics that the shipyard did not intend to seriously pursue significant amounts of commercial work, since high overhead is a major impediment to the shipyard's competitiveness in commercial markets.

35. Congress cancelled the third Seawolf in the early 1990s. Its revival in the mid-1990s may have had much to do with shipyard lobbying of a more defense-friendly Congress. See the discussion in chapter 1.

36. Estimates are derived from the Virginia Employment Commission's "Employer Information for Defense Contractors" list, the Virginia Employment Commission's ES-202 employment data file for 1993 (see note 22), adjusted with establishment data provided by the U.S. Census Bureau's *County Business Patterns* for Virginia, 1988. The calculations were performed by the author.

37. The following companies were represented in Hampton Roads as of 1994: American Management Systems, American Systems Corporation, American Systems Engineering Corporation, Computer Sciences Corporation, Electronic Data Systems, AFS Inc., IBM, Loral Aerospace, Martin Marietta, Northrop, Paramax Systems, QED Systems, Raytheon, Resource Consultants, Rockwell International, SAIC, Tracor-Vitro, TRW, VSE Corporation, and Westinghouse Electric.

38. AMSEC is headquartered in Baltimore and is a subsidiary of Science Applications International Corporation (SAIC), headquartered in La Jolla, California. SAIC employs 16,000 persons in 300 offices worldwide. Seventy percent of its work is with the federal government, and two-thirds of that amount is in defense. The AMSEC subsidiary employs about 1,000 persons near U.S. Navy bases.

39. As noted previously, the Hampton Roads Chamber of Commerce established its own private-sector-led economic-development agency in the mid-1980s, because it had grown frustrated with what it perceived to be the inability of local governments to cooperate effectively to promote economic development in the area. Therefore it is not surprising that the chamber would initiate a visioning process without direct participation by the public sector.

40. Nevertheless, Plan 2007 organizers did inform local public officials of the upcoming process by visiting the monthly meeting of the mayors, chairs, and city managers group, an informal gathering of the chief officers of all 15 Hampton Roads jurisdictions that has existed since about 1990. Also, the chamber sought the active participation and research support of two nonbusiness organizations—local universities and the Hampton Roads Planning District Commission (PDC), a regional-planning agency that serves all 15 jurisdictions. John Whaley, chief economist of the PDC, served as chief economic staff to the Plan 2007 process.

41. The state did provide a nominal amount of money to help PATC rent office space on the campus of Thomas Nelson Community College, a state institution.

42. Several informed observers found these statements consistent with the shipyard's tradition of keeping its subcontractors loyal by discouraging them from doing work for

others. And at least one federal official surmised that the shipyard succeeded in convincing Congress that its survival is crucial to the U.S. defense-industrial base, as evidenced by Congress's continued support for the CVN and CVX carrier programs and its decision to allow Newport News to share work with General Dynamics on the development of the new attack submarine.

43. This is a frequent and important criticism of high-technology stimulation efforts that, it is argued, ignore the needs of the existing manufacturing base in favor of futuristic visions of technology.

44. In addition to providing basic business-development services, PATC continued to pursue its vision of effectively linking workers with jobs. It conducted a survey of business-skill needs during the summer of 1995 to facilitate more rapid reemployment of dislocated workers. As part of this effort, PATC also organized a Peninsula Training Consortium to ascertain business-training needs and to identify training capacities whereby some businesses might provide training services to others. PATC also initiated an effort to make engineering course credits transferable among the five higher education institutions in the Hampton Roads region.

45. Jack Dorsey and Dale Eisman, "Oceana Comes Out a Winner." *Virginian-Pilot* (March 1, 1995).

46. Hampton Roads Planning District Commission Staff, "The Hampton Roads Military Complex." Unpublished paper, November 21, 1994.

47. "Anticipating BRAC'95" Conference, April 13, 1994, Norfolk, Virginia, sponsored by the Tidewater Association of Service Contractors.

48. Oceana will receive 56 F-14 Tomcat fighters from California, as well as 135 F/A-18 Hornet aircraft from Cecil Field in Florida. "Gains Top Losses." *Richmond Times-Dispatch* (March 1, 1995), pp. A1, A8; Hampton Roads Planning District Commission Staff, "Selected Impacts from the 1996–1999 Oceana Expansion," June 1996, p. 1.

49. "Everyone's Fighting Base Closing: Suddenly, a Megabase." *Virginian-Pilot* (January 23, 1995). Still, the jurisdictions continued to fight fiercely over other issues such as water supply and business recruitment.

50. Anderson, "Capturing a Labor Force for Virginia's Growth Industries."

51. It should be noted that Virginia is a right-to-work state, so unions are neither strong nor accepted by most company management. This weakness certainly doesn't give the unions a strong foundation upon which to argue for conversion, but unions at defense employers throughout the country generally have been reluctant to back conversion initiatives, choosing instead to support their employers' calls for more defense spending.

52. A small Peninsula Peace Education Center held a meeting about conversion early in 1992, but it did not follow the issue thereafter. The Norfolk Catholic Worker organization conducts occasional small demonstrations at military-ship launchings, but it is a tiny organization with no paid staff and its concerns are directed at the inhumanity of the war machine, not at alternative economic-development efforts.

53. The low wages are primarily the result of the tourist, local-service, branch plant, and military enlisted-personnel jobs. Military officer pay, however, is considerably above the national average.

54. For example, in 1999 Hampton Roads became the first American community to adopt a "citistate regional flag." *First U.S. Citistate Regional Flag* (http://www.citistates.com/hampton.htm). See Tom Shean, "Q & A: James F. Babcock Retired Banker: Regionalism Still a Huge Issue." *Virginian-Pilot* (August 2, 1998), p. D1.

55. See, for example, *Virginian-Pilot*, "Low Wages: What's Holding Us Back? Hampton Roads Still Far Below National Average." Editorial (March 14, 1999), p. J4.

1. ARLINGTON:

- Pentagon (7th Communications Group), D
- Naval Supply Systems Command, N
- Naval Sea Systems Command, N
- Naval Air Systems Command, N
- Bureau of Naval Personnel, N
- Henderson Hall, M
- Fort Meyer, A

2. ALEXANDRIA:

- Defense Mapping Agency, D
- Naval Facilities Engineering HQ, N
- Cameron Station, A

3. FAIRFAX:

- Fort Belvoir, A
- Defense Mapping Agency, D

4. PRINCE WILLIAM:

- Henry Diamond Labs, A

5. FAUQUIER:

- Vint Hill Farms Station, A

6. STAFFORD (FAUQUIER, PRINCE WILLIAM):

- Quantico Marine Corps. Combat Development Command, M

7. KING GEORGE:

- Dahlgren Naval Surface Warfare Center, N

8. CAROLINE:

- Fort A.P. Hill, A

Northern Virginia
Military Bases and Installations

A=Army, D=Department of Defense, M=Marines, N=Navy. Map adapted from: "Major Military Bases and Installations," *Governor's Commission: Base Retention and Defense Adjustment*, 1994.

4

The New Face of Defense: Systems Engineers and Bureaucrats in Northern Virginia

THE RISE OF THE HIGH-TECH DEFENSE ECONOMY

Unlike Hampton Roads, whose defense economy has undermined its economic performance, Northern Virginia has used defense and other government markets to launch a vibrant high-tech economy. Thus, post–Cold War federal procurement policies affected this community differently than they did Hampton Roads. Nevertheless, Northern Virginia growth interests and elected officials shaped the community's responses to defense-spending cutbacks, much as they did in Hampton Roads. This chapter describes those responses. To understand Northern Virginia, however, one must first understand something of the economy of the entire Washington, D.C. metropolitan area, and one must appreciate the forces that have, in the space of about 50 years, transformed this essentially placid community into one of the most dynamic areas in the world.

Since its origins at the beginning of the nineteenth century, the Washington, D.C. economy has had little else than the federal government's administrative offices as an export base. Commercial manufacturing never gained a foothold here, and even military-related production did not flourish.[1] Although the Washington Navy Yard was established in 1806, it never played a significant role in shipbuilding and repair because the navy believed it was too far from the sea.[2] For most of its history the federal bureaucracy was relatively small, so the District remained small as well. Its hinterland, with the exception of a couple of small towns such as Alexandria across the Potomac River, consisted of farms, rolling hills, and swamps.

That began to change in the 1930s with the establishment of President Roosevelt's New Deal programs and through other developments that expanded the federal bureaucracy. The trend continued in the 1940s as the War Department and, after passage of the National Security Act in 1947, the Defense Department, swelled to 23,000 employees. By the 1950s population and employment were spilling into the surrounding countryside. Although the District itself began to lose population, growth in the new suburbs accelerated and, during the 1980s, skyrocketed. By 1992 the District metropolitan area's population had topped four million.[3]

Several factors, including Cold War defense spending, are responsible for this explosive growth. Expansion of the federal government's administrative apparatus is one cause. By 1988, the federal government employed 390,320 civilians and 94,690 military personnel in the area.[4] The growth of special interest and lobbying organizations added many thousands of workers to that number. Also, the growth of the global economy drew foreign and domestic corporate offices and business-support activities that worked with foreign-mission staff and U.S. government representatives to develop international-trade opportunities. By 1989 the District was surpassed only by New York as a location for headquarters of international banking, finance, scientific, cultural, educational, humanitarian, and charitable organizations. And by the late 1980s, tourism accounted for a large portion of the region's revenues as well.[5]

But it is the rise of the computer, avionics, and the Internet that have contributed most to the amazing growth of the District-area economy. This new high-tech business base became established because it enjoyed strong and growing demand from a large market—the federal government. Although military spending has accounted for a large portion of this demand, other federal agencies have been frequent customers also.

High-tech services sold to the federal government can be broken down into two categories: information systems and weapon systems. Information-systems services are sold to virtually all government agencies, defense and civilian alike. They include data-processing and analytic services, design and integration of high-speed telecommunications networks, and software engineering. Their growth in the Washington area can be traced to the privatization of many information-management functions in the 1980s, coupled with the rapid development of information technology. During the 1990s the major information-technology growth engine in the area was the Internet—a Pentagon invention during the Cold War used to link universities, contractors, and procurement officials. The opening of the Internet to civilian use in the early 1990s generated a torrent of activity, further stimulating what was already a thriving software- and network-development industry.

Because it began as a government service-provider, the network industry has been concentrated in the District of Columbia area. It remains concentrated there now because the federal government is still the world's largest producer of information and because of the important role of federal government policy in shaping the industry. Thus, the area to the west, north, and east of the District, in a 25-mile arc around the city, has come to be known as the "Netplex," because of the concentration of computer-network firms there. Already by 1994, the Netplex was a close second to Silicon Valley in the number of high-tech companies, with the likes of America Online, MCI, Northern Telecom, General Electric Information Services, PSI, UUNET, and Metropolitan Fiber Systems headquartered there and many others such as Sprint, GTE, Hughes, and Intelsat doing business there.[6]

Weapon systems constitute the second major type of high-tech services sold to the government in the Washington, D.C. area. They are indeed *services*, not weapons per se. As Markusen et al. (1991) note, the primary product of this work is not equipment that will be deployed in battle, but software, that eventually "will be used to navigate spacecraft, eavesdrop on conversations in distant places and record faraway events, anticipate and monitor attacks by hostile powers, and perhaps destroy missiles in space . . . but . . . [production of the weapons themselves] will happen in distant locations. . . ."[7] Weapon-system prototypes also are developed here but, again, final production occurs elsewhere. A related function performed by the so-called systems houses in the area is the development of entire procurement systems for weapons, including specifications of equipment and software to be used.

Several factors seem to be accountable for this separation of production from design in weapon systems, with the location of the latter function in the D.C. area: One is the fierce rivalry among the armed forces, which leads each to develop and fund as many of its own weapon systems as it can, despite the resulting system redundancies. A second factor is the increasing technological sophistication of modern weaponry; specifically, the use of very complicated and costly electronic components in all weapon systems, which has lengthened development times and increased the number of personnel who must be involved in guiding the systems through their multiyear development processes. This has spawned a Pentagon bureaucracy attached to the management, logistics, and engineering of weapon systems. As explained in chapter 1, weapon-system cost increases, coupled with interservice rivalry, have also resulted in slower production schedules and in smaller numbers of units actually produced, but not in less research and development (R&D). Indeed, half of the dramatic Defense Department budget increase of the 1981–1985 period was for R&D and new weapons development.[8] Thus defense contractors have found it necessary to cluster near the Pentagon, where weapon-system decisions are made. As a contractor explained to Markusen et al.:

"To be successful in competing later, you have to be involved as a contractor from the very front end of that requirements definition until the time they actually go on the street with the request for proposals. . . . If you aren't involved in it from the beginning, you might as well forget it because you have to understand what the air force really wants." Often, that may involve a shop near the operational bases. More and more, however, it also means a presence near the seat of high-level strategic thinking.[9]

Pentagon decisions are not the only important ones, however. A third factor that explains the concentration of defense contractors in the Washington, D.C. area is the increasing congressional scrutiny of the weapons-procurement process, which has induced both the Pentagon and contractors to step up their efforts to influence federal legislators. To this end, most major defense contractors have established at least government-relations offices in the area and many, such as General Dynamics, have established their corporate headquarters there as well.

This high-tech economy did not grow up inside the District but, for the most part, in the surrounding area. Beginning with the construction of the Pentagon in sparsely settled Arlington County in 1943, the high-tech civilian and defense sectors moved into the undeveloped areas surrounding the city, especially Northern Virginia. By 1993 there were 791,930 civilian and military jobs in the Northern Virginia suburbs. The region's major industries were business services and communications (the high-tech defense and civilian contractors) and the federal government (both civilians and military). This economic structure had remained relatively constant since 1979, indicating that the region had, from the beginning of its growth period, been dependent upon the federal government.[10]

It is difficult to describe Northern Virginia's defense dependence with precision, however, since many high-tech information-systems firms produce services for the Department of Defense as well as for nondefense and, in some cases, even nongovernment markets. Even some of the companies that design weapon systems may also produce for nondefense government agencies. (This, of course, is a strength of the Northern Virginia economy and it indicates how smoothly some firms may be able to move from defense to civilian work, at least within the government market, but it makes defense-dependency analysis somewhat difficult.) Based upon the estimates of Robert Griffis of the Virginia Employment Commission, roughly 20 percent of Northern Virginia's 791,930 jobs were in defense prime or subcontractors in 1993. Assuming an economic base multiplier of 2, whereby each defense-related job supports one additional local retail or service job, 40 percent of area jobs could be regarded as defense dependent.[11]

The business-services industry comprises two-thirds of Northern Virginia's defense-procurement work, while manufacturing and telecommunications each account for about 15 percent. As previously described, business services involves either developing and integrating computerized management and information systems that may link organizational entities, or weapon-systems software, such as flight simulators or submarine-warfare simulation. These and related industries are sometimes called the "CCI industry"—computer, communications, and information.[12] The bulk of the defense-manufacturing employment is in office, computing and accounting machines, instruments and supplies, other transportation equipment, and radio, television, and communications equipment.[13]

In 1991 over 300 prime contractors in the business- and engineering- and management-services industries were located in Northern Virginia. Some of the nation's largest companies with Northern Virginia defense-contractor offices include Electronic Data Systems, Mitre Corporation, IBM, Grumman Aerospace (now Northrop-Grumman), SAIC, Honeywell, TRW, BDM International, Unisys, Boeing, PRC, CACI, VSE Corporation, Raytheon, Dyncorp, Magnavox, Martin Marietta (now Lockheed-Martin), and Xerox. Within the durable-goods manufacturing industries, especially office computing and accounting machinery, instruments and supplies, and radio, television, and communication equipment, Northern Virginia had almost 90 prime contractors in 1991, including Unisys, Honeywell, Contel, Federal Computer Corporation, SMS Data Products Group, Zenith, Xerox, Navcom Systems, SAIC, McDonnell Douglas (now part of Boeing), Magnavox, TRW, PRC, Federal Systems, and Hughes. Most defense contractors are located in office parks in Fairfax County, which, as of 1993, had about 45 percent of Northern Virginia's total jobs. Indeed, Fairfax annually captures about one-third of Virginia's total defense-procurement dollars. Arlington County also had a significant concentration of defense contractors, mostly near the Pentagon, in office complexes such as Crystal City.[14]

In addition to defense contractors, in 1993 the Northern Virginia area was home to 80,340 Department of Defense employees (33,166 military personnel and 47,174 civilians). Over one-half of these persons (43,003) were located in Arlington, at the Pentagon (26,000), the Crystal City office complex (16,000 navy military and civilian employees), and Fort Meyer (2,622 personnel, mostly army). Alexandria hosted 11,870 army personnel. Fort Belvoir in southern Fairfax County had 7,863, mostly army, personnel, and the Quantico Reservation in southern Prince William County had 8,773 personnel, most of whom were navy–marine military and civilians. The Vint Hill Farms Army Intelligence Station in rural Fauquier County had about 1,400 personnel in 1993. These are "station strength" employment numbers, which include only full-time, permanently assigned military and civilian personnel. Part-time, temporary, and transitional personnel as well as national guard and military reserves are excluded.[15]

COMMUNITY CONTEXT: SUBURBANIZATION AND GROWTH INTERESTS

As population and employment grew in the suburbs of Northern Virginia, they created a local political culture that constitutes the context in which defense cutbacks are interpreted and responses fashioned. To appreciate that context, it is necessary to briefly describe the suburbanization process itself. The suburbanization of the Washington, D.C. area followed a path similar to that of communities across America during the post–World War II period. In each case, federal mortgage insurance and federal highway building encouraged young couples to spend their pent-up wartime savings on new, single-family tract housing outside the city and to commute to work. In most communities, development grew along major transportation arteries built with federal and state funds, and from there it spread, like a tree's root system, farther into the undeveloped area. The resultant growth pattern looked like spokes of a wheel radiating outward, with rings of denser development nearer the city. Sometimes a major employment center (a factory or office) would find a suburban location first, to be followed by housing and then retail and commercial development. Sometimes housing was the first new use to be developed. Development did not spread evenly, of course, but clustered, to some extent, at nodes where highways crossed. This gave rise to the now-infamous "edge cities"—dense clusters of office and retail establishments that sprang up to challenge the dominance of the central city.

By the 1970s two important spokes connected the District with its hinterland: I-270, leading north to Hagerstown, Maryland; and the Pentagon–Dulles Airport corridor, leading westward from Arlington through Fairfax to Loudoun County. They and other spokes were connected by I-495, Washington's well-known Beltway. By this time an inner ring of suburban jurisdictions—Arlington, Alexandria, and Fairfax in Virginia and Montgomery in Maryland—had begun to grow. Between 1930 and 1990 the population of Fairfax County increased from 23,155 to 818,623. By 1996 Fairfax County had an estimated 911,300 residents, about 55 percent of the Northern Virginia total. Arlington County had 180,600 and the city of Alexandria, 115,000. By 1996 a second ring of suburbs, farther out from the city, had developed. Prince William County had 247,700 residents and was growing rapidly, Loudoun County had 125,500, Fauquier County, 51,200, the city of Manassas, 32,600, and Culpeper County, 31,700[16] (see map at beginning of chapter).

As in other American communities, growth interests—developers, financiers, real estate brokers, and construction companies—drove the development process in the Washington suburbs. Usually they were well ahead of efforts to plan for or channel growth into designated areas where adequate services could be provided or where transportation networks could be laid out, or to save areas for open space and recreation. The infamous William "Til" Hazel, for example, whose development company built a significant amount of suburban Northern Virginia, worked indefatigably to overturn every local government attempt to plan, channel, or slow growth.[17] Due in part to Hazel's success, Northern Virginia's (especially Fairfax County's) road system is ill equipped to serve the traffic that uses it. As a local planning director quipped: "Northern Virginia starts where the traffic stops." Indeed, Northern Virginia has become a textbook example of both the sprawl (low-density, land-intensive, automobile-oriented development) that is synonymous with American suburbs, and congestion, a problem that heretofore has afflicted mainly central cities.

Hazel's success produced another result as well. It helped to galvanize an aggressive environmental-preservation movement, comprised of well-heeled estate owners in the outer suburbs and recent middle-class suburban immigrants who watched as increasing congestion turned their suburban dreams into nightmares. During the 1990s Northern Virginia's environmental coalition won one battle after another with growth interests (even as sprawl continued), derailing a plan to move the Washington Redskins professional football team to an old railyard in Alexandria, defeating a proposed Disney theme park to be built on a Civil War battlefield site at Manassas, and stopping a large retail development by Hazel himself at another site near Manassas. Each case pitted environmental interests not only against a development company, but against the usual array of growth interests—chambers of commerce and local governments. Local government, however, approached these conflicts with considerable ambivalence, since some elected officials needed antigrowth votes and some local government agencies, such as planning departments, wanted to channel and regulate growth. Nevertheless, the dominant sentiment in local governments was supportive of development projects, especially ones that promised to increase real estate and sales tax revenues, which would enable them to pay for the services demanded by their growing populations. This growth–no growth war is an important contextual feature in Northern Virginia and it played a significant role in the community's responses to defense-spending cutbacks.

Other than the environmental and pro-growth interests (which include the local chambers of commerce and the Greater Washington Board of Trade—a regional chamber of commerce—and its research arm, the Greater Washington Research Center), Northern Virginia had few organized interests during the early to mid-1990s. Organized labor was, with the exception of local public schools, completely absent. Although two high-technology business-promotion groups— the Northern Virginia High-Technology Council and the Potomac Knowledge Way Project—would rise to prominence during the 1990s (in part due to concerns about industry dependence upon the federal government), they would play no role in the response to defense-spending cutbacks during the early to mid-1990s.[18] Thus the assessment of a local defense-business observer in 1995 seems quite apt: "We're a suburb of the federal government. There's no cohesive business community or local focus here. Rather, there are national and global companies, each with its own direct feed into the Defense Department."

The public sector also lacked regional cohesion, notwithstanding the work of a few regional public organizations. One of these is the Washington Council of Governments (WashCOG), which was founded in the 1980s to develop transportation plans that help the region reduce air pollution caused by automobiles. The Northern Virginia Planning District Commission (PDC) serves the inner-ring suburbs and the Rappahannock–Rapidan PDC serves several of the outer-ring ones, but, unlike the Hampton Roads PDC, neither body maintains a high profile. Also, during the mid-1990s, the Greater Washington Board of Trade (the regional chamber of commerce), at the urging of the state, formed the Greater Washington Marketing Partnership to attract new businesses to the region. Nevertheless, by the end of the 1990s Northern Virginia's local governments remained almost completely focused on increasing their own tax bases, even when this meant attracting businesses from Washington or from locations in the increasingly expensive inner-suburban ring. This competition also played a role in local responses to defense-spending cutbacks.

DEFENSE CUTBACKS AND LOCAL RESPONSES

Employment losses from defense-spending cutbacks had only modest impacts on the Northern Virginia economy in the 1990s, despite both Defense Department force reductions and contractor layoffs. But the employment losses that did occur were experienced unevenly throughout the region, at different times during the period, in some cases causing considerable dislocation and hardship. Defense Department employment in Northern Virginia decreased from 87,441 in 1989 to 80,340 in 1993, a loss of 7,101, or about 8 percent over the five-year period. Arlington, Alexandria, and Fort Belvoir suffered most of the loss. Three major facilities were closed or vacated through the Base Realignment and Closure (BRAC) process. Cameron Station, which employed about 867 workers in 1988, was slated for closing by BRAC'88; the closure process was completed during the mid-1990s. BRAC'93 targeted the Vint Hill Farms Army Intelligence Station (1,410 employees) in Fauquier County for closing by 1997 and it also approved the layoff of 4,000 and the transfer of 12,000 navy personnel from the Crystal City office complex in Arlington by 1997. And in 1994 the army's small Woodbridge Research Facility in Prince William County, which employed 60 persons, was closed. The BRAC'95 process did not bring significant new cutbacks to the region.

On the procurement side, the picture is more complex. Real (inflation-adjusted) defense-procurement spending in Northern Virginia decreased in all but one year between 1985 and 1989.[19] Between 1989 and 1994, however, real defense-procurement spending in the region, for both information systems and weapon systems, increased steadily. However, since some large defense companies maintain only small proposal-writing staffs or headquarters operations in the area and send the procurement dollars to their facilities in other states, the amount of defense procurement spending that remains in the Washington metropolitan area cannot be stated with precision (nor is it known how many local firms serve as subcontractors to prime contractors in other states[20]). Nevertheless, one regional economist estimated that overall, less than 20 percent of procurement amounts leaks out of the region.[21] Aggregate employment data shed more light on the subject. Employment data for 1979, 1989, and 1993 show steady increases in the region's largest defense industries—business services and engineering and management services. However, in electronic-equipment manufacturing, instruments and related products, transportation equipment and communication, employment increased significantly from 1979 to 1989, but then declined somewhat from 1989 to 1993.[22]

Some officials who administer the federal Economic Dislocation and Worker Adjustment Assistance program (EDWAA) at various locations in the region contended that there was substantial defense-related worker dislocation between 1989 and 1993.[23] Analysis by the author of Worker Adjustment and Retraining Notification (WARN) Act notices filed by companies laying off 50 or more workers showed that 3,567 private-sector defense-related dislocations occurred in Northern Virginia between January 1, 1991 and October 31, 1993, mostly from the Federal Systems Corporation in Manassas. Local EDWAA officials estimated that an additional 1,500 jobs were lost from firms that employed less than 50 workers and thus were not covered by the provisions of the WARN Act. This would bring the total to 5,067. These 5,067 private-sector jobs, coupled with the 7,101 Department of Defense jobs lost from 1989 to 1993, constitute a sizable number, although they account for only about 1.5 percent of the 791,930 jobs in Northern Virginia. Assuming an economic base multiplier of 2, about 3 percent of total jobs were lost due to defense cuts.

Moreover, the 1989–1993 period, and especially the years 1990–1992, were recession years in the region, during which many workers in real estate, construction, and banking lost their jobs. Furthermore, defense-related job losses constituted only part of the employment cutbacks in the federal government. Between 1993 and 1995, for instance, the number of executive-branch workers in the region dropped from 316,000 to 302,000, as the Clinton administration reduced the size of the federal bureaucracy. Thus it is easy to understand why EDWAA officials, who assist dislocated workers, perceived there to be a significant problem.

On the other hand, the region's unemployment rate remained at least two percentage points below the state's low rate throughout the 1990s, only briefly rising as high as 4 percent during the trough of the 1990–1992 recession.[24] And by the end of the decade most dislocated workers were having little difficulty finding replacement jobs. Indeed, by 1998, Northern Virginia companies were reporting 23,000 vacancies in the information-technology and telecommunications industries alone.[25] Therefore the picture that emerges is one of a turbulent labor market, especially in defense-related industries, where workers faced significant job insecurity and dislocation. Nevertheless, they also enjoyed some reemployment opportunities during the first half of the decade, and many more during the latter half.[26]

Defense-Contractor Responses

Beginning in the 1980s and continuing into the late-1990s, Northern Virginia's defense contractors exhibited responses similar to those of Hampton Roads contractors, as well as to those defense contractors elsewhere in the nation. These include downsizing, merging with other companies, and cutting back on subcontracting. Within both the services and manufacturing sectors many large contractors cut back on subcontracting so as to continue to employ as many of their own workers as possible. Westinghouse (electrical equipment), Boeing (computer-programming services), VSE (engineering services), and SAIC (commercial physical research) are good examples of this strategy. Some of the nation's largest defense contractors merged; examples include Lockheed and Martin Marietta, Northrop and Grumman, and Loral and IBM and Unisys. Downsizing is a strategy that most companies pursued, with or without mergers; General Dynamics is perhaps the most well-known example of a company that moved its headquarters to Northern Virginia, only to divest many of its divisions. Another example is Federal Systems Corporation, located in Manassas. Federal Systems (which was sold by IBM to the Loral Corporation in 1994 and then to Lockheed Martin in 1996) makes military computer networks and anti-submarine-warfare technologies for the navy. Between 1990 and 1994, Federal Systems reduced its 5,200-member workforce by 62 percent, down to less than 2,000 workers.

Some Northern Virginia companies tried to diversify out of defense work into other government contracting and, in some cases, commercial work. In both cases, diversification often was achieved by acquiring new individuals or entire companies with the expertise to do the new work. DynCorp is an example of this strategy. It added to its competence in maintaining U.S. enemy-submarine-monitoring ships by starting to operate ships that respond to oil spills. Also, the company won a contract with the U.S. Department of Energy to maintain and operate the nation's strategic-petroleum reserve, and it designed a computer-based sorting system for the U.S. Postal Service. Similarly, BDM Corporation, an engineering- and professional-services firm, used its military technology to manufacture lead-acid batteries for electric cars; it also converted its air force air-traffic-control system into one for the Federal Aviation Administration and used its enemy-detection software to create traffic-simulation software for the U.S. Department of Transportation. In addition, BDM acquired several nondefense professional-services firms as subsidiaries.[27] Another example is the Computer Sciences Corporation, a large data-processing firm that by 1990 had begun to diversify out of defense work into processing environmental-contamination claims for the U.S. Department of the Interior.[28]

As these examples show and as many observers confirmed, diversification for these firms (like the business- and engineering-services firms in Hampton Roads) meant working with other federal government agencies and, increasingly, state and local governments as well. Several reasons account for this: One is that the efforts of some large defense contractors to move into nongovernment, commercial markets were unsuccessful, because they could not reduce their overhead costs enough to be competitive with smaller companies or with those that are used to working in mass markets. Also, some defense firms' products or services had no direct commercial equivalents, and the project-specific nature of some of the services and products provided by defense contractors differs markedly from the mass-market nature of many commercial markets. Thus large firms that were not willing to commit substantial time and resources could not enter nongovernment commercial markets. The growth of Defense Department procurement spending in Northern Virginia after 1989 and, perhaps more importantly, the continuing growth of federal, state, and local government demand for information-technology services convinced some large firms that they did not need to convert to nongovernment markets.[29]

Small firms in the software-engineering and computer integrated-systems industries suffered adverse effects from the decrease in subcontract work from the larger firms, as well as from the entry of larger firms into the smaller firms' markets. Some were knocked out of business entirely, while others found that they could only stay in business by focusing on other federal agency contracts, such as with the Environmental Protection Agency. Some small firms were acquired by prime contractors who wanted the innovative technology that many small contractors possess. In the computer hardware (electronic-equipment) industry, rising production costs and falling sale prices forced all but the largest companies out of the market. Within other industries, however, such as contract construction, small defense contractors were able to find work with state and local government agencies, much as larger contractors did.

COMMUNITY RESPONSES TO PROCUREMENT CUTBACKS

Individual Localities

As discussed previously, regional cooperation is not an established norm in Northern Virginia. Although some amount of interjurisdictional cooperation characterized public responses to Base Realignment and Closure Commission decisions, localities handled procurement cutbacks on their own, or not at all. The efforts of Fairfax and Arlington counties and the city of Manassas are the most noteworthy. All three jurisdictions practice traditional strategies of growth promotion through business recruitment. Defense-spending cutbacks did not cause them to reconsider these strategies—only to redouble them. None of these localities tried to help defense companies convert to civilian markets by retraining their workers, and no organized groups asked them to do so.[30] Yet, professionals administering services to dislocated workers complained that these services were insufficient to meet the demand. These complaints called forth only small and belated responses, however.

Fairfax County

In 1989, James Scampavia, the research director of the Fairfax County Economic Development Authority, conducted a study of the nature, magnitude, and probable impacts of defense procurement-spending cutbacks on Fairfax businesses. Scampavia was concerned that declining procurement might have a serious impact on county economic activity. Using an input–output model and surveys of a few defense contractors, Scampavia concluded that few negative employment effects were likely.[31] Interviews with defense contractors conducted by Scampavia indicated that, as one put it: "Defense contractors were already practicing good business [principles]," planning and seeking out new markets to substitute for declining defense contracts. Nevertheless, between about 1990 and 1992, Fairfax economic-development staff monitored the activities of large corporations with offices in the county, mostly through newspapers. They noticed that some of these companies were downsizing their operations elsewhere in the United States, but not in Fairfax. These monitoring efforts ceased in 1992, after which time the county used its business-call program (through which staff visit about 200 firms per year) and liaisons to the 14 subchambers of commerce in the county to keep tabs on defense contractors.

Although this was a pragmatic way of handling defense-procurement issues, economic-development philosophy also played a role. Asked whether the authority would consider providing conversion assistance or information to small contractors who were squeezed out of defense markets by large firms, one official responded that it would be inconsistent with the authority's philosophy to do so. Rather, Fairfax County's approach to economic development is to build a climate conducive to business investment rather than to facilitate internal business development, in contrast, say, to the Peninsula Advanced Technology Center. How the county would have responded to a significant loss of employment through defense cutbacks is not clear, but Arlington County's actions may provide a clue.

Arlington County

In 1993 the Arlington Board of Supervisors established the Arlington Economic Futures Committee, a county-wide economic-visioning and strategy-formation group comprised of business leaders, citizens, and county officials. A couple of key events provided the impetus. A decision by the 1993 Base Realignment and Closure Commission to approve the navy's plan to transfer or lay off 16,000 personnel from Arlington's Crystal City office complex caused alarm among real estate interests in the Arlington Chamber of Commerce. Also, for years the chamber had been asking the County to reduce business taxes and offer subsidies to both attract new businesses and keep existing businesses from moving to Fairfax County. According to a chamber official, his organization's economic summit in the summer of 1993 embarrassed the county and induced it to form the Economic Futures Committee. A county official acknowledged a need to adopt new approaches to stimulate more development. The committee reviewed the county's approach to economic development and suggested a more aggressive strategy. In response, the county made several changes, including the adoption of more flexible procedures for dealing with developers and a lowering of the business-license tax rate. Thus, in the context of interjurisdictional rivalry, defense cutbacks provided a rationale for growth interests to make a case for more growth-friendly policies.

Manassas

Noteworthy by virtue of its inaction is the city of Manassas in Prince William County, which probably faced more defense-related job loss per capita than any other Northern Virginia community. Manassas is the home of the Federal Systems Company, which, during its transition from ownership by IBM to Loral between 1990 and 1994, reduced its 5,200-member workforce down to less than 2,000 workers. Although the Flory Small Business Development Center in Manassas and the state's dislocated-worker services centers helped laid-off workers, they were not able to meet the demand for services. Neither the city of Manassas nor Prince William County, which surrounds it, responded to this downsizing or to defense-spending cuts generally. They did, however, continue with ongoing efforts to develop the tax base of this bedroom community by attracting new companies to the area. In 1995 their efforts appeared to bear fruit as IBM and Toshiba America Information Systems announced a joint venture to invest $1.2 billion in a vacant IBM computer-chip plant and employ about 1,200 persons.[32] Citing this announcement and the recruitment of a new biotechnology plant earlier in the year, officials downplayed the impact of defense cutbacks and described the area as "booming."

Region-Wide Dislocated-Worker Services

Although none of the local jurisdictions responded to procurement cutbacks, state-funded agencies offered assistance to displaced workers. The Northern Virginia Manpower Consortium, located in Fairfax County, coordinates the region's Rapid Response system for responding to worker lay offs of 50 employees or more from a single company.[33] According to the federal Worker Adjustment and Retraining Notification (WARN) Act of 1988, firms are required to announce lay offs of this magnitude 60 days in advance. Rapid Response includes worker needs assessment and seminars at the work site, as well as job-search assistance through the state's local job-service offices. Typically, 30 percent of those separated from jobs in Northern Virginia in the early 1990s required job training and placement services funded by the Economic Dislocation and Worker Adjustment Assistance Act (EDWAA).[34] Many dislocations occurred at smaller firms or in numbers of less than 50; in such cases, employers were not required to file WARN notices or to allow Rapid Response staff onto their premises to provide assistance to workers.

As noted above, over 5,000 civilian defense-company employees and 7,000 military personnel were estimated to have lost their jobs during the 1991–1993 period, in addition to the thousands who were forced out of work by the recession of 1990–1992. The existing employment services were not sufficient to meet the combined demand from dislocated workers in the defense and banking industries. In order to address the large number of displaced professional workers, a special Professional Resource Center was established in Fairfax. Demand for the Center's job search and related services was so strong that the director stopped advertising it in 1994, with plans to open an additional Professional Resource Center in Alexandria at a later date.

Small-Business Development Centers

Northern Virginia, like other parts of the commonwealth, has been served since 1990 by small-business development centers (SBDCs) that are funded by the federal Small Business Administration, the Commonwealth of Virginia, and local governments and universities. Northern Virginia has two SBDCs. In the early 1990s, the Flory SBDC in Manassas had a budget of about $200,000 and a staff of five full- and part-time professional and administrative persons. Like the dislocated-worker services in the area, this SBDC faced waves of clients during the early 1990s as the Federal Systems Corporation downsized. As one staff person put it: "We had grown men in here crying." Many of these clients were professional workers with innovative product ideas, but the SBDC's meager resources made it difficult to serve them well. To overcome this barrier, the SBDC worked hard but unsuccessfully to garner additional funds from Virginia's General Assembly. Eventually, the federal Small Business Administration awarded this SBDC $300,000, to be shared with the Radford and Hampton Roads SBDCs, to increase the staff that assisted dislocated defense workers wanting to start their own businesses.

RESPONSES TO THE BRAC PROCESS: RESISTANCE AND REUSE PLANNING

Three major facilities and one small research-lab complex were closed or vacated through the Base Realignment and Closure (BRAC) process. Cameron Station, which employed about 867 workers in 1988, was slated for closing by BRAC'88; the closure process was completed during the mid-1990s. BRAC'93 targeted the Vint Hill Farms Army Intelligence Station (1,410 employees) in Fauquier County for closing by 1997 and also called for the laying off of 4,000 and transfer of 12,000 navy personnel from Arlington's Crystal City office complex. And in 1994 the army's Woodbridge Research Facility in Prince William County, which employed 60 persons, was closed. Just as growth interests forced Arlington County to respond to procurement cutbacks (albeit not with conversion), so too did they call for community responses to the BRAC process, both before and after decisions were taken. The Crystal City case provides an excellent example of this and illustrates the risks that local government officials take when they are perceived to be unsupportive of growth advocates' efforts.

The Crystal City Office Complex and Arlington County Task Force

Crystal City is a huge commercial development in southeastern Arlington County, near Washington's National Airport. It includes more than 11,000,000 square feet of office space, 275,000 square feet of retail shops, and several major hotels. The primary developer of the complex is the Charles E. Smith Companies, one of the largest developers in the United States. Smith owns and manages about 6.8 million square feet of the space, while Harvard University and the Zell Corporation own some of the other buildings. Among the complex's many tenants were four of the U.S. navy's largest commands,[35] occupying a total of 2.5 million square feet (much of it in Harvard and Zell buildings) and employing 16,000 military and civilian personnel. Also, 8,500 defense-contractor employees occupied 1.5 million square feet of space owned by the Smith Companies. These contractors were located at Crystal City because of the Pentagon's demand that they be close to the armed services with which they do business and because, as described previously, they needed to be close to Pentagon weapons-development decision-making to compete for weapon-system contracts later.

In March 1993 the preliminary base closure and realignment list appeared. It included the laying off of 4,000 and the transfer of the remaining 12,000 navy civilian and military personnel from the Crystal City office complex to other locations.[36] Sources differed in their assessment of the probable impacts of the navy's departure from Crystal City. One regional economist stated that its departure would actually help Crystal City's owners, as they would be able to upgrade the properties and then lease them at higher rents to higher-income tenants such as lawyers and other federal agencies. However, he believed that it would not be politically feasible for Arlington County officials to say so publicly. Rather, they would have to express outrage at the loss of jobs and economic activity, he explained. A representative of the Charles E. Smith Companies countered that Crystal City could find new tenants, but that the navy was a no-risk leaseholder, that keeping it at Crystal City would mean no "down time" for the space and thus no loss of cash flow and, most importantly, that lawyers would have less need to locate at Crystal City if the navy and most of the defense contractors moved out. In short, lawyers follow contractors, and contractors follow the navy. Chamber of commerce sources argued that the move would have a strong, negative impact on Arlington's economy, since the total job loss from the departure of most of the navy's 16,000 personnel at the site, as well as many of the 8,500 defense contractor employees[37] and thousands of jobs in hotels and retail establishments, could easily top 25,000, and might reach as high as 30,000.

Most local, state, and federal elected officials expressed surprise at the announcement that the navy would leave Crystal City. Since Crystal City is not a base, they did not expect it to be included in the BRAC process at all. But this was not the first time the navy had expressed dissatisfaction with its facilities at Crystal City or stated a desire to move. Beginning in 1984, the navy had periodically declared its intention to consolidate its commands in other facilities such as the Washington navy yard in the District of Columbia. Each time, Arlington County, the chamber of commerce, and the Charles E. Smith Companies marshaled forces to convince the navy (and Congress) to keep the commands at Crystal City—a pattern similar to that of Hampton Roads growth interests and boosters. The navy was particularly dissatisfied with the poor maintenance of the Harvard- and Zell Corporation-owned buildings that it occupied. In 1990 the Charles E. Smith Companies won a competition to develop a new complex for the navy at Pentagon City (also in Arlington, near Crystal City), but the plan reportedly foundered due to the opposition of a Pennsylvania congressman. According to several sources, the plan also lacked the support of Arlington County officials, since the navy would not be paying real property taxes.[38] Therefore a number of observers expected another attempt by the navy to leave Crystal City.

Soon after the March 1993 announcement that the Crystal City departure was under consideration by the BRAC Commission, a Crystal City Task Force was organized to fight the move. The task force was organized by U.S. Representative Moran, the area's congressman, because, as one observer put it, "[i]t's become politically astute to be near a closure."[39] In other words, the congressman was dutifully showing his concern for local jobs. Moran's committee included government officials and chamber of commerce representatives from Arlington, Fairfax, and Alexandria, as well as representatives of the Northern Virginia High Technology Council, the Commonwealth of Virginia,[40] and U.S. Senators Robb and Warner. Perhaps the most active participant in the fight to remove Crystal City from the BRAC list was the Charles E. Smith Companies. The Smith Companies financed much of the effort, including weekly meetings, trips to the areas where the Crystal City commands would be transferred, letter-writing campaigns to Congress, and research. The Smith Companies even sued the federal government (unsuccessfully) over the action and encouraged Arlington County to do so as well (they declined).[41]

After President Clinton signed the BRAC Commission list, Congressman Moran reconvened the Crystal City group to begin planning for the transition of the complex (as was typical in BRAC base-closing processes). The committee became the Arlington County Task Force and was chaired by the finance director of Arlington County. Its membership remained largely the same, but now also included the District of Columbia, small businesses, and the Washington Board of Trade. Beginning in August 1993 and for several months thereafter, the Task Force met monthly, focusing on three issues: (1) How to keep defense contractors at Crystal City after the navy commands left for other parts of the metro area; (2) identifying other activities, such as convention business, that could enable Crystal City's hotel industry, which employed about 5,000 workers, to continue to operate at full capacity; and (3) convincing the navy to reverse its decision to leave. The BRAC'93 process had uncharacteristically allowed for the possibility that the navy might strike a deal with Crystal City building owners such as Harvard, who reportedly wanted to sell its property to the navy. Under the provisions of an amendment to the 1994 Defense Authorization bill attached by Senator Warner and Congressman Moran, the navy was to review such options and make an official report by May 1, 1994. Many observers expected the navy to work out some arrangement to stay at Crystal City, but in late June it announced that it had completed its review of the options and would proceed with its planned move to White Oak, Maryland.

Nevertheless, the Smith Companies continued to press their case through connections in the Pentagon. On October 31 it appeared that these efforts might have some success when Deputy Defense Secretary John Deutch asked the navy to review its cost estimates for moving the Naval Sea Systems Command (NAVSEA) from Crystal City to White Oak.[42] Still, the review did not undo the navy's decision to leave Crystal City nor did proposals organized by Congressman Moran's office to sell some Crystal City buildings to the navy do so. Instead, the Pentagon recommended to the 1995 Base Realignment and Closure Commission that the Naval Sea Systems Command be transferred to the Washington navy yard in the southeast corner of the District of Columbia, instead of to White Oak, and that the Naval Surface Warfare Center in White Oak (which employs about 200 persons) be closed.[43]

The Crystal City case shows local growth interests in action: Organizing chambers of commerce as well as federal and state officials to resist a military departure and to continue fighting even after seemingly final decisions have been made. It also illustrates some of the ambivalence that local government officials may feel about the military, because, at least in facilities that the military owns (such as the proposed navy complex at Pentagon City), it demands services but does not pay property taxes. When Arlington County officials did not respond aggressively to the navy's proposed departure, however, growth interests pushed them to do so.

Cameron Station, Alexandria

The decision of BRAC'88 to close the army's Cameron Station is, no doubt, one of the few base closures in America that was welcomed by dominant interests in the community. The facility once employed as many as 4,000 civilians and 330 military personnel,[44] but city officials and the chamber of commerce were happy to see it closed, since 88 percent of its personnel reportedly did not live in the city and since, as a military installation, it paid no taxes to the locality. Moreover, developers and city officials alike viewed it as a prime site for new development. The 164-acre camp, which first opened as a supply depot in 1869, was built up during World War II as a temporary base and never received a clear mission. Instead, it became what one source called "Camp Odds and Ends," eventually housing 24 facilities, including the Defense Logistics Agency. Some of the camp's larger functions, such as the commissary and base exchange, were transferred to Fort Belvoir in Southern Fairfax County, but others were slated to leave the state.

Shortly after the closing announcement in 1988, a local citizen-activist and retired Pentagon long-range planner asked the city to constitute the Cameron Station Closing and Reuse Task Force, to which he was appointed chair. The task force included two city councilpersons and other interested citizens, including engineers, architects, business persons, and retirees, as well as an army liaison. During the next three years the task force developed a land-use and zoning plan for the base, which included a 50-acre park, 1,910 units of moderate-to-upper income townhouses and condominiums, 4,000 square feet of office space, and up to 80,000 square feet of retail space.[45] The land-use plan easily won city council approval, although a couple of environmental issues (e.g., removal of geese from the area) generated opposition from environmental interests. In January 1995 the Army Corps of Engineers began taking bids on 93 acres that were zoned for residential and commercial use.

The closing was to have been completed by January 1995, but the McKinney Homeless Act process, during which time developers of housing for the homeless and other low-income persons may propose development projects, took longer than expected. In July 1994 the Abundant Life Christian Outreach Ministries sought about 700,000 square feet of the base's warehouse space to house and provide education, medical services, child care, and counseling to homeless persons. However, Alexandria city officials, backed by Congressman Moran, staunchly opposed the proposal, claiming that such a facility would deter investment in the remainder of the complex. The federal Department of Health and Human Services eventually denied Abundant Life's request on the grounds that the organization did not have the financial resources to make the plan work. However, the department did approve proposals by another shelter and a food bank, each of which received one building on the perimeter of the base where they would not lower property values.[46]

Unfortunately, in the rush to transform Cameron Station into a high-quality living environment with valuable real estate and local tax revenues, the needs of some workers at the facility were overlooked. Even though Cameron Station was slated for closing in 1988, a workforce Transition Assistance Center reportedly was not established there until June 1994. As a result, many workers, especially the Hispanic and other minority food-service workers at the commissary, reportedly did not receive needed services in a timely fashion. Although some eventually were offered transfers to other facilities, others, such as the sales baggers in the commissary, reportedly received no reemployment assistance.[47]

Vint Hill Farms Station, Fauquier County

The Vint Hill Farms Station closing provides another example of the growth coalition in action as it planned the reuse of a facility slated for closure. It also sheds light on other reuse-planning issues, specifically the barriers to the inclusion of workers in base transition-planning efforts and the problem of poor coordination between the base, federal agencies, and state government in closing and reuse planning. Vint Hill Farms Station was an army intelligence listening post with 1,410 personnel in 1995, comprised of 1,010 civilians and 400 soldiers.[48] Established in World War II because of the area's rare magnetic-interference-free qualities, the station was reportedly so powerful that it could pick up conversations of German taxicab drivers during the war. It was located in still-rural but, by the 1990s, rapidly growing Fauquier County in southwestern Northern Virginia, and was the county's second-largest employer. BRAC'93 decided to close the installation by September 1997. About 780 of the civilians were offered the opportunity to transfer to a facility in Monmouth, New Jersey, which would take on Vint Hill Farms's mission, and the remaining 230 were to be laid off. The Intelligence Battalion of 450 military personnel was transferred to Fort Gordon, Georgia, in late 1994, and another group of 100 soldiers and 25 civilians was moved to Pennsylvania in early 1995. In addition to civilian and military personnel, the base also supported approximately 450 contractor employees who worked with a great variety of firms, from engineering services to facilities management.[49]

Apparently, no one in Fauquier County expected or made plans for the closing prior to the BRAC'93 action. Unlike the Norfolk Naval Base, which is venerated by the community, few people in Fauquier County even knew of Vint Hill Farms's existence until the spy station celebrated its 50th anniversary in 1992. After the BRAC'93 closing announcement, however, local reuse planning of the site proceeded swiftly. As at Cameron Station and other facilities, however, the process of planning for the reuse of the site was conducted separately from the process of planning new activities for the workers. Therefore base-reuse possibilities that would employ the existing workforce were not seriously considered.

In August 1993 the county constituted the Economic Adjustment Task Force, chaired by the president of the Fauquier National Bank, to coordinate reuse planning for the site. Other participants included officials of Fauquier County, the town of Warrenton and Prince William County, Congressman Frank Wolf and State Delegate Wood, the Virginia Power Company, the Defense Department's Office of Economic Adjustment, the army's Transition Coordinator, and staff from the Northern Virginia Planning District Commission and the Virginia Department of Economic Development.

The task force studied the buildings and grounds, it applied for and received a Defense Department Office of Economic Adjustment planning grant, it hired a full-time executive director and retained a consulting firm that developed four alternative base-reuse proposals. By June 1994 the task force had given preliminary consideration to various alternative uses for the site, including an expression of strong opposition to a proposal to locate a prison there. It then held public hearings to discuss various reuse ideas. By June 1995 the task force had endorsed a reuse plan for approval by the Faquier County Board of Supervisors. The plan would maintain the same mix of uses that already existed at Vint Hill Farms: housing, education, recreation (pool and gym), offices, and warehousing. The plan called for reuse of the base's magnetic interference-free qualities as well as its extensive network of antennas, microwave and radio towers, telephone wires, and fiber-optic cables for a high-tech office park or similar use. The plan included the creation of a local reuse-implementing authority that would receive the property from the federal government and market it to developers.

Although a majority of task force members voted to endorse the reuse plan, environmental interests opposed it. Organizations such as Keep Faquier Clean and the Piedmont Environmental Council that in 1994 had joined with many others to dissuade the Disney Corporation from building a historical theme park a few miles from Vint Hill Farms now voiced strong opposition to the use of Vint Hill Farms as an economic-development engine. In particular, they opposed use of the base's substantial excess-sewer capacity to support growth in the area, and many also opposed using the base for low-income housing. Some opposed the creation of the local reuse authority to manage redevelopment of the base, because, they believed, any government-affiliated entity would allow too much growth in the area. Nevertheless, after concessions were made to the environmental-protection interests, the reuse plan was approved by a 3–2 vote of the Fauquier Board of Supervisors. As a concession to environmental interests, the new Vint Hill Economic-Development Authority would not receive tax revenues to support its marketing and redevelopment of the area, no county-elected officials would be allowed to serve on the authority's board, and the authority would automatically dissolve after the redevelopment plan was implemented. Moreover, the plan pledged to retain not only the existing mix of uses at the facility, but also the existing population and employment numbers (but not the workers).

The worker-transition and -adjustment process was handled separately from the base reuse-planning process, by the base's transition office, under the Vint Hill Farms Directorate of Community and Family Activities.[50] The transition office received a special Defense Department grant of $100,000 per year to support these efforts. After considerable effort on the part of the directorate and Virginia state agencies, the office was able to access federal EDWAA retraining funds for some workers prior to their being laid off from the base so that they could stay in the community (rather than transfer to New Jersey) without enduring a long period of unemployment.[51] Such incumbent-worker training occurred in only a few communities across the country.

Although the transition office provided a wide array of services to base employees, these services were geared towards providing workers with employment opportunities away from the base. There was no formal connection between the real estate planning process carried out by the Fauquier County Task Force and reemployment for the workforce.[52] In fact, the two planning processes were funded by two separate federal agencies. The Department of Labor funded (part of) the workforce-transition process; the Defense Department's Office of Economic Adjustment funded the base reuse-planning process, but it did not encourage worker involvement in the planning process. The Fauquier County Task Force included neither army nor contractor employees. However, in the fall of 1994, the Directorate of Community and Family Activities formally requested that the reuse task force explicitly consider the existing workforce in its planning process. According to task force members, the workforce was then considered. Still, no attempts were made to constitute a structured workforce-led base-reuse planning process or to build explicit worker involvement into the reuse-planning process.[53] Thus initiatives that would link base reuse with worker reemployment, such as a plan to have a number of Vint Hill Farms personnel become transition-office trainers, received no hearing in the Fauquier County Task Force. Nor were other, possibly better ideas developed to minimize worker dislocation through viable enterprises.

Lack of coordination between federal programs that supported employer conversion and those that supported worker retraining plagued the defense-downsizing process nationwide, at both bases and defense contractors.[54] Several factors seem to account for the lack of inclusion of workforce reemployment in the base reuse-planning process, at least at Vint Hill Farms: One, of course, is the fact that there is no institutional linkage between the Defense Department's Office of Economic Adjustment process and the Department of Labor's worker-adjustment programs, and the purposes of the two programs do not dovetail. The Office of Economic Adjustment encourages local reuse committees to include all relevant local stakeholders as participants, but the determination of the identities of the local stakeholders is left to the local government and dominant interests. Therefore the Vint Hill Farms Task Force included public officials and growth interests, but neither worker nor environmental interests. A second factor is that the community at large was not concerned about the workforce or jobs at the base. This probably was due to the fact that few area residents knew much about the secretive installation. A third factor is that the base employees did not ask to be included in the base reuse-planning process. They were not offered the chance to participate and the army focused their attention on transferring to Monmouth, New Jersey. Defense Department workers do have strong incentives for staying in the department until retirement. Federal retirement benefits are generous and the Defense Department provides helpful relocation assistance, including moving costs, the sale of one's previous home, and employment services for spouses in the new location. Moreover, because the transfer of workers to Monmouth would take place at one time, in September 1997, rather than gradually, Vint Hill Farms really could not be marketed to new users until after the army had completely vacated (i.e., after all the workers had gone). Thus a worker who might have wanted to stay at Vint Hill Farms rather than transfer to New Jersey assumed a considerable risk of waiting months or years for a new job and, perhaps, of not finding any suitable new job at the facility.

In addition to the difficulty of keeping skilled workers employed in Fauquier County, the base reuse-planning process suffered from other problems that resulted from an absence of institutional coordination between the army high command, the local base commander, and the community. With the exception of environmental clean-up provisions, the Defense Department reportedly had no clear policies on base closings and did not proactively address problems or opportunities. As a case in point, the Defense Department's Office of Economic Adjustment requires that the reuse-planning process be completed in a certain number of months, which happens to be well before the army's environmental assessment of the property typically is completed. Therefore an entire reuse plan could be invalidated if the army's environmental assessment showed problems that were not accounted for in the plan. (Fortunately for Vint Hill Farms, the environmental assessment did not identify new problems.) Also, once the 1993 BRAC process was concluded in August of that year, Pentagon agencies began to cut needed services for Vint Hill Farms even though the base was not to close until 1997. There appeared to be a lack of communication between the Defense Department, the Commerce Department, and the Department of Labor on base-closing issues. Within the Vint Hill Farms command itself, there was confusion about how dislocated-worker problems and opportunities should be addressed. Moreover, on many issues there was lack of communication between the Commonwealth of Virginia and the armed services. For example, the Rapid Response program, which informs workers who are going to be laid off about public programs available to them, had no official standing with base commanders; workers were not required nor even encouraged to consider using these services. Where services were provided, it seemed to be more a result of committed individuals in the transition office breaking through barriers and building new bridges than the result of clear policies. Despite the good work of the individual federal, state, and local agencies involved, the suboptimal results of the process highlight the need for more comprehensive federal conversion and adjustment policies.

CONCLUSION

A community with an economic base resting primarily upon growing industries that enjoy strong demand from a relatively stable market is in a good position to weather the effects of defense downsizing, especially when the downsizing itself is moderate. Indeed, Northern Virginia provides an excellent example of a modern, technology-driven economy and the military spending that is a significant part of that economy. It bears repeating that the rise of Northern Virginia's information-technology industry, not to mention weapons technology, is due in large part to government demand. Therefore defense contractors were able to shift out of defense spending when procurement cuts came, but they needed to go only as far as other government agencies, not to the more competitive nongovernment commercial market. Of course, commercial-market demand for information technology has grown dramatically and many Northern Virginia firms serve it as well as defense markets.[55] Nevertheless, the lesson is that government markets can play an important role in smoothing the transition from defense to a civilian economy.

At the community level, company conversion-assistance efforts were not considered. The closest that the community came to the ideals of conversion planning was in the efforts of state-funded agencies to assist dislocated workers, through counseling and retraining grants and through help in establishing their own businesses. These efforts were important but do not constitute a conversion program. Moreover, they were underfunded; only a portion of the dislocated workers who needed assistance received it. The dominant philosophy of how the community should deal with business in Northern Virginia is the traditional growth model rooted in land development and new business recruitment, as propounded by the local chambers of commerce and for the most part by local governments. This philosophy guided the community's responses to the BRAC process, both its resistance to closures and its efforts to plan for the reuse of facilities being closed. In this respect it acted in ways similar to its Hampton Roads counterpart. It resisted most military-facility closures, but after the closure decisions were finalized, it led the reuse-planning efforts. By and large, the growth coalition's interests were reflected in the reuse plans.

Nevertheless, throughout the 1990s the growth model was challenged by environmental interests. They not only succeeded in thwarting some commercial-development projects, but also in determining the reuse of a small military facility. The army's Woodbridge Research Facility, a 580-acre complex at the confluence of the Occoquan and Potomac rivers in Prince William County, was viewed by county officials and business interests as an economic-development site. But environmental interests persuaded Congress to turn the property over to the Department of the Interior for a wildlife refuge.[56] Environmental interests also influenced the Vint Hill Farms reuse plan. Thus, as discussed in chapter 2, organized opposition groups can challenge growth-interest objectives.

As in Hampton Roads, the nature and strength of local interests determined the nature of local responses to defense-spending cutbacks. The lack of an organized conversion or defense-worker interest insured that there would be no conversion planning in the area, outside of the diversification efforts of individual firms. The presence of professional dislocated-worker advocates at Vint Hill Farms, at the Flory Small Business Development Center in Manassas, and in the Job Service Centers did ensure that worker interests would not be entirely neglected. But in the case of Vint Hill Farms, they were not able to overcome institutional barriers to a stronger worker role in reuse planning.

NOTES

1. Constance McLaughlin Green, *American Cities in the Growth of the Nation.* New York: Harper & Row, 1957.

2. Ann Markusen, Peter Hall, Scott Campbell, and Sabina Deitrick, *The Rise of the Gunbelt: The Military Remapping of Industrial America.* New York: Oxford University Press, 1991, p. 214.

3. James Woodwell and Adrian Overton, *Economic Trends in Metropolitan Washington.* Washington, DC: Metropolitan Washington Council of Governments, December 8, 1993, p. 6.

4. Stephen S. Fuller, "The Internationalization of the Washington, DC, Area Economy," in ed. Richard V. Knight, *Cities in a Global Society*, vol. 35, *Urban Affairs Annual Reviews.* Newbury Park, CA: Sage Publications, 1989, p. 111.

5. Fuller, "The Internationalization of the Washington, DC, Area Economy," p. 116.

6. Thomas A. Stewart, "The Netplex: It's a New Silicon Valley." *Fortune* (March 7, 1994).

7. Markusen et al., *The Rise of the Gunbelt*, p. 213.

8. Ibid., p. 216.

9. Ibid., p. 220.

10. Virginia Employment Commission, *Covered Employment and Wages by 2-Digit SIC Industry, 1979, 1989, 1993*; U.S. Department of Labor, *Employment and Earnings, 1979, 1989, 1993*; Robert J. Griffis and Timothy O. Kestner, *Department of Defense Employment Military and Civilian, by Service Branch and Region, 1989–92.* Richmond: Virginia Employment Commission, September 1993; Robert J. Griffis, Ann D. Lang, and Timothy O. Kestner, *Department of Defense Employment Military and Civilian, by Service Branch and Region, 1993–94.* Richmond: Virginia Employment Commission, July 1995.

11. Robert J. Griffis, *Estimated Private Sector Defense Employment by Industry and Region in Virginia.* Richmond: Virginia Employment Commission, February 1993; Virginia Employment Commission, *Employer Information for Defense Contractors as of December 1992.*

12. Virginia Secretary of Economic Development, *A Case Study of the Impact of Defense Cuts on Northern Virginia's Economy.* Commonwealth of Virginia, October 12, 1990.

13. Robert J. Griffis, *Listing of Virginia's Prime Defense Contractors Ranked by Contract Amount, 1991.* Richmond: Virginia Employment Commission, February 1993; Robert J. Griffis, Ann D. Lang, and Michael A. Thacker, *Listing of Virginia's Prime Defense Contractors Ranked by Contract Amount, 1993.* Richmond: Virginia Employment Commission, September 1994; Griffis and Kestner, *Department of Defense Employment Military and Civilian, 1989–92*; Griffis, Lang, and Kestner, *Department of Defense Employment Military and Civilian, 1993–94.*

14. Woodwell and Overton, *Economic Trends in Metropolitan Washington*, pp. 74–78; Griffis, *Listing of Virginia's Prime Defense Contractors Ranked by Contract Amount, 1991*; Griffis, Lang, and Thacker, *Listing of Virginia's Prime Defense Contractors Ranked by Contract Amount, 1993*; Virginia Employment Commission, *Employer Information for Defense Contractors as of December 1992*; Robert J. Griffis, Ann D. Lang, and Timothy O. Kestner, *Defense Expenditures in Virginia.* Richmond: Virginia Employment Commission, June 1995.

15. Given the large number of trainees and transitional personnel at locations such as

Fort Belvoir and the Pentagon, the employment numbers given here can be regarded as an undercount. See Griffis and Kestner, *Department of Defense Employment Military and Civilian, 1989–92*; and Griffis, Lang, and Kestner, *Department of Defense Employment Military and Civilian, 1993–94*.

16. Laura L. Clauser and John L. Knapp, "Northern Virginia: Planning District Number 8. Table 2: Population of the Northern Virginia PD, 1990–96," in *Virginia's Local Economies 1998 Edition* (Charlottesville: University of Virginia, Weldon Cooper Center for Public Service, 1998); see also Clauser and Knapp, "Rappahannock–Rapidan: Planning District Number 9. Table 2: Population of the Rappahannock–Rapidan PD," in *Virginia's Local Economies 1998 Edition*.

17. See Joel Garreau, *Edge City: Life on the New Frontier.* New York: Doubleday, 1991.

18. The Northern Virginia High-Technology Council was founded in 1991, but it initially had a small membership base and did not play a significant role in local or state politics. By 1998, however, the organization had 750 company members representing 100,000 employees, a budget of $1.75 million, and a staff of 11. It had begun to successfully advocate for high-technology businesses with the Virginia General Assembly in Richmond. See James Schultz, "The Great Communicators." *Golden Egg* 1 (Herndon: Virginia Center for Innovative Technology, 1998). The Potomac Knowledge Way Project was launched late in 1994 by the Moreno Institute (a local foundation). It also advocated the development of a strong economic and social infrastructure for high-tech development in the region. It was created explicitly to expand the area's high-tech industries into the nongovernment, commercial sector. Its efforts to date include advocating for more computer usage by youth and for a greater recognition among the public at large of the importance of high technology in today's economy.

19. Timothy F. Canan, *Economic Trends in Metropolitan Washington.* Washington, DC: Metropolitan Washington Council of Governments, August 1991.

20. The picture is further complicated by the wave of mergers and restructuring of firms in defense industries, which affected a number of Northern Virginia firms. Loral Corporation's acquisitions of IBM federal systems in Manassas and Unisys defense systems in McLean and subsequent sale to Lockheed-Martin, as well as Raytheon's purchase of E-Systems, Inc., with 3,300 employees in the Washington area, are but two cases in point. In some cases, such as Loral's acquisition of IBM federal systems, the mergers resulted in substantial local job loss. See John Mintz, "Another Addition to the Loral Corral." *Washington Post* (March 22, 1995); and Mintz, "Raytheon to Acquire E-Systems, $2.3 Billion Merger Continues Trend." *Washington Post* (April 4, 1995). See also the discussion of defense-company mergers in chapter 1.

21. Fuller, "The Internationalization of the Washington, D.C., Area Economy."

22. Virginia Employment Commission, *Covered Employment and Wages by 2-Digit SIC Industry, 1979, 1989, 1993.*

23. Title III of the federal Job Training Partnership Act, called the Economic Dislocation and Worker Adjustment Assistance (EDWAA) Act, is administered through service-delivery areas throughout the state, including the Northern Virginia area (which has three offices) and the Alexandria/Arlington area (which has one office). In addition to EDWAA, these offices also administer other titles in the Job Training Partnership Act, including the large Title II for disadvantaged persons. Services include skills and preference assessment, occupational-skills training, on-the-job training, supportive services, and employability development.

24. Clauser and Knapp, *Northern Virginia*, p. 17.

25. Courtney Anderson, "Capturing a Labor Force for Virginia's Growth Industries." *Virginia News Letter* (Charlottesville: University of Virginia, Weldon Cooper Center for Public Service) 75, no. 5 (May 1999).

26. Peter Behr, "Federal Cuts Give the Private Sector a Paramount Role." *Washington Post* (April 4, 1995).

27. Kelly Jackson Higgins, "A New Vision for Virginia's Defense Industry." *Virginia Business* (May 1993).

28. Very few contractors appeared to have pursued foreign exports. In fact, only one Northern Virginia defense contractor, Booz Allen Hamilton, which is doing some work in Russia, could be identified as having engaged in exporting as a diversification strategy.

29. This finding is partially at odds with the results of a study of Washington-area federal government contractors conducted by Stephen Fuller of George Washington University in 1990, which found that 80 percent of the firms had nonfederal clients, often in the private sector, and that the products or services they sold to nonfederal clients were very nearly the same as those they sold to the federal government. See Stephen S. Fuller, "Federal Contractors in the Washington Area: Who Are They? How Have They Been Affected by Reductions in Federal Procurement? What is Their Future Outlook?" Unpublished paper, Association of Collegiate Schools of Planning (November 1990). See also Fuller, *Federal Purchases in Greater Washington.* Washington, DC: Greater Washington Research Center, December 1989; and James Scampavia, "Fairfax County Defense Industry Phase One and Phase Two Survey Results." Executive Summaries. Fairfax County, VA: Fairfax County Economic Development Authority, April and October 1990.

30. The following incident exemplifies local government attitudes toward conversion. When in 1993 the Virginia Department of Economic Development called a meeting in Northern Virginia to explain the federal Technology Reinvestment Project and offer assistance to companies and localities that might want to apply for funds, no local government representatives came to the meeting.

31. See also Fuller, "Federal Contractors in the Washington Area."

32. Paul Bradley, "Manassas to Get IBM–Toshiba Deal." *Richmond Times-Dispatch* (August 8, 1995); and Bradley, "Chips Outshine Magic Kingdom." *Richmond Times-Dispatch* (August 9, 1995).

33. Rapid Response is one of the dislocated-worker programs funded under Title III of the federal Job Training Partnership Act. Although Rapid Response is administered by the states, other portions of Title III, notably the Economic Dislocation and Worker Adjustment Assistance Act (EDWAA) as well as Title II (the largest portion, which serves disadvantaged persons), are administered by local service-delivery areas with minimal state supervision. Thus, while Rapid Response draws, in part, upon the services of the EDWAA training program, it is not always able to do so easily. See also note 51, below.

34. EDWAA is included in Title III of the federal Job Training Partnership Act (JTPA).

35. The major commands include Naval Sea Systems, Naval Air Systems, the Space and Naval Warfare Systems Command, and the Bureau of Personnel.

36. Naval Sea Systems, the largest command at Crystal City with about 3,800 workers, was slated to go to White Oak, Maryland. Naval Air Systems, the second largest command with 2,700 employees, would go to the Patuxent River in rural southern Maryland, where new facilities would be built. The Bureau of Personnel would go to Millington, Tennessee.

37. As of June 1994 the Arlington County Task Force had planned to ascertain the total magnitude of job loss through a survey of defense contractors, funded by an Office of Economic Adjustment grant. The outcome of that survey is not known.

38. At the time, says one observer, office-vacancy rates in Arlington were only 2 percent, which, in his view, caused the county to take the navy's long-term presence there for granted.

39. It may also be an indication of the absence of a strong, region-wide organization that could coordinate a regional response, such as the Hampton Roads Planning District Commission or Forward Hampton Roads. However, it should be noted that some existing regional organizations such as the Greater Washington Board of Trade and Wash COG could not become involved in the opposition because the interests of the Northern Virginia jurisdictions conflict with those of the Maryland jurisdictions.

40. One participant complained that the Commonwealth of Virginia was not particularly helpful and that a powerful state legislator from Hampton Roads had even suggested "sacrificing" Crystal City so that bases in Hampton Roads might be spared.

41. According to one knowledgeable source, Arlington blundered in turning the Crystal City "defense" effort over to the Charles E. Smith Companies, who, in turn, hired a leading accounting firm to develop the strategy. This firm, the source charged, did not follow the military value criteria used in the BRAC process, so its case was weak. Otherwise, the Smith Companies might have prevailed in their BRAC defense effort.

42. The cost of $74.5 million estimated during the BRAC'93 process was revised to $218 million in an April 1994 navy study. That fact, combined with a General Accounting Office report released in Fall 1994 that projected severe budgetary shortfalls in the Department of Defense, as well as prodding from Senator Robb, triggered the review. See "Navy Rethinks Move." *Arlington Journal* (November 2, 1994), pp. 1–2.

43. Northern Virginia officials and Congressman Moran agreed that this decision would ease the blow to Crystal City since, they stated, the thousands of Northern Virginians who work at the Naval Sea Systems Command could easily commute to the Washington navy yard, and the thousands of private contractors who work with the Naval Sea Systems Command could remain at Crystal City and still be physically close to the navy. However, one small-business-development official reported in August 1995 that contractors were already beginning to leave Crystal City and that many more would do so, now that the navy commands were slated to move.

44. Cameron Station employed about 876 workers in 1988 according to DOD data. (However, others stated that the facility employed 3,700 workers in 1988, a discrepancy that could be explained, in part, by the possible existence of trainees and other temporary personnel at the base.)

45. Steve Bates, "Cameron Station Plans Submitted." *Washington Post* (February 1, 1996), p. V1.

46. Steve Bates, "Homeless Groups Favored in Army Base Duel." *Washington Post* (July 4, 1994); Bates, "Charity Loses Bid for Army Post in VA." *Washington Post* (August 5, 1994); n.a., "Army Solicits Bids for Most of Base." *Washington Post* (January 26, 1995); n.a., "Alexandria Can't Wait for This Base to Close." *Richmond Times-Dispatch* (March 12, 1995).

47. Alexandria City officials reportedly began to sharpen their focus on the potential worker-dislocation problem that might result from increased layoffs in the area, although not necessarily from Cameron Station.

48. This estimate is derived from Defense Department "station strength" estimates (distilled by Robert Griffis of the Virginia Employment Commission) and was verified in interviews with base personnel. Nevertheless, it conflicts with news accounts of upwards of 3,000 employees. Most likely, the additional workers are accounted for by the many

private-contract workers on the base. See Spencer Hsu, "Army Facility Could Become Office Park." *Washington Post* (November 15, 1994).

49. The former included SAIC, DynCorp, Vitro, Raytheon, Hughes, Quest-Tech, and Mantech.

50. The transition office had a comfortable facility on the base, with five computer stations, a small library, and training rooms. Its services included the use of job data banks, employer networking services, job-search assistance, and employment workshops that provided assistance in preparing federal Civil Service applications, resume-writing skills, interview training, personal-change management, and other skills.

51. Usually, workers can only receive EDWAA-supported services after they have received formal layoff notices (usually only a few months before they become unemployed). This posed a hardship for workers who wanted to stay in the community rather than transfer to Monmouth, New Jersey, but who did not want to endure many months of unemployment while they retrained. Fortunately, the Virginia Employment Commission and the Governor's Employment and Training Department (which oversees the local service-delivery areas that administer EDWAA) adopted a policy in the fall of 1993 to allow base employees to enroll in EDWAA-supported training services if their names appeared on a list drawn up by the base and if the workers signed statements that they would not leave the area following training. As late as July 1994, however, few Vint Hill Farms workers had availed themselves of this opportunity, because their decision to do so depended upon the BRAC'95 process in which the army might have decided to close the Monmouth facility. By August 1995 most (but not all) workers and contract employees reportedly had accepted the inevitability of the Vint Hill Farms closure. In neighboring Culpeper County, 100 Vint Hill employees had applied for early EDWAA assistance. After a "Relocation to Monmouth Fair" was held in May 1995, a number of employees stated that they would choose to transfer.

52. However, one participant in the reuse-planning process stated that the committee identified reemployment of Faquier County residents as a goal early in its deliberations, and this goal was reaffirmed after it determined that the facility should be reused for high-tech purposes, since many existing workers have skills in electronics engineering, logistics, and related areas. The institutional problems discussed in the following paragraphs, however, proved daunting.

53. Moreover, the Fauquier community seemed to be unconcerned about reemploying the workforce. At the first public hearing in the fall of 1994, nine community residents reportedly asked about saving the pool, but only one person asked about jobs at the base.

54. See Laura Powers and Ann Markusen, *A Just Transition? Lessons from Defense Worker Adjustment in the 1990s.* Washington, DC: Economic Policy Institute Technical Paper No. 237, April 1999.

55. See Fuller, "Federal Contractors in the Washington Area."

56. Charles Ashby, "Army Lab Site Set to Become Wildlife Refuge." *Potomac News* (August 1994), p. A1.

Other Virginia Locations
Military Bases and Installations

1. CHARLOTTESVILLE
- Foreign Science and Technology Center, A
- Judge Advocate General's School, A

2. RADFORD
- Radford Army Ammunition Plant, A

3. RICHMOND
- Defense Supply Center Richmond, DL
- Sandston Air National Guard Station, NG

4. PETERSBURG
- Fort Lee, A
- Defense Commissary Agency, JS

5. DINWIDDIE, NOTTOWAY, BRUNSWICK
- Fort Pickett, A

ALBEMARLE

CHARLOTTESVILLE

BOUNDARY OF
NEW RIVER
VALLEY

MONT-
GOMERY

ROANOKE

ROANOKE
CITY

PULASKI

RADFORD

WYTHE

WYTHEVILLE

RICHMOND

PETERSBURG

NOTTOWAY

DINWIDDIE

BLACKSTONE

BRUNSWICK

OTHER
VIRGINIA
LOCATIONS

NO SCALE

A=Army, AF=Air Force, DL=Defense Logistics, JS=Joint Services, NG=National Guard. Map adapted from: "Major Military Bases and Installations," *Governor's Commission: Base Retention and Defense Adjustment*, 1994.

5

Rural Areas and Small Cities: Dependency, Adjustment, and Conversion

Chapters 3 and 4 examined the process of mobilizing resistance and adaptation to defense-spending cutbacks in large metropolitan areas; one with a traditional economic base of shipbuilding and military bases, the other with a modern high-tech base. Both communities had well-organized growth interests and export-oriented industries as well as other groups that advocated alternative approaches to development—environmental advocates in Northern Virginia and a "technology interest" in Hampton Roads. This chapter discusses the responses in rural areas and small cities. Because of their small size and narrow economic bases, one might imagine that they would be unable to challenge defense cutbacks and unable to devise alternative sources of economic activity. Yet, as discussed in previous chapters, the nature of the response depends primarily upon the nature of the community's dominant interests, as well as its prior experiences with economic dislocation. Even in small communities, elected officials, following their mandates to react to visible job loss, lead aggressive campaigns to avoid defense cutbacks. And once cutbacks occur, the cases in this chapter show that even relatively small communities can devise ways to adapt to them. Nevertheless, growth coalitions are largely absent in rural settings, so groups that might, in urban settings, be only marginal players, may be able to influence small-community responses.

The first case concerns a downsizing at the Radford Army Ammunition Plant in the Appalachian foothills of southwestern Virginia. It illustrates the effect of prior experience with economic dislocation on a community's response to defense downsizing. It also describes how problems in the organization of conversion efforts at the federal level undermine local responses. The second case focuses on a BRAC'95 decision to realign an army training fort in southside

Virginia, despite the spirited opposition of the community, led by federal, state, and local politicians. Here, too, in the absence of a strong growth coalition, political leaders organized a credible reuse effort after the closure decision was finalized. The chapter also briefly discusses a response to the end of the Cold War in the small city of Charlottesville—the only Virginia community in which a pro-active community economic-conversion plan was developed (see map at beginning of chapter).

ECONOMIC DISLOCATION IN APPALACHIA: THE RADFORD ARMY AMMUNITION PLANT

Background

Economic dislocation is nothing new in Appalachia. Never truly prosperous, northern Appalachia's coal miners and farmers suffered as much as the rest of the country during the Great Depression. Thus, when in August 1940 the U.S. Army chose tiny Radford in Virginia's fertile New River Valley as the site for one of its 29 new, inland armaments factories, it set in motion a process that would transform the town.[1] During the next eight months, the army spent $44 million and employed 23,000 construction workers, building 100 buildings on 6,000 acres. The Radford Army Ammunition Plant, dubbed "the arsenal" by local residents, would be a government-owned, contractor-operated (GOCO) facility managed by a private contractor—the Hercules Corporation—to make and package explosive propellant into mortar shells, rockets, missiles, and other weapons. Despite the dangers associated with the work, the Radford Army Ammunition Plant was, in many ways, the community's best employer. It offered wages and benefits that were two-to-three times higher than those of other employers in the region, and it offered opportunities for promotion through internal career ladders. People commuted from as far as a hundred miles away and they stayed at the arsenal for their entire working lives if they could. The high wages and benefits and the secrecy of their work bred an intense loyalty among workers toward one another and toward the company. This, in turn, reinforced their sense of national patriotism and support for the country's military policies. As one company official stated in 1975: "We have no pacifists working here."[2] Nevertheless, like the defense facilities in Hampton Roads and elsewhere, the arsenal's employment level would spike with each war and decline thereafter. Production employment reached 9,200 in 1945, 8,600 at the height of the Korean War, 9,300 during the Vietnam War, and 4,728 during the Reagan arms build-up. During the interwar years employment fell: To as low as 150 after World War II, to 2,575 after the Korean War, 2,500 after the Vietnam War, and 1,250 by 1996.[3] Thus, like the shipyard workers in Hampton Roads, workers at the arsenal learned to live with the cyclical nature of defense employment.

In the meantime the local economy grew somewhat as manufacturing branch plants came to the Valley, but the arsenal would remain the largest employer until the 1980s. By 1989 employment in the New River Valley planning district, which includes the small city of Radford, as well as Pulaski, Montgomery, Giles, and Floyd counties, had reached 58,167 and population had climbed to 152,680. And by 1989 the army Ammunition Plant was no longer the largest employer in the New River Valley, having been overtaken by Virginia Polytechnic Institute and State University (Virginia Tech), a land-grant university with 6,000 employees. By 1997 Radford University, with 1,600 employees, had also surpassed the shrinking arsenal. The growth of these universities, as well as two community colleges in the area, signified a partial shift from an economy based upon agriculture, coal mining, and manufacturing to a more professional, high-tech-based economy, but the shift was just that—partial. With the exception of higher education, the community's economic base remained dependent upon manufacturing, particularly mature industries and assembly operations such as chemicals (the ammunition plant), furniture, textiles, apparel, stone clay and glass products, truck assembly, and electric and electronic equipment.[4] Unfortunately, none of these plants managed to spin off new activities in related fields. Each was owned by a company that was either too small to develop spin-offs or else had its headquarters and research and development (R&D) operations elsewhere. Hercules, for example, has its headquarters and R&D staff in Delaware.

As in other mature industrial regions, workers who lose their jobs to sagging demand or mechanization in the coal industry, to layoffs at the arsenal, or to departing branch plants do not find jobs in higher education. Rather, they join the ranks of the unemployed or discouraged until work picks up in existing manufacturing plants or until new plants are recruited. Thus the New River Valley, much like the areas to its immediate north, west, and south, has been locked in a perennial struggle for economic stability. Unemployment rates throughout the region are usually above the statewide average, and laborforce participation rates are lower. But work in the "informal" sector, which is believed to be substantial, supports only a subsistence existence. Few college graduates remain in the area after they receive their degrees. Nevertheless, residents place a high value on the region's quality of life, particularly its mountains, low crime rates, and other rural amenities.

A by-product of the region's quest for economic stability has been a vibrant economic-development industry. As one local observer said: "You won't find a community with more economic-development organizations than this one. It's a result of frustration with the area's slow growth. People criticize existing organizations for not getting the job done, then they form a new one that carves out a niche for itself." Virtually every county and city in the area has an economic-development commission or department, many of which focus on some aspect of new-business recruitment.

A number of community-wide economic-development organizations also serve the area. One of these is the New River Valley Planning District Commission (PDC), which serves Radford, Montgomery, Pulaski, Floyd, and Giles. Like the PDCs in Northern Virginia and Hampton Roads, it produces regional transportation and infrastructure plans and studies of local economic conditions and provides assistance to local planning agencies. Unlike these other PDCs, however, the New River Valley PDC has for many years played an aggressive role in economic development, stimulating the creation of a number of region-wide organizations such as the New River Valley Economic Development Alliance, which focuses on attracting new firms to the area.[5]

Chronic economic dislocation has also sparked the formation of many grass-roots organizations, some of which focus on economic-development issues.[6] Unfortunately, these groups usually do not participate in the community's many government-sponsored economic-development planning initiatives. To some extent this is due to a failure by local officials to solicit community-organization participation on economic-development boards (although such participation is solicited for broader planning exercises). It is also due to a long-held skepticism on the part of some community groups that government-sponsored efforts will meet their needs. Thus community organizations have little direct influence on local policy, but their existence does help to keep the issue of job development on the public agenda.

The business community in the New River Valley is relatively unorganized. Most of the dominant businesses are export-oriented branch plants with head-quarters elsewhere and they are relatively unconcerned with local development. Local growth-oriented businesses such as banks, developers, and grocery-store chains, are small—a common feature of rural and small city areas. The universities and community colleges support growth but, as in big cities, they are not the primary growth boosters. Thus, even though every city and county in the area has a chamber of commerce that belongs to the New River Valley Chamber Coalition, the coalition does not sponsor initiatives or programs. Rather, economic-development initiatives generally emanate from the public sector, which then seeks support from local businesses. Because the Chamber Coalition is weak, it cannot organize or speak for the business community, so public agencies must secure business support one business at a time. The lack of a growth coalition appears to account for the fact that the New River Valley's economic-development initiatives generally focus on job and workforce development rather than real estate development projects. The same is true of the Mount Rogers planning district to the south and southwest of the New River Valley. Although business recruitment is still the dominant economic-development technique in these communities, it is more deliberately linked with workforce training efforts. Roanoke, on the other hand, which is a small metropolitan area (1990 population: 224,589) that borders the New River Valley to the east, has a strong chamber of commerce that functions much as the Hampton Roads chamber does.

Labor unions represent the workforces in a number of manufacturing companies in the New River Valley and also farther south and west in the coalfields. However, Virginia is a right-to-work state and the climate does not favor proactive union work. Local community activists claimed that businesses and local officials in the area are antiunion. As one case in point, they noted that one local chamber of commerce advertised the area's workforce as "docile." Also, they alleged that it is a common business practice in the area to raise worker wages if any threat of unionization appears. Nevertheless, the Oil, Chemical, and Atomic

Workers (OCAW) International Union, Local 3-495 in Radford, has represented most of the workforce at the Radford Army Ammunition Plant for many years with relative success. The OCAW is a member of a Radford Army Ammunition Plant Readjustment Task Force that has planned new uses for the Arsenal. However, trade-union organizations generally have not been active participants in, much less initiators of, regional or local economic-development efforts. Rather, they have followed a "business union" approach, restricting their activities to managing the grievance and contract-negotiating processes within their plants. When asked by the author about the community's economic-development efforts, local labor leaders expressed skepticism that these efforts would find jobs for laid-off workers in the area.

Defense Dependency and Cutbacks

The Radford Army Ammunition Plant is the largest defense employer in the New River Valley. Indeed, it is the largest Virginia defense employer west of Richmond. In 1989 its 3,700 remaining employees (down from 4,718 in 1987) constituted over 6 percent of the total employment in the New River Valley. However, when the Cold War ended the army reduced its total demand for propellant and also began to buy it from lower-cost foreign firms. As a result, some of the nation's 29 army ammunition plants closed, and all plants reduced their workforces. Employment at the Radford arsenal dropped to 1,250 by 1996. The fifteen remaining ammunition plants, including the Radford arsenal, also implemented cost-cutting measures and engaged in a partial facility reuse-planning process.[7]

The Radford Army Ammunition Plant is not the only defense contractor in the area. According to a survey conducted in 1993 by the New River Valley Planning District Commission (PDC), 39 manufacturing and related firms worked as defense prime- or subcontractors sometime between 1988 and 1993. With the exception of the Army Ammunition Plant and Virginia Tech (which conducted research for the Defense Department), most of the firms employed less than 200 workers. Also, most firms did less than 50 percent of their work with the Defense Department. Their products included conveyers and conveying equipment, motors and generators, slip rings, radio and television communications equipment, computers and peripherals, facilities support services, parachute material, fiber optics, wood products, electric motors and actuators, military maps/covers, bagtags for identity containers, security systems and components, drydock blocks, heat-flux sensors, military housing-design services, boilers, grading and excavating services, and thermal remediation of contaminated soil.[8] In short, most firms produced materials with both military and civilian uses and were not highly dependent upon defense contracts.[9]

Thus the loss of over 3,000 jobs from the Radford arsenal accounted for the largest defense-related employment losses in the New River Valley during the 1989–1994 period. Assuming an employment multiplier of 1.75,[10] the loss of 3,000 jobs from the ammunition plant during the period 1987 to 1993 resulted in an additional loss of 1,687 jobs in the area—for a total loss of 4,687 jobs, or about 8.1 percent of the 1989 New River Valley employment. This overstates the impact slightly, since the high wages at the Army Ammunition Plant attracted workers residing as far as 100 miles away. However, the primary impact of the arsenal job losses was on the New River Valley, which was also reeling from the departure of an AT&T microelectronics plant employing 1,000 workers, and the loss of 620 jobs due to force reductions at Virginia Tech and at a Sara Lee Bakery.[11] Between 1989 and 1993 total employment in the New River Valley declined by 3.4 percent. The June 1994 unemployment rate topped 10 percent.

Nearby regions suffered defense cuts as well. In the Mount Rogers region to the south and southwest of the New River Valley, Brunswick Corporation, a maker of plastics, filaments, and ceramics for Patriot missile nosecones and advanced composites for airplane wingflaps, cut its employment from 1,200 to 600, but this amounted to less than 1 percent of total community employment.[12] In the Roanoke metropolitan statistical area (MSA), which borders the New River Valley on the east, the ITT Electro-Optical Products Division cut its employment from 1,100 to 650 when the army did not place a repeat order for its Generation II night-vision goggles, but this had a negligible impact on the local economy. Greater hardship and concern were caused by layoffs in banking and other industries and by the Roanoke community's continued reliance on mature, low-wage manufacturing industries for much of its export base. In the meantime, however, ITT diversified its products and began to make night-vision goggles for civilian use also.[13]

Thus cutbacks in procurement orders for the region's large companies resulted in layoffs, especially at the Radford Army Ammunition Plant. In the case of ITT and some smaller firms, it also resulted in conversion into civilian markets. Neither the contractors nor the community offered public resistance to these cutbacks. Indeed, as these were U.S. Defense Department procurement decisions and not congressional-funding decisions, there was no obvious public pressure point. Instead, the community moved directly into efforts to adapt to the cutbacks.

Community-Wide Initiatives

As discussed above, the New River Valley has many economic-development organizations, which were created for the most part as responses to the economic dislocations the area has suffered over the years. Many of these organizations, such as the New River Valley Economic Development Alliance, simply redoubled their business-recruitment efforts. The following account focuses mostly on the new initiatives in the New River Valley community, initiatives whose explicit purpose was to address defense-employment cutbacks.

New River Valley Economic Adjustment Strategy

One of the most active economic-development organizations in the New River Valley is the New River Valley Planning District Commission (PDC). In

September 1992 the Montgomery County Regional Economic Development Commission, citing employment losses at the Radford Army Ammunition Plant as well as economic dislocation throughout southwestern Virginia, called upon the PDC to prepare a plan to help companies and workers affected by these events.[14] The PDC applied for a $197,800 planning and adjustment grant from the Defense Department's Office of Economic Adjustment (OEA) (matched with $31,000 of state and local money) that was finally disbursed in August 1993.[15] The OEA funds were used to purchase consultant studies and to fund the New River Valley Economic Adjustment Strategy, a region-wide planning process that took place in 1993 and 1994.[16] The initiative was overseen by a steering committee, whose members included each local government in the New River Valley, the New River Valley Economic Development Alliance, Hercules Incorporated (the operator of the arsenal), the U.S. Army, U.S. Representative Boucher (who represents the New River Valley), the Oil, Chemical, and Atomic Workers Union Local 3-495, local colleges and universities, and three state agencies. With the exception of the universities, this committee did not include any traditional local growth interests, which, as noted above, are not well developed in the New River Valley.[17]

By June 1994 an adjustment strategy with the following elements had been developed: Region-wide education and training initiatives, with an emphasis on the interface between training and industrial development; stimulation and support of local entrepreneurship; expansion of basic (export) employment and support services by attracting and developing new businesses and improving existing business competitiveness; physical infrastructure improvements; preservation and promotion of the natural and cultural environment for recreation, tourism, and enhanced quality of life; and improved human-services-delivery mechanisms. The strategy was widely discussed through community forums and published in April 1995 as the "New River Valley Vision 2020." Like the Plan 2007 process in Hampton Roads, the Vision 2020 report did not address the issue of displaced workers, nor did it suggest vehicles to implement the visions.[18] Nevertheless, various New River Valley officials expressed an expectation that leadership to implement the adjustment strategy would emerge in 1995. Indeed, over the next several years localities in the New River Valley undertook initiatives that were encouraged by the Vision 2020 report. They established small-business incubators, improved their public infrastructure, and redoubled their business-recruitment efforts. The community colleges introduced new worker-training initiatives. By 1998 the unemployment rate had been cut to 3.4 percent, thanks in part to a booming national and state economy that helped attract new branch plants to the area.[19]

Although the new jobs had appeared largely through old business-recruitment methods, the Economic Adjustment Strategy process created some new economic-development institutions that improved local economic-development capacity. For example, the Corporate Roundtable committee, a group of 30 representatives from the largest (mostly export-oriented) businesses in the New River Valley, was created to identify ways to assist existing industries and to promote economic development generally. As a result of the roundtable's deliberations, the PDC applied for a $3 million grant through the federal Empowerment

Zone/Enterprise Community program to capitalize a revolving-loan program, of which $2 million would assist existing companies in their retooling efforts; the remainder would support microenterprises and high-tech industrial entrepreneurship. The roundtable also explored ways to provide companies with worker training at the company site as well as other services to enhance competitiveness, such as ISO 9000 certification. This kind of business retention and expansion effort constituted a significant innovation for the New River Valley. Thus the roundtable began the important process of integrating workforce skill-upgrading with company technology development.

Converting the Radford Army Ammunition Plant

The community's most direct response to the loss of jobs at the arsenal was to create the Radford Army Ammunition Plant (RAAP) Task Force. Organized by the New River Valley PDC to influence the disposition of the arsenal, it was comprised of representatives of the army command at the arsenal, the New River Valley PDC, the Oil, Chemical, and Atomic Workers Union, the New River Valley Economic Development Alliance, Congressman Boucher, and Hercules Incorporated (replaced by Alliant Techsystems in March 1995). Although only Hercules and the army had formal authority to decide the fate of the arsenal, the RAAP Task Force had some influence. It focused on the following issues: "Inside the fence" development, to convert part of the facility to commercial use; marketing of RAAP facilities to prospective commercial ventures; small-business assistance to companies that might locate in the facility; labor–management relations, including cooperative initiatives to cut costs; and public representation at the U.S. Army's national Public–Private Task Force on the disposition of army ammunition plants nationwide.[20]

As this list suggests, much of the work of responding to downsizing at the arsenal involved an effort to convert part of the facility to commercial uses. This focus was the result of both local interest and explicit national policy, specified in the federal Armament Retooling and Manufacturing Support (ARMS) Initiative of 1992, developed with assistance from Congressman Boucher, and passed as part of the FY1993 Defense Authorization Act. The stated purpose of the initiative was "to ensure a continued industrial base for the manufacture of ammunition by encouraging the peacetime use of government-owned ammunition-manufacturing facilities for military and nonmilitary commercial manufacturing."[21] The Act covered the 15 army-owned, contractor-operated ammunition facilities that were still active as of 1993, all of which had excess capacity.[22] Under the terms of the initiative, contractors who had previously produced munitions for the U.S. Army and managed the facilities under cost-plus contracts were given the opportunity to become leasing agents of the now-unutilized portions of that property, responsible for payments to the army for using the facilities. The army would promote this effort through various incentives: marketing; use of land, buildings, and equipment; environmental-baseline studies; state and federal permits; loan guarantees; planning grants; and employment incentives.[23] Those parts of the facility that were still in use to produce munitions for the army would function much as they did in the past, with the army paying the contractor to manage the facility and produce munitions. However, cost-plus contracting would no longer be used. Instead, the contractor would compete with other U.S. and foreign plants for the army's business on a fixed-price basis. Some parts of the facilities were mothballed for later use if the need for more munitions arose. Thus the ARMS Act was quite consistent with much of the Bush and Clinton administrations' brand of reuse and conversion policy. It sought to preserve and enhance the defense industrial base by setting aside parts of the army's ammunition plants for production use at a later date. It also sought to ensure the overall viability of the plants by introducing commercial operations whose rent payments could help to defray the high overhead costs associated with the maintenance of an ammunition plant.

To encourage the contractors and potential commercial enterprises to use the facilities in this way, Congress earmarked $200 million, to be drawn down during FY1993 and FY1994. Of the $200 million, approximately $140 million was reserved for incentive payments, including loan guarantees, to lure firms into the facilities, and the rest was made available to administer the initiative and to demonstrate new and innovative incentive programs. To oversee implementation, Congress established a national Public–Private Task Force, comprised of about 20 persons, almost all of whom were representatives of the army and the munitions-plant contractors. The ARMS Initiative did not require community or worker participation in the local facility-reuse planning process, but the New River Valley PDC established the RAAP Task Force to attempt to influence it.

Over the next several years the RAAP Task Force and particularly the New River Valley PDC worked hard to overcome various bureaucratic and technical barriers to make conversion of the arsenal a reality. The key barrier was an opinion rendered by the army's legal staff that the army had no authority to administer the financial incentives to companies that agreed to locate in the plants, particularly the loan-guarantee funds. Without such location incentives, however, the added costs of doing business in an army-owned facility, in 50-year-old buildings, would make the location uncompetitive with other facilities. Although language in the ARMS Initiative anticipated the possibility that special authorization might be required for the army to administer the loan guarantees and other financial incentives and called upon the Secretary of the Army to move swiftly to secure such authorization, swift action did not occur. Indeed, it took almost a year just to constitute the national Public–Private Task Force that oversees implementation of the initiative. As late as July 1994, the national Public–Private Task Force had met only four times. To get the process moving, New River Valley representatives worked with key members of the Senate and House of Representatives to secure their willingness to pass an amendment that would explicitly give the army authority to administer the Initiative. This was accomplished as part of the FY1995 Defense Appropriations Act. This Act also extended the ARMS Initiative through FY1996.

Another implementation problem concerned the facilities-use contract called for in the ARMS Initiative. Under the Initiative, Hercules, Inc. was required to sign a contract with the army that set forth the terms under which it would operate each portion of the plant, including the areas to be used for commercial work by Hercules or by new companies. Several issues slowed the process of negotiations, including the question of environmental indemnity (would the army or Hercules be held legally responsible, and for what periods of time?); the payment of postretirement benefits to company personnel (previously, the army had paid); and the overarching issue of whether the army would treat the ARMS Initiative as an investment in the arsenal from which it would expect a competitive return in the form of payments from Hercules, or whether it would lower its expectations to simply reducing the losses it would incur from continuing to maintain the plant without tenants. Without a facilities-use contract, ARMS funds would not flow and conversion would not proceed at the Radford Arsenal.

ARMS Initiative implementation problems caused even conversion planning to move slowly. The initiative called for strategic planning to determine what parts of the facility would remain in service for munitions production for the army, what ones would be turned over to the contractor-operator for commercial and other military-production purposes, and what ones would be mothballed or taken down. The ARMS Initiative allowed for up to $1.5 million to be spent at each ammunition plant for planning and marketing, yet no funds had been disbursed as of June 1994. In anticipation that it would receive the funds retroactively Hercules began to spend money for assessment and planning activities, but the army's commitment to reimburse all of these costs became uncertain during the spring of 1994. In response, Hercules slowed its planning and assessment activities considerably. By July 1994 the RAAP Task Force had stopped meeting, except for occasional briefings with Congressman Boucher. As one disenchanted labor participant put it: "It's a lot of talk. Nothing's happened for two years."

The spirits of some parties improved in October 1994 when the army and Hercules signed the facilities-use contract, paving the way for partial conversion of the plant to civilian use. When Alliant Techsystems took over the plant in March 1995, it also signed a facilities-use contract with the army. But as late as the spring of 1995 it appeared that Congress would not reauthorize the Act, thus allowing it to die in 1996. Fortunately, a massive lobbying campaign organized by New River Valley PDC staff and other community leaders, joined by ammunition-plant communities and contractors around the nation, led to the passage of legislation to reauthorize the Act at $45–$60 million for an additional two years. Congress continued to extend the Act into subsequent years and, as of August 1999, appeared to be ready to continue funding the initiative in FY2000.

However, knowledgeable observers detected more than bureaucratic problems with the ARMS Initiative—problems such as its dual-use premise for the ammunition plants. As long as the army owned and regulated the use of the facilities, the costs of the associated red tape would either prevent the contractors from making money by leasing the facilities, or they would be so high as to drive away most companies that might consider locating on them. One source complained that the initiative failed to take into account major issues such as the fact that the Radford facility was 50 years old and "not in pristine condition." Another observer explained that the costs of installing new water or sewer lines that might connect with an interior part of the plant to the space occupied by a new commercial company were very high, given the maze of pipes that covered the plant, but these costs had not been calculated.[24]

The local economic context also posed a challenge to successful conversion of the arsenal. Throughout the 1990s the community had many industrial parks operating below capacity, as well as vacant industrial buildings. Although Hercules and later, Alliant Techsystems, targeted their marketing efforts at firms that were best suited for munitions plants such as fireworks manufacturers, competition between the arsenal and the other industrial spaces was a potential problem.

Given these problems, it seemed unlikely that the ARMS Initiative would succeed at the Radford Arsenal. Still, in August 1995 Alliant Techsystems announced that it would bring its commercial powder operation from New Jersey to Radford, which was worth about 150 jobs initially and up to 250 eventually. By March 1996 Carillion Health Systems of Roanoke had signed a contract to operate the Radford facility's wellness center, employing about 50 persons. Shortly thereafter Alliant recruited Fireworks by Grucci, a maker of pyrotechnics and fireworks displays. By 1998 Alliant had added a commercial propellant manufacturer, a machine shop, and an industrial equipment supplier. It had also leased space to Virginia Tech to store coal supplies for the university's power plant. Over $48 million in ARMS funds had been spent to refurbish parts of the arsenal and attract the new firms (although 44 contaminated sites remained to be cleaned up). Nevertheless, the new firms employed a total of only a couple hundred workers—a small fraction of the 3,500 that had lost their jobs at the arsenal during the previous decade.

Clearly, the ARMS Initiative was not a cost-effective way to reemploy laid-off defense workers, but that unfortunately was not its purpose. Whether it proves to be a cost-effective way to keep the arsenal ready for future military build-ups by defraying overhead costs with private company rents, however, remains to be seen.[25] In the meantime, workers laid off from the arsenal were gradually using up their two years of unemployment benefits and retraining funds through the federal Trade Adjustment Act. Although a number of these workers reportedly found jobs (albeit at lower wages) in some of the region's expanding companies, many others joined the ranks of the structurally unemployed and discouraged.

Dislocated Worker Services

As in Hampton Roads and Northern Virginia, local offices of the Virginia Employment Commission's (VEC) job service and local service-delivery area administrators of Economic Dislocation and Worker Adjustment Assistance (EDWAA) programs responded to the dislocated-worker problem resulting from the layoffs at the arsenal and elsewhere. The VEC's job-service office in Radford administered the federal Trade Readjustment Assistance program whereby workers who lost their jobs to foreign competition were eligible for up to two years of unemployment insurance payments and up to two years of retraining.

According to VEC job-service staff in Radford, ascertaining the status of dislocated workers proved difficult (a view that was shared by job-service staff elsewhere in Virginia). Of those laid off from the arsenal, some retired, some left the area, some sought reemployment on their own, and some applied for benefits with the VEC office. For a variety of reasons, including fear and mistrust of traditional institutions, many workers did not enroll in retraining programs. Of those who did begin retraining, some did not complete the programs, either because they grew discouraged or because meanwhile they found employment. Although the VEC sent letters to workers 60 and 90 days after they completed their training to learn if they had found jobs, some did not reply.

Using partial information, officials at the Radford office estimated in June 1994 that upwards of 2,000 Radford Arsenal workers were still receiving Trade Readjustment Act benefits. Moreover, officials estimated that upwards of 6,000 persons remained unemployed in the New River Valley region, with many more underemployed or out of the labor force entirely. Nevertheless, job opportunities were increasing and more workers were being placed daily, as companies in manufacturing, construction, and trucking expanded. Unfortunately, the jobs did not pay as well as those at the Radford Arsenal, where workers had been compensated for the high risks of the work and had shared in the federal government's cost-plus contract largess. Indeed, most new jobs in the area paid only 50 percent of the average arsenal wage. Similarly, officials in contact with workers who had been laid off from the Brunswick Corporation in Marion found that these workers, although they generally had higher skills than arsenal workers, could not find jobs in the region that paid anywhere near the money they earned at Brunswick. Thus for most workers the process of adjusting from defense to civilian production was anything but smooth.

Nevertheless, the VEC's dislocated-worker services were well integrated with the area's economic-development system (unlike the situations in Northern Virginia, Hampton Roads, and in many other communities across the United States). The director of the VEC's Radford job-service office was a member of the board of directors of the New River Valley Economic Development Alliance, as well as the RAAP Task Force. Through these and other forums he met frequently with economic-development officials. Moreover, the staff of the New River Valley Economic Development Alliance used a frequently updated list of dislocated-worker skills when working with prospective companies. There were also linkages between economic-development entities and education and training brokers and providers. For example, Wytheville Community College (45 miles south of Radford) maintained a team of counselors, instructors, and financial-aid staff that visited companies laying off workers, the president of the college sat on the local industrial-development authority, and the college had its own economic-development council that watched for plant closings, force reductions, and other economic events that might require a proactive community-college response.

The chief shortcoming in the dislocated-worker service system was that effective tracking of workers after they received services was not pursued, except for the 60- and 90-day follow-up letters. One grass-roots community-organization representative claimed that it was easy for workers, especially those who might be fearful of the education system, to fall through the cracks and join the ranks of discouraged workers. According to VEC and community-college staff, however, budgets and staffing levels did not permit closer tracking or more intensive interventions with discouraged or alienated workers. The lack of a more effective tracking system proved costly to the community. When the New River Valley PDC tried to survey unemployed and dislocated persons to prove the need for a federal Department of Labor-funded one-stop training shop, it found that neither the Oil, Chemical, and Atomic Workers union local nor Hercules had information about dislocated workers from the Radford Army Ammunition Plant. The PDC obtained a list of about 600 persons (less than one-fourth the number of dislocated workers estimated to be living in the region) from the Virginia Employment Commission, but only 60 of those returned the surveys. The poor response reportedly convinced the Department of Labor not to fund the one-stop shop.

Other Community Initiatives

Throughout the region, concerns about the Radford Army Ammunition Plant downsizing and other layoffs caused by defense cutbacks were used to help generate support for other economic-development initiatives, just as similar concerns in Hampton Roads and Northern Virginia were tapped to create support for the Peninsula Advanced Technology Center and the Arlington Economic Futures Committee. The most well known of these are the three described here, which are initiatives that were organized by groups who approached the problem from different philosophical perspectives. One was the Southwestern Virginia Advanced Manufacturing Technology Center. Similar in some ways to the Peninsula Advanced Technology Center, this initiative was inspired by an industrial engineer and sponsored by five community colleges in southwestern Virginia. Rather than recruit new branch plants to the area, this center sought to develop the economy by helping small manufacturers, including small defense contractors wishing to move into civilian markets, to improve their products and production processes through problem-solving and technology-upgrading assistance. Its target market was the 660 small manufacturers (most of whom did not do defense work) within a two-hour drive of the center's location at Wytheville Community College.[26]

Like the Peninsula Center, the Southwestern Virginia Advanced Manufacturing Technology Center planned to function as a one-stop shop for a variety of business and laborforce services. These included technology-transfer services provided through the Virginia Center for Innovative Technology, whereby new products or processes developed at Virginia universities would be marketed to firms and entrepreneurs for commercialization. The center also planned to tap the services of the Small Business Development Center already housed at the college and to add a number of continuing education and training services. Also included was a mobile training unit, through which workers and managers could learn the basics of computer-aided design and computer-integrated manufacturing. Although this center failed to receive federal Technology Reinvestment Project funds, it did receive money from the Appalachian Regional Commission, the Tennessee Valley Authority, and later from the Commonwealth of Virginia. By 1998 the center had become established as a permanent presence at Wytheville Community College.

A hundred miles south of Wytheville, in the Clinch Valley, a regional consortium of grass-roots, community-based organizations, small businesses, and public agencies took an even more innovative approach to addressing economic dislocation in southwestern Virginia and northeast Tennessee. Citing the loss of employment in coal mining, textiles, apparel production, and defense contracting as well as environmental damage through coal mining, clear-cut logging, and landfill operations, in 1994 the Clinch-Powell Sustainable Development Forum produced an economic-development plan.[27] The plan called for the employment of local residents in environmentally benign industries such as sustainable logging and wood products, sustainable home construction, nature tourism, and sustainable agriculture. It recommended the creation of new institutions such as a regional information bank that would improve cooperation among local chambers of commerce, and a network of local businesses that would develop methods for reusing or recycling currently discarded products and creating new, energy-efficient ones. The plan also envisioned the development of microenterprises, incubators, and flexible manufacturing networks.[28] By 1998 the group had received funding and the plan was in the process of being implemented. Here, as in the New River Valley, the absence of a growth coalition allowed other interests to emerge and begin to influence economic development.

Unlike both the Clinch Valley and New River Valley, the Roanoke MSA has a traditional growth coalition organized through its chamber of commerce, the Roanoke Business Council. In 1994 this group, led by the president of Carrillion Health Care System, began a two-year region-wide visioning initiative, called the New Century Council. "Region-wide" in this case meant the jurisdictions of the small Roanoke metropolitan area (1990 population: 224,589) and those of the New River Valley (1990 population: 152,680). The stated purpose of the council was to respond to the economic dislocations caused by downsizing of the Radford Arsenal and the ITT Electro-Optical Products Corporation as well as at nondefense businesses both in Roanoke and in the New River Valley. But an equally strong motive for Roanoke was the opportunity to work with Virginia Tech. Roanoke growth interests had long sought to establish closer ties with Virginia Tech, and the New Century Council provided such an opportunity.

In both its leadership and scope of work, the New Century Council bore a striking resemblance to the Plan 2007 initiative in Hampton Roads. The effort was organized and guided by the chamber of commerce, with local government officials in nonleadership roles. The work effort was organized through teams of volunteers who were asked to work on the issue areas of economy, education, quality of life/environment, health and safety, infrastructure, governance, and leadership. The council's 1995 report also resembled growth-coalition plans in other communities. It focused on broad initiatives, not on the details of bringing them about. It called for the establishment of regional commerce parks, to be developed by flattening hills in areas that would not impinge upon the region's tourist industry and quality of life. It also called for merging the region's economic-development entities and for convening an annual regional political summit to prepare for the Virginia General Assembly session.[29] The report proposed no initiatives to assist dislocated defense workers or to improve the competitiveness of existing companies.

Although the process initially received state funding and drew appearances by state legislators, the report's economic-development recommendations drew criticism. And some accused the process itself of duplicating efforts already underway in the New River Valley and elsewhere in the region. Although the New Century Council helped to promote a fiber-optic "smart highway" linking the university with Roanoke and other initiatives, it appeared to have little overall impact. In 1997 it officially closed its office, stating that it had fulfilled its objectives.

TROOPS, TEXTILES, AND TOBACCO IN SOUTHSIDE VIRGINIA: THE FORT PICKETT ARMY BASE

Fort Pickett is located in rural southside Virginia, in the Piedmont planning district approximately 45 miles southwest of Richmond. The planning district's 1996 population was 90,700, which constitutes one of the lowest population densities (number of persons per square mile) in the state. Until the 1960s this region relied almost solely upon agricultural products—flue-cured tobacco, poultry, and dairy products—for its livelihood. In recent decades the area has developed a small-manufacturing base comprised mainly of textiles, lumber and wood products, and furniture—generally nonunion branch plant operations that pay low-to-moderate wages. Poverty and unemployment rates have generally been well above statewide rates, and education and laborforce participation levels have typically been below statewide levels.[30]

The larger communities around Fort Pickett have chambers of commerce and industrial-development authorities that seek to attract new business to the community. But, as in the New River Valley, the chambers are not large enough to initiate development programs on their own. Moreover, traditional growth-oriented businesses such as banks and developers are underrepresented in the local economy, so local governments pursue employment growth through recruitment of new businesses and the chambers support and encourage them. Other interests such as organized labor, environmental advocates, or citizen groups that advocate for specific economic-development policies do not exist here.

Fort Pickett's Functions

Since its establishment in 1941 Fort Pickett has served as a training and maneuvers base for active and reserve components of the army and other armed services, including marines, navy SEALs, and the air force. Its facilities include the Virginia Army National Guard Mobilization and Training Equipment Site and (until 1997) the 80th Army Division Equipment Concentration Site. Almost 93 percent of its 45,160 acres serve as operations areas for live tank and artillery-firing training and as a 16-building mock city used for urban-warfare training.[31] During World War II Fort Pickett housed as many as 50,000 troops and, in the years since then, the fort has annually trained as many as 90,000 persons. Although employment and training activities decreased in the early 1990s, the fort continued to employ upwards of 425 civilians and 50 military personnel on a permanent, year-round basis and annually trained at least 50,000 troops.[32] Even prior to the 1997 realignment, almost a half of the training activity at Fort Pickett was devoted to national guard units from Virginia, Pennsylvania, and Maryland. The guard employed 120 to 130 persons full-time at Fort Pickett to maintain heavy weapons and equipment such as tanks and armored personnel carriers for training purposes.[33]

Economic Impact

In the early 1990s Fort Pickett was one of the largest employers in the region, with about 250 full-time, year-round workers and hundreds more seasonal and part-time workers. Its direct economic impact (measured by commuting patterns) extended in a radius of 25 miles from the fort.[34] An impact analysis conducted by the Virginia Employment Commission in 1995 found that the fort's operations accounted for an estimated 1,126 jobs in the adjacent counties of Nottoway and Lunenburg (including the town of Blackstone) and $38.4 million in total output in 1994.[35] The 1,126 jobs accounted for roughly 9 percent of total employment in Nottoway and Lunenburg, but far more than that in the town of Blackstone (1996 population: 3,691), which is situated in Nottoway County just two miles west of Fort Pickett. Indeed, one observer called Blackstone "a giant off-base trading post."[36] Fort Pickett manages Blackstone's airfield, water and sewer systems, and is the location of the town's only movie theater and bowling alley. Under its Wildlife Management Program, the fort allows the general public to engage in hunting, fishing, and other recreational activities on about 40,000 acres of its property.[37] Thus Fort Pickett is the economic and cultural focal point of this rural community. When the fort closed briefly in 1946 and again in 1954, the town of Blackstone essentially closed with it.[38]

Efforts to Enhance the Fort

When the army began considering closing Fort Pickett in the 1980s, members of Virginia's congressional delegation—Senator John Warner (at the time, a member of the Senate Armed Services Committee) and Representatives Lewis F. Payne, Jr. and Norman Sisisky (a House Armed Services Committee member)— began working with local government and Fort Pickett officials to enhance and thereby protect the fort. In the early 1980s they encouraged the army to refurbish one of four runways at the Blackstone–Fort Pickett Air Base so that it could accommodate the army's new C-130 and C-141 cargo aircraft. The restored runway would be a joint military/civilian facility. In 1985 the Piedmont Planning District Commission reported that the regional economic impacts of such a project would be quite favorable.[39] In June 1988 Senator Warner secured funds to conduct a formal study of the project. The refurbishment project was not funded, but Representative Sisisky convinced the 82nd Airborne Division at Fort Bragg, North Carolina, to make greater use of Fort Pickett for paratrooper training. He also succeeded in bringing other new facilities to the base.[40] Apparently, their efforts helped to keep Fort Pickett off the base-closing list in the 1988 and 1991 Base Realignment and Closure processes. On January 6, 1993, the commander of Fort Pickett publicly described the many improvements he was making to the fort, improvements that he believed would demonstrate its continued military value.[41]

An Effort to Diversify the Fort

Although most of the energy expended on Fort Pickett over the years consisted of efforts to maintain and enhance its military value, it was the object of one commercial economic-development proposal. In 1990 Colonel Maynard Austin, retired commander of Fort Pickett who was then executive director of the Nottoway Economic Development Commission, proposed the establishment of a major agricultural export–import center at the fort. The center would have a 10,000-foot runway that could accommodate 747-size cargo airplanes, a livestock-holding facility, refrigeration facilities, and a free-trade-zone designation (whereby import duties are waived for companies importing goods into the zone that are then exported elsewhere and not sold in the United States). Development of the center would require a substantial upgrade of one of the runways at the Blackstone–Fort Pickett airport. Funds to develop the facility were to be requested from the Federal Aviation Administration's pool for joint-use military airports, created in the federal Budget Reconciliation Act of 1991. By January 1992 all of the county governments in the region reportedly had approved Austin's proposal to establish a Southside Regional Airport Authority to oversee the export center, and legislation to create the body had been introduced in the Virginia General Assembly.[42] Ultimately, the authority was not created and plans for the export center were shelved. In August 1995 one local official commented that the idea had been analyzed and found infeasible. Another observer stated that personality conflicts with Austin had scuttled the plan. Others noted that in a community that was striving to enhance and retain its military facility, there was a fear that entertaining the notion of diversifying it to partial civilian use would send the wrong message to the Pentagon and BRAC Commission. As one local government official stated: "We're trying to keep it, not convert it." This fear was not unique to the Fort Pickett community. As discussed in chapter 3, it played a role in Newport News Shipyard's opposition to the Peninsula Advanced Technology Center and in the Hampton Roads BRAC'95 defense effort. And it was observed in communities around the country during the BRAC process. It constitutes at least one reason why proactive alternative-use planning for military facilities, regardless of economic viability, may not be politically feasible.

Defending the Fort in the BRAC'95 Process

Despite attempts to enhance Fort Pickett's military value, the fort did appear on the base-closure list submitted by the Defense Department in March 1995. The Pentagon also recommended that the Virginia Army National Guard study the prospect of taking over the facility and maintaining a skeletal force there so it could continue to be used for national guard training (a recommendation made for other forts as well).[43] Reactions by Virginia state, local, and congressional officials as well as by the local chambers of commerce were swift and negative. "This will not be Pickett's last charge. We're going to win," vowed Congressman Sisisky to a supportive crowd in Blackstone on March 4, 1995.[44] A Fort Pickett Support Group, comprised primarily of Virginia congressional, state, and local government representatives and some chamber of commerce members, was quickly formed to mount a defense of the base.[45] To assist in developing a strategy to defend the fort, the group retained a retired army colonel who was also helping to defend Fort Lee (near Petersburg) and the Defense General Supply Center (near Richmond) from closure. The group also retained the services of another retired army colonel (an Arlington, Virginia, attorney) to be the principal coordinator of the strategy to save the fort.[46]

As was typical in such efforts, the support group focused on arguments that the army had erred in assigning a low military value to Fort Pickett. The group maintained that the army had failed to recognize that all branches of the armed services trained at the base, which facilitated the interservice cooperation stressed by the Pentagon. The group also argued that the army had disregarded the fact that Fort Pickett featured almost 46,000 acres of unrestricted training space, including one of the few artillery ranges on the East Coast. Because of its ample space and absence of environmental-encroachment issues, Fort Pickett provided training space for nearby Fort Bragg, North Carolina, which was "environmentally constrained" because of the presence there of the rare red-cockaded woodpecker. Moreover, claimed Senator Warner, the army's plan called for shifting several thousand trainees from Pickett to Bragg, a position he called "contradictory."[47] In response to the army's assertion that Fort Pickett's airfield was militarily inadequate, Congressman Sisisky arranged to have one of the air force's new C-17 transport planes flown in to demonstrate the airfield's adequacy. (Thenceforth the air force began using the airstrip for training missions with the C-17.[48]) The support group made its case to a BRAC Committee member in March and before a full commission hearing in Baltimore in May 1995. BRAC Commission members visited the fort on two occasions during the decision-making process, but in July the commission voted to uphold the Pentagon's recommendation to realign the fort. Over 40,000 acres would be retained for military training, but be managed by the Virginia National Guard instead of the army.[49] The nature of the training and even the number of troops trained each year would not change. The remainder of the fort (about 3,600 acres) would be made available to the community.

Reuse Planning

Shortly after the BRAC Commission's decision, a Fort Pickett Local Reuse Authority was constituted. Its steering committee was comprised of representatives from the town of Blackstone and five surrounding counties. Its advisory committee included representatives of the Virginia congressional staff, the Governor's Office of Base Retention and Adjustment, the Virginia National Guard, a base-reuse consultant, the army's Base Transition Coordinator, the army's Directorate of Engineering and Housing, and the Commander of Fort Pickett. As was true of reuse-planning efforts at Vint Hill Farms and elsewhere in the nation, the committees did not include employees of Fort Pickett. The steering committee applied for federal Office of Economic Adjustment funds to support the planning process.

Because the BRAC decision split the fort into two components, the reuse-planning and -organizing process proceeded along two tracks: One entailed efforts to plan the mission of the national guard, which assumed command in October 1997. Since very few of the former army employees chose to leave the area, the Local Reuse Authority arranged to have some army employees rehired by the Virginia National Guard with full state-employee benefits, but at somewhat lower salaries than they had been paid in the army. In the meantime, a new function was being added to the national guard post at Fort Pickett. In July 1995 Governor George Allen was persuaded (possibly by a member of the Local Reuse Authority) to propose the relocation of the Virginia Department of Military Affairs, which includes the headquarters of the Virginia National Guard, from Richmond to Fort Pickett.[50] The Department of Military Affairs employed about 270 persons, most of whom were expected to make the 45-minute commute from Richmond to Fort Pickett and some of whom, it was hoped, would move to the area.[51] Strong opposition by the Richmond delegation to the General Assembly and by employees of the Department of Military Affairs caused the General Assembly to refuse to fund the relocation in 1997, but the 1998 General Assembly assented and in December of that year the move was completed. Although the relocated Department of Military Affairs did not hire unemployed Fort Pickett personnel, it did increase economic activity around the fort. Thus it was strongly supported by the local chambers of commerce, which took steps to welcome the new workers and encourage them to move to the area.

The second track entailed planning for reuse of the roughly 3,600 acres of the fort that the army had deemed expendable, all of which lay in Nottoway County. The steering committee of the Local Reuse Authority determined that about 1,200 acres already in use by Virginia Tech's Agricultural Research and Education Center would continue in that use and that the university could take title of the land in 30 years. The Blackstone Army Airfield, which occupied about 500 acres, would be transferred to the town of Blackstone or jointly to Blackstone and the national guard.[52] The remainder, about 1,600 acres, would be transferred to Nottoway County and zoned for light-to-heavy industrial use. This phase of the planning process generated conflict on the steering committee, however. In a region with chronic under-utilization of industrial land, neighboring counties worried that the Fort Pickett property, with its excellent infrastructure of roads, utilities, and the nearby airfield, would attract companies that would otherwise locate in their industrial parks and pay property taxes there.

Nevertheless, by 1999, the issue had been settled and new businesses had located on the property. These included a trucking company, a maker of herbs and spices, a metal spray company, and a small textile manufacturer. An ambulance company had rented the old fire station and several houses and cottages had been rented to weekly commuters from Richmond who worked at the relocated Department of Military Affairs offices. Some of the new companies reportedly employed former army personnel, albeit at lower wages than they had previously earned. A local government official ascribed the quick success of the redevelopment to the booming economy during the late 1990s and to Fort Pickett's location near the urban fringe. It is only 20 miles from the Richmond–Petersburg metropolitan area and only 45 miles from the city of Richmond itself. It is situated on a major state highway and near an interstate highway, and both land and labor costs are low.

DEFENSE-CONVERSION PLANNING IN THEORY: THE RESPONSE IN CHARLOTTESVILLE

Charlottesville is the only Virginia community in which a peace group advocated defense conversion by developing a community defense-conversion plan and encouraging local governments to implement it. Although the plan itself ultimately went unheeded, the circumstances under which it came about are noteworthy because they did not exist elsewhere in Virginia.

Background

The Charlottesville metropolitan statistical area (MSA) is situated in the foothills of the Blue Ridge Mountains about 70 miles northwest of Richmond. It comprises four jurisdictions: the city of Charlottesville, and the counties of Albemarle, Fluvanna, and Greene. As of 1996 the MSA's population was 147,208, having registered an increase of 16 percent from 1980 to 1990, and an additional 12 percent from 1990 to 1996.[53] Almost all of this increase took place in Albemarle County, which surrounds the city, while the city of Charlottesville's population declined slightly.

For most of its history Charlottesville was an agricultural area and, since its founding by Thomas Jefferson in 1819, the home of the University of Virginia (UVA). In later years the area would establish a modest amount of textile and food-products manufacturing, but the dominant activity remained the University of Virginia. By 1993 UVA (including its hospital) employed 10,000 persons—by far the largest employer in the region. Other industries in the economic base included electrical and electronic equipment manufacturing, hotels, printing and publishing, furniture stores, and communication services, most of which had grown up in the area because of the university. The Charlottesville MSA employed 47,540 persons in 1979 and 67,444 in 1993. Thus employment grew by 37 percent from 1979 to 1989, and by almost 3 percent from 1989 to 1993, despite the recession of 1990–1992.[54] Unemployment rates in the region have typically remained below statewide rates despite pockets of poverty in the city and in the rural counties.

One of Charlottesville's major issues is management of the sprawling growth and congestion created by the university and its ancillary services. Another issue is city–county relations. Charlottesville's fiscal health has deteriorated as Albemarle has grown, even though the university is located in the city. The city of Charlottesville manifests many characteristics of a typical college town, including somewhat more liberal political attitudes than those that characterize other parts of the state. This is the basis upon which the defense-conversion plan was developed.

Defense Dependency, Cutbacks, and Community Responses

Charlottesville has less defense dependency than the other Virginia communities discussed in this book. Of the dozen defense-related employers, very few are large, and fewer still rely upon defense work for much of their revenue. In 1990 the University of Virginia employed about 55 persons on military-related research grants; a number that remained fairly stable over several years.[55]

Private contractors included a manufacturer of desk telephones that sold about 5 percent of its total output to the Defense Department, as well as a 1,000-employee company that produces navigational equipment for marine and aerospace users. Half its work was in military sales in 1990. By 1994 it had laid off several hundred workers. Three other defense contractors—an avionics-components supplier, a record-management-services company, and a maker of audio components—laid off a total of about 400 workers between 1990 and 1994. The army's Foreign Science and Technology Center, whose 535 workers collect and analyze military-intelligence information, did not lay off many workers. The army also maintains the Judge Advocate General's School in Charlottesville to educate government-affiliated attorneys. The school reportedly is not sensitive to defense budgeting. Thus the maximum possible number of jobs lost due to defense cutbacks in the area between 1989 and 1994 was about 750. Assuming a multiplier of 2, whereby each defense-related job would support one additional local service job, the total job loss would amount to 1,500, or about 2.2 percent of total employment in 1989. In view of the fact that total employment in the area grew by over 2,000 jobs between 1989 and 1993, it appears that the area was more than able to absorb the impacts of the slight defense downsizing that occurred.

Community Responses to Defense Dependency

In 1990, however, the nature and magnitude of coming defense-spending cutbacks was not yet known. Throughout the country, many businesses and defense-dependent communities were worried and many defense-conversion advocates were optimistic about the impending cutbacks. In this climate, the Charlottesville Peace Education Center formed the Charlottesville–Albemarle Taskforce on Economic Conversion. Like other economic-conversion groups in the United States, the taskforce hoped to encourage the conversion of the military economy toward peacetime activities by facilitating such a transformation at the local level. The group wrote a report entitled "Preparing for Reduced Military Spending," which included a list of the defense contractors and military facilities discussed above, as well as results of interviews with most of the organizations about the extent of their vulnerability to defense cutbacks. The taskforce's report recommended that Charlottesville and Albemarle consider adopting economic-conversion ordinances that would establish economic conversion as a purposeful, constructive local process. It recommended the creation of an environment conducive to the development of new enterprises that would make use of the experience and skills that had been developed in the defense industry. To further this aim, the report suggested that the skills of at-risk workers be inventoried and that existing worker-retraining programs be reviewed to determine if they could meet the needs of defense workers. The report also recommended support for new business development through start-up capital and loan-guarantee funds. It identified state and federal government funding sources that might facilitate these goals as well as state and local institutions such as the University of Virginia that could retrain dislocated workers and assist those wishing to start their own businesses.[56]

The taskforce presented its report to both the Albemarle County Board of Supervisors and the Charlottesville City Council, who thanked the taskforce for its work and stated their intention to follow the issues more closely. Some officials openly endorsed the report and its call for assistance to help companies convert to civilian production.[57] Some, however, expressed skepticism that the issue warranted concerted attention from the public sector. By September 1994 the skeptics had been vindicated. The defense-related dislocations that occurred were small, isolated events that appeared to have little disruptive effect on the Charlottesville-area economy.[58] Nevertheless, at least several hundred defense workers were affected by the cutbacks and it is not known if they were able to find new jobs in the area at comparable wages.

In 1994 officials from the city of Charlottesville and Albemarle County expressed the opinion that defense cutbacks in their area were not a problem and were not expected to become one. They were knowledgeable about the fortunes of the defense contractors mentioned above, but they believed that the situations at these companies did not warrant special attention. They stated that they had ignored the report of the Charlottesville–Albemarle Taskforce on Economic Conversion, since they believed that there was little that government could or should do about defense-spending cutbacks when they did occur, especially when such cutbacks in the Charlottesville area had such a small local impact.

CONCLUSION

The Radford Arsenal and Fort Pickett cases share several common features. Both are southern, rural areas with economies based, to some extent, on agriculture and low-wage manufacturing. Both have relatively weak chambers of commerce, so local public agencies play leading roles in economic development. In the New River Valley, a history of economic dislocation spawned a number of active public economic-development organizations. Nevertheless, both areas focus primarily on traditional branch-plant-recruitment strategies. Both communities faced serious economic dislocation as a result of the downsizing of their major defense facilities. In both cases, elected officials demonstrated concern for local job loss. In the BRAC'95 realignment of Fort Pickett, politicians led the opposition at least as vigorously as did their urban counterparts in Hampton Roads. Although this option was not open to the New River Valley because of the nature of the decision, Congressman Boucher kept a high profile as he worked on issues concerning the Radford Arsenal downsizing. However, it is noteworthy that neither he nor local elected officials nor the Oil, Chemical, and Atomic Workers Union local begged the army to favor the Radford Plant over others, although this is precisely what politicians did in the BRAC process. The BRAC process is apparently too public and too political in nature for politicians to ignore it, whereas the Radford-downsizing decision was less publicly visible. Moreover, the Radford-downsizing process, like defense-contractor downsizing in Hampton Roads, in Northern Virginia, and elsewhere, had the aura of an economic decision as opposed to a political one. Hence it was more acceptable to an essentially conservative community and to conservative politicians.

No one—not politicians and not even the union—encouraged the arsenal contractor, Hercules, to moderate layoffs through job-sharing arrangements or to help arrange some type of employment bridge to new jobs for arsenal workers. Indeed, neither Hercules nor the union apparently even kept track of their laid-off workers. It appears that, despite decades of economic dislocation and a resultant well-developed local capacity to pursue economic development, labor's weakness has prevented the New River Valley community from pursuing more labor-friendly development initiatives.

Both the New River Valley and Fort Pickett responded with aggressive efforts to adjust to the cutbacks once they occurred. Elected officials played visible leadership roles here as well. Local businesses, including chambers of commerce, supported and participated in these efforts, but, except in Roanoke, they did not play leadership roles. In the New River Valley, the absence of a strong growth coalition as well as the history of economic dislocation and activism seem to have allowed space for the community to focus more attention on job and workforce development than on real estate projects. The crisis atmosphere and history of economic dislocation in the greater New River Valley area also created opportunities for a technology interest and a sustainable development interest to put forward alternative economic-development approaches that generated enough support to survive.

The Radford Army Ammunition Plant story illustrates the difficulty of converting such a facility to partial civilian use, especially given the limitations of the ARMS Initiative's dual-use strictures and sluggish army implementation. Nevertheless, as a New River Valley PDC staff person pointed out, the ARMS Initiative did provide significant funding to refurbish the plant and market it to new users. No conversion could have taken place without such funding, nor could any conversion of the arsenal have taken place without the dogged determination of the New River Valley PDC, which had to continually educate the army and Congress about the ARMS Initiative's shortcomings and work to improve it and keep the funds flowing. Nevertheless, these efforts were insufficient to employ more than a small fraction of the laid-off arsenal workers. Indeed, reemployment of laid-off arsenal workers was not the purpose of the ARMS Initiative. In neither the New River Valley nor in the Fort Pickett area did displaced workers generally fare well, although at Fort Pickett some workers were at least able to convert directly from army service to national guard service. And both communities, especially the New River Valley, certainly tried to link displaced workers with job opportunities in newly recruited businesses.

Other than its small size, the Charlottesville community has little in common with the Fort Pickett and New River Valley areas. Charlottesville is a college town with a healthy economy and relatively little defense dependency. It is noteworthy, however, that although several hundred defense workers were laid off, local politicians expressed no concern about them and took no actions to assist them. This outcome provides yet another example of the pattern identified earlier: namely, that politicians know they must respond only to visible job loss, not job loss per se. (In fairness, however, it should be noted that local leaders assumed that such small amounts of laborforce dislocation could be easily handled by the labor market without government intervention.)

The experience of the Charlottesville–Albemarle Taskforce on Economic Conversion shows that unless peace-advocacy groups are able to organize community-wide conversion-planning processes, their efforts are likely to be ignored. But, as discussed in chapter 2, such organizing is only likely to succeed when the community faces an economic crisis that established interests appear unable to satisfactorily solve. Charlottesville perceived no economic crisis, so it felt no need to pursue alternative approaches to local economic-development policy. Chapter 7 provides examples of successful organizing and community-wide planning efforts by peace-advocacy organizations.

NOTES

1. The population of Radford at the time numbered only 6,828. See Robert Freis, "A Stern Necessity." *Roanoke Times On-Line* <http://www.newrivervalley.com/news/features/raap1.html> (circa 1997).

2. Robert Freis, "Behind the Gates." *Roanoke Times On-Line* <http://www.newrivervalley.com/news/features/raap3.html> (circa 1997).

3. Freis, "A Stern Necessity"; see also Freis, "Behind the Gates."

4. Virginia Employment Commission, *Covered Employment and Wages in Virginia by 2-Digit SIC Industry (ES-202)*, 1979, 1989, 1993.

5. Some of the other region-wide economic-development organizations include the Mount Rogers Development Partnership; Blue Ridge Region of Virginia, Inc., a forum for linking the New River Valley Alliance with the Roanoke Valley Economic Development Partnership and with Lynchburg's Region 2000 strategy; Forward Southwest Virginia, a forum that focuses economic-development issues for action by the state General Assembly; New River Valley HOSTS, a regional organization promoting tourism development; Showcasing Southwest Virginia, U.S. Representative Boucher's vehicle for bringing leading U.S. and international company representatives to the area; and the Southwest Virginia Economic Developer's Association, an economic-development professionals organization. Other groups that have economic-development-related functions include the New River Valley Development Corporation; the New River Valley Community Vision 2020, an annual community-wide discussion of important planning and economic-development issues; the I-81 Corridor Council; the New River Valley Response Team; the Blue Ridge Small Business Development Center (funded by the federal Small Business Administration and the state of Virginia); Economic Development Administration overall economic-development planning committees; a variety of study commissions; and other private groups. The Commonwealth of Virginia's Department of Economic Development maintains a local office, as does the Virginia Employment Commission.

6. These include New River Community Action in Radford, Pulaski Encouraging Progress in Pulaski, and Floyd County's Neighbor for Neighbor. Organizations in the Mount Rogers district just south of the New River Valley include People Incorporated in Abingdon, the Appalachian Office of Justice and Peace (a region-wide, church-affiliated group located in Abingdon), the Clinch Powell Sustainable Development Forum, and the Ivanhoe Civic League, which conducts GED classes and advocates for local economic development. For insight into the nature and workings of grass-roots economic-development groups in Appalachia, see John Gaventa, Barbara Ellen Smith, and Alex Willingham, eds., *Communities in Economic Crisis: Appalachia and the South.* Philadelphia: Temple University Press, 1990.

7. Robert Freis, "Swords into Plowshares." *Roanoke Times On-Line* <http://www.newrivervalley.com/news/features/raap4.html> (circa 1997); ARMS National Marketing Program, Operation Enterprise, *The Arms Program: Opportunity for Business Growth and Expansion* <http://www.openterprise.comarms/armover.html> (1996–1998); Virginia Employment Commission, *Employer Information for Defense Contractors as of December 1992*; Virginia Employment Commission, *Employer Information for Defense Contractors as of March 1994.*

8. Virginia Tech Center for Survey Research, "New River Valley Economic Adjustment Strategy Corporate Survey" (Prepared for the New River Valley Planning District Commission, October 1993); Virginia Employment Commission, *Employer Information*

for Defense Contractors as of December 1992; Virginia Employment Commission, *Employer Information for Defense Contractors as of March 1994.*

9. Virginia Tech Center for Survey Research, *New River Valley Economic Adjustment Strategy Corporate Survey.* Nevertheless, 11 of these firms reported that they had experienced layoffs related to defense cutbacks. Virginia Tech experienced an 85 percent decline in defense contracts from 1987 to 1991, but the university was able to replace this work with other research contracts.

10. This multiplier was used by Robert Griffis of the Virginia Employment Commission to calculate the impact of employment loss at the Radford Army Ammunition Plant. Communication from Jeffrey A. Windom, Director of the Virginia Employment Commission to Holly Lesko of New River Valley PDC on March 26, 1993.

11. The AT&T plant had employed as many as 4,000 workers a few years earlier.

12. *Roanoke Times and World News*, "Cuts Hurt Western Virginia Workers Too" (March 10, 1993).

13. Greg Edwards, "ITT Makes Deal: Begins New Product Line." *Roanoke Times and World News* (August 24, 1994).

14. *Roanoke Times and World News*, "Montgomery Wants Plan to Ease Arsenal Cuts' Impact" (September 26, 1992).

15. The PDC had been planning to apply for federal Economic Development Administration (EDA) funds to support a region-wide planning process in the aftermath of the AT&T plant closing in Pulaski County in 1989. The layoffs at the Radford Arsenal added legitimacy to the grant application. However, the Office of Economic Adjustment (OEA) was eventually chosen as the grant agency, which precluded receipt of the EDA funds. The PDC was able to secure more money from the OEA than would have been available from the EDA, but they had to wait an additional year to receive the money. The PDC later received money from the EDA for other purposes, including preparation of the area's Overall Economic Development Plan.

16. See, for example, Thomas G. Johnson et al., "An Economic Opportunity Analysis for the New River Valley." Virginia Polytechnic Institute and State University, Program in Agricultural Economics, March 1994. Johnson's team identified new industries, including import substitution opportunities for the region.

17. Within the Adjustment Strategy planning process, six committees reported to the steering committee—the corporate roundtable, physical infrastructure, human infrastructure, quality of life, economic infrastructure, and the Radford Army Ammunition Plant Task Force. *Source*: New River Valley Planning District Commission documents provided to the author, January 1994.

18. New River Valley Planning District Commission, "New River Valley Vision 2020," April 1995.

19. New River Valley Planning District Commission, "New River Valley News & Views," October–November 1998 <http://crusher.bev.net/blacksburg/pdc/octo98.html>.

20. New River Valley Planning District Commission documents, January 1994.

21. United States Public Law 102-484, October 23, 1992, 106 STAT. 2315, FY1993, Defense Authorization Act, Subtitle H, Armament Retooling and Manufacturing Support Initiative.

22. The facilities are located in Baraboo, Wisconsin; Charlestown, Indiana; Middletown, Iowa; Parsons, Kansas; Independence, Missouri; Texarkana, Texas; Karknack, Texas; Shreveport, Louisiana; Milan, Tennessee; Stennis Space Center, Mississippi; Radford, Virginia; Riverbank, California; Scranton, Pennsylvania; De Soto, Kansas; and

Chattanooga Tennessee. ARMS National Marketing Program, Operation Enterprise: Facility Amenities <http://www.openterprise.com/facam.html> (1996–1998).

23. Commander, U.S. Army, Armament Munitions and Chemical Command brochure, "Armament Retooling and Manufacturing Support Initiative," circa 1993.

24. One person even stated that the loan-guarantee mechanism that was the primary attraction for commercial enterprises could founder. Since the facility and, in some cases, the equipment, were owned by the army, the company would have no collateral to secure the loan guarantee.

25. The ARMS Initiative was not the only reaction to layoffs at the Radford Arsenal. In response to the end of cost-plus contracting arrangements and, more importantly, the Radford Arsenal's failure to win a portion of the army's shrinking demand for propellant contracts from foreign producers that resulted in the massive layoffs, Hercules, Inc., began a program of cost cutting in 1993. The program entailed the layoff of many salaried personnel and the initiation of a labor–management cooperation effort with the Oil, Chemical, and Atomic Workers Union (OCAW). The latter initiative, which began in December 1993, consisted of problem-solving teams comprised of Hercules management, OCAW representatives, and army officials. The teams addressed safety and environmental issues, communications, and cost-saving ideas. By June 1994 accomplishments included efforts to eliminate oil spills and explosions. Although layoffs continued through 1995, the labor–management cooperation effort continued as well.

26. "Southwestern Virginia Advanced Manufacturing Technology Center," Technology Reinvestment Program Proposal, May 1993, in *Commonwealth of Virginia Technology Reinvestment Program Applications.*

27. The defense-company layoffs that most affected the region were those at the Radford Army Ammunition Plant, the Brunswick Company in Marion, Virginia, and the Raytheon Corporation in Bristol, Tennessee.

28. Clinch Powell Sustainable Development Forum, "Sustainable Development for Northeast Tennessee and Southwest Virginia." Abingdon, VA, April 1994.

29. Associated Press, "Making Prosperity Blend with the Scenery." *Richmond Times-Dispatch* (July 18, 1995).

30. Piedmont Planning District Commission, "Fort Pickett: The Economic Impact on the Piedmont Planning District," December 15, 1988. See also Brian P. McManus and John L. Knapp, *Piedmont Planning District Number 14.* Charlottesville: University of Virginia, Weldon Cooper Center for Public Service, 1998.

31. Piedmont Planning District Commission, "Fort Pickett"; Timothy Petrie, "A Reuse Plan for Fort Pickett Army Base," Department of Urban Studies and Planning, Virginia Commonwealth University, April 1992, p. 9; see also Associated Press, "Base-Closing List Galvanizes Support for Fort Pickett; State and Local Leaders Begin a Campaign to Keep the Army Facility from Closing." *Virginian-Pilot* (March 6, 1995).

32. Robert Little, "Blackstone's Fort Pickett; A Town, a Fort, a Future?" *Virginian-Pilot* (March 12, 1995). These employment figures conflict with a more modest estimate given in the Associated Press article cited above (note 31), but they are closer to prior year totals. The Virginia Employment Commission put the employment total at 502 in 1992 and Petrie ("A Reuse Plan for Fort Pickett Army Base") determined that about 480 civilians worked at the base in 1992. Part of the discrepancy can be traced to the fact that the base employed a substantial number of workers on a temporary basis, to assist when large numbers of trainees are on base. A June 1991 story in the *Richmond Times-Dispatch* cited Lennice Thompson, a spokesperson for the fort, who reported that the Fort had 100 mili-

tary personnel and 600 to 800 civilians, depending upon the season. Ms. Thompson also stated that almost 90,000 troops had trained at Fort Pickett in 1990. See William Ruberry, "A.P. Hill, Pickett, Put on List of Bases that U.S. May Shut." *Richmond Times-Dispatch* (June 1, 1991).

33. Peter Bacque and Jamie C. Ruff, "State Guard Studies Taking Over Pickett." *Richmond Times-Dispatch* (March 3, 1995).

34. Piedmont Planning District, *The Economic Impact on the Piedmont Planning District.*

35. This includes the direct effects of the fort's training operations and reservist-trainee expenditures, as well as indirect and induced spending and employment in the surrounding community. The size of the impact was due in part to the above-average wages that Fort Pickett paid. See Virginia Employment Commission, *A Revised Impact Analysis of Fort Pickett*, March 1995.

36. Little, "Blackstone's Fort Pickett."

37. Petrie, "A Reuse Plan for Fort Pickett Army Base," p. 15.

38. Little, "Blackstone's Fort Pickett."

39. Piedmont Planning District Commission, "Restoration and Enhancement of the Blackstone–Fort Pickett Army Air Base: Assessment and Recommendations," February 25, 1985.

40. Ruberry, "A.P. Hill, Pickett, Put on List of Bases that U.S. May Shut"; see also William Ruberry, "Personnel at Bases Edgy Over 'Hit List.'" *Richmond Times-Dispatch* (December 1988).

41. Public statement made at the Virginia Commission on Defense Conversion and Economic Adjustment hearing, Radford, Virginia, January 6, 1993.

42. Susan Winiecki, "Major Export–Import Center Proposed for Southside." *Richmond Times-Dispatch* (January 17, 1992).

43. Through the BRAC'95 process the army also assigned Forts Chafee (Arkansas), McClellan (Alabama), and Indiantown Gap (Pennsylvania) to the Army National Guard. National Guard Association of the United States, "Washington Focus" <http://www.ngaus.org/washfoc/99brac.htm>.

44. *Virginian-Pilot*, "Base-Closing List Galvanizes Support for Fort Pickett."

45. The Fort Pickett Support Group was chaired by William A. Armbruster, a retired U.S. Navy Captain and member of the Blackstone Town Council, Ginna Bauhan of the Governor's Office of Base Retention and Defense Adjustment, Charles Burgess, Jr., Dinwiddie County administrator, James Harris, MD, Jack E. Hughton, Director of the Piedmont Planning District Commission, R. L. Mann, Manager, Crewe Municipal Airport, Earl Moore, Owner of the Burkeville Market, Garland Redford, Mayor of the town of Crewe, Ronald Roark, Nottoway County administrator, Gary Simmons, Vice President of Simmons Monument Co., J. A. S. Wilson, president of Citizens Bank and Trust, Macon Booker, Amelia County Supervisor, Jim Eanes, publisher of the *Crewe–Burkeville Journal*, J. C. Higgenbotham, Crewe town manager, Jeffrey Johnson, Brunswick County administrator, Harrison Moody, farmer, J. Larry Palmore, Blackstone town manager, Charles Rickers II, sales representative, J. Howard Settle, retired from the Farm Credit Bank, Sherman Vaughan, assistant superintendent of Nottoway County Schools, Stanley Worsham, Jr., Finance Manager, Southside Electric Cooperative.

46. *Virginian-Pilot*, "BRAC Commander to Visit Fort Pickett in Virginia" (March 19, 1995).

47. Ibid.

48. Dale Eisman, "N.C. Plans a Dogfight This Week for Navy Jets." *Virginian-Pilot* (May 2, 1995).

49. The army also assigned Forts Chafee (Arkansas), McClellan (Alabama), and Indiantown Gap (Pennsylvania) to the Army National Guard. See National Guard Association of the United States, "Washington Focus."

50. Michael Hardy and Mike Allen, "Allen Offers Plan to Offset Pickett Closure." *Richmond Times-Dispatch* (July 15, 1995).

51. At Governor Allen's request, the Virginia General Assembly commissioned a feasibility study of the proposed relocation in March 1996, which determined that the move would save the state $500,000 per year because the Fort Pickett facilities would be cheaper than the Richmond office building.

52. As of August 1999 this issue had not been settled.

53. The Virginia Employment Commission projected a 12 percent population growth rate from 1990 to 2000. Virginia Employment Commission, *Virginia Population Projections, 2010*, June 1993.

54. Virginia Employment Commission, *Covered Employment and Wages in Virginia by 2-Digit Industry (ES-202), 1979, 1989, 1993.*

55. The Charlottesville–Albemarle Taskforce on Economic Conversion, "Preparing for Reduced Military Spending," unpublished report, February 12, 1991. Also, tabulations supplied to the author by John L. Knapp, professor and research director, University of Virginia, Weldon Cooper Center for Public Service, September 1994.

56. The Charlottesville–Albemarle Taskforce on Economic Conversion, "Preparing for Reduced Military Spending," February 12, 1991.

57. The report and the positive responses of local officials were featured in a 30-minute televised program on defense conversion produced by the Center for Defense Information in Washington, D.C., and aired nationally in 1991.

58. Un-weighted averages calculated by the author from unemployment data supplied by William H. Mezger, chief economist, Virginia Employment Commission, 1995.

6

The State Politics of Defense Restructuring: Adjustment and Resistance

Previous chapters have described the sources of resistance and adjustment to defense-spending cutbacks in Virginia's defense-dependent communities. Resistance arose primarily during the base-closure process, but also when major defense-system contractors such as Newport News Shipyard faced contract cutbacks. (Recall, for example, the shipyard's congressional letter-writing campaign to secure funding of the CVN-76 carrier.[1]) The primary source of resistance to base closures was public officials, whose unwritten job descriptions include the necessity to at least show concern and possibly take action when local jobs are threatened.[2] A secondary source of local resistance to base closures was local growth interests. And in several Virginia communities, local public officials and chambers of commerce mobilized jobholders at military installations and citizens-at-large to appear at BRAC Commission hearings and argue for retaining their military facilities.[3]

Adaptive responses arose both after procurement cutbacks and after base closures. In Virginia communities, at least, the primary source of adaptive response to procurement cutbacks was contractors who needed to keep their companies afloat. Local growth interests also needed to replace lost economic activity, but they played prominent roles only in adjustments to base closings, not contractor layoffs. Local politicians had to replace lost jobs and develop sources of real estate tax revenues, so they were a primary source of adaptive response to base closings. But they only assisted defense companies in the New River Valley area, where the traditional growth interests are weak. Another source of adaptive response to procurement cutbacks was the "technology-development interest," whose promoters developed the Peninsula Advanced Technology Center and the Southwestern Virginia Advanced Manufacturing

Technology Center. Also, professional staff at the Small Business Development Centers and the dislocated-workforce services centers in Hampton Roads, Northern Virginia, and the New River Valley articulated the need for better services for their clients. With the exception of Charlottesville's peace-education center, neither peace advocates nor organized labor were able to promote adaptive responses to cutbacks.

Virginia state policy reflected dominant local interests, so it did not mitigate the effects of procurement cutbacks, and it resisted base closings. To be sure, a gubernatorial commission that met in 1992 and 1993 recommended adaptive responses to procurement cutbacks. These recommendations were technically sound and represented standard practice in defense conversion, but they lacked a direct connection to the Virginia General Assembly that was asked to approve them. They were neither drafted by legislators nor supported by an organized grass-roots constituency that would urge the General Assembly to pass them into law. Hence the General Assembly rejected them. When the 1993 BRAC Commission accepted the Pentagon's recommendation to close the Norfolk Naval Aviation Depot, Vint Hill Farms Station, and the Suffolk Undersea Warfare Center and to move 12,000 navy employees out of the Crystal City office complex, the forces of resistance to base closures quickly mobilized. This chapter describes the unsuccessful attempt to develop an adaptive response at the state level and the subsequent state campaign to resist base closures.

MONITORING AND ADAPTING TO PROCUREMENT CUTBACKS: 1990–1993

Research and Monitoring Activities

As discussed in the chapter on the response in Northern Virginia, that region began to suffer the effects of defense-procurement cutbacks as early as 1987 (which came on the heels of several years of unprecedented peacetime defense-expenditure increases). As those cutbacks continued and as the Cold War ended, observers began to voice concerns about the potential fallout in Virginia.[4] These concerns led to research and analysis of defense dependency. James Scampavia of the Fairfax Economic Development Authority and Stephen Fuller of the Greater Washington Research Center began studying the effects of cutbacks on companies in 1989, and John Whaley of the Hampton Roads Planning District Commission produced reports on that community's military economy. Also, an assistant to the Virginia Secretary of Economic Development studied the impact of defense cutbacks on Northern Virginia's economy.[5] Other analysts focused on the entire state. In 1990, for example, Nestor Terlekyj of NPA Data Services, Inc., analyzed the state's vulnerability to defense-spending cutbacks. In 1991 the Virginia Joint Legislative Audit and Review Commission published *Possible Impacts of Defense Cutbacks on Virginia's Economy*, and in 1992 John Knapp of the University of Virginia published "The Impact of Defense Spending on Virginia's Economy."[6]

The most comprehensive studies of the nature and impact of defense-spending in Virginia were conducted by chief economist Robert J. Griffis of the Virginia Employment Commission, under the auspices of an Inter-Agency Task Force on Defense Conversion and Economic Adjustment, created in 1990 by Governor L. Douglas Wilder. The task force was comprised of ten state-agency representatives and the state's Washington, D.C., liaison office.[7] From 1991 to 1995 Griffis published numerous reports, including annual analyses of defense expenditures by type and region, lists of Virginia's defense prime contractors, Department of Defense military and civilian employment in Virginia, and estimated private-sector defense employment in Virginia. He also conducted analyses of the regional economic impacts of military installations targeted for possible closure by the Base Realignment and Closure Commission. Communities relied upon these studies to help defend their bases before the commission.[8]

Griffis's attempts to create lists of defense subcontractors, however, so that he could describe defense dependency more accurately and so that state programs to assist small businesses could be developed, were unsuccessful. The reasons for this shed light on the barriers to proactive defense adjustment and conversion. The U.S. Defense Department does not require prime contractors to report their subcontractors, so there is no standard format or central list of such firms. In 1991 Griffis's staff tried to survey firms listed with the State Office of Minority Business Enterprise about their subcontract status, but no surveys were returned. Between 1990 and 1993 the Virginia Secretary of Economic Development (now Commerce and Trade) made several requests of Newport News Shipyard to provide a list of its subcontractors in Virginia, but it never complied with the request, despite the fact that one of its officials was a member of Governor Wilder's Commission on Defense Conversion and Economic Adjustment.[9]

Despite Virginia's timely entry into defense research and monitoring activities, it took considerably longer to begin conversion and adjustment planning. Several factors seem to be responsible: First, neither the 1988 nor 1991 BRAC rounds cut into Virginia's military employment to a noticeable degree (although procurement cutbacks certainly affected the Northern Virginia economy in the 1980s and the Hampton Roads economy in the early 1990s). The only base closure that Virginia experienced was that of Cameron Station in Alexandria, a move welcomed by dominant interests in the community and that took until 1995 to complete. Second, most of those who analyzed Virginia's defense dependency in the early 1990s concluded that, with the exception of Newport News Shipyard, Virginia would not experience significant defense-procurement-spending cutbacks beyond those already encountered in Northern Virginia in the late 1980s, nor would it, they expected, suffer significant job losses in the 1993 or 1995 BRAC rounds. In the former case, they reasoned, Northern Virginia's communication- and information-technology industry products and services were slated for defense-spending increases. Also, they expected defense cutbacks to reconsolidate military commands, especially the navy's, back to ports such as Hampton Roads from which they had been dispersed during the defense build-up of the 1980s. However, these studies focused mostly on aggregate trends, not on the dislocations that defense workers and small businesses might suffer. Third, Virginia has traditionally eschewed proactive, interventionist economic policies. Economic-development policies have generally been limited to the recruitment of businesses from the Northeast and abroad. Unlike some states, particularly Rust Belt states that suffered substantial dislocation in the 1970s and 1980s, Virginia officials have generally taken restructuring and business out-migration in stride rather than adopt policies to assist existing businesses or retrain dislocated workers. Thus, until 1992 at least, simply monitoring the situation seemed to fit best with Virginia's traditional approach to the economy. As late as May 1992, Virginia officials maintained that they did not expect severe cutbacks, that Virginia had already taken steps to diversify its economy, and that it had long since created appropriate business-recruitment programs that would counteract any negative effects of defense downsizing.[10]

But pressures for a more activist approach were beginning to build. The recession of 1990–1992, which hit the state particularly hard and resulted in state tax-revenue shortfalls, provoked concerns about the economy. In this environment, the prospect of more defense cuts led to calls for state action. By January 1992 legislative study commissions on economic policy were recommending state assistance to localities affected by defense reductions.[11] Defense-conversion and -adjustment discussions began to receive more publicity as well. In 1991 the Charlottesville–Albemarle Taskforce on Economic Conversion publicized its report and, in the spring of 1992, Virginia Polytechnic Institute and State University organized a public forum in Hampton Roads to discuss the issue of defense cutbacks and appropriate state-government responses.[12] News media in Hampton Roads had begun to focus on the issue also. During the summer and fall of 1991 the National Governors' Association conducted a study of defense dependency and conversion policies in four states, including Virginia. Its report, *A Governor's Guide to Economic Conversion*, was published in early 1992 and recommended that Virginia continue research efforts, increase public awareness of the issues, and establish a single point of contact in state government on defense-conversion and economic-adjustment issues.[13]

Following up on the National Governor's Association study and the recommendations of a legislative study commission, Robert Griffis drafted a "Virginia Economic Conversion and Adjustment Plan" in January 1992 for consideration by the General Assembly (which meets in January and February). The plan called for the creation of an intersecretarial and interagency committee to coordinate state policy on conversion and adjustment, with a staff of one full-time and one part-time person. It also suggested continuing research and analysis of defense spending and the impacts of cutbacks, a community education and outreach program, and assistance to communities, firms, and workers.[14] The General Assembly failed to pass the budget amendment that would have funded the plan.

Defense Conversion and Adjustment Planning:
The Wilder Commission

In March 1992 the Secretary of Economic Development persuaded Governor Wilder to create a gubernatorial study commission on Defense Conversion and Economic Adjustment.[15] The commission's mission was to "recommend and promote principles, policies, and structures to assure the integration of state and federal programs and employment of fiscal and human resources necessary to aid in the conversion and diversification of defense-dependent industries, to include separating defense employees, in support of long-term economic development of the Commonwealth of Virginia."[16] Commission members were named in August 1992. The commission was chaired by Cathleen Magennis, Secretary of Economic Development (now called Commerce and Trade) and General John Loh, Commander of the Air Force Air Combat Command housed at Langley Air Force Base in Hampton. (Loh was also a founder of the Peninsula Advanced Technology Center and a champion of measures to enhance the defense industrial base.) Membership primarily comprised representatives of defense contractors and technology-development experts as well as the Virginia AFL-CIO and the Richmond Federal Reserve Bank.[17] Others included Robert Templin of Thomas Nelson Community College (also a founder of the Peninsula Advanced Technology Center) and representatives of Northern Virginia Congressman James Moran and of U.S. Senator John Warner. The largely nonpolitical, technical and business backgrounds of the committee reflected the commission's primary focus on defense industry and community conversion and adjustment as well as the technical focus of staff to the process, such as that of Robert Griffis, who assisted in the commission's member-selection process.

The commission met five times between September 1992 and November 1993. It conducted local public hearings and toured local bases and contractor facilities. It issued three reports during the course of its 16-month tenure. Each report contained summaries of Robert Griffis's reports on Virginia's defense economy, as well as on cutbacks and employment losses throughout the state. Inventories of federal and state economic-development and worker-retraining programs were included in the reports as well. Most important, each report contained commission recommendations for state administrative and legislative actions—54 in all. These recommendations can be grouped into the following categories: (1) Continued data collection, analysis, and dissemination of reports on the status of defense industries and Department of Defense employment in Virginia; (2) measures to help defense-dependent businesses convert or diversify to civilian products and services; (3) measures to retrain or employ dislocated defense workers, especially those being discharged from the military; (4) new institutions or staff positions; and (5) minority and women-owned business recommendations.

Some of the commission's recommendations were implemented by administrative action, without General Assembly approval. Those recommendations that required funding or additional staff, however, had to be approved by the

General Assembly. But almost none of these legislative recommendations were approved. Some observers cited the sour relations between Democratic Governor Wilder and the Democratic-led General Assembly as the primary reason for the latter's refusal to enact the recommendations. There is considerable truth in this observation. Also, some General Assembly members reportedly were irked that none of their members had been asked to serve on the commission. No doubt, Governor Wilder's failure to place any General Assembly members on the commission ensured that no legislator's support was guaranteed. Also important were the results of the BRAC'93 process and the divergent philosophies of the commission and General Assembly members about economic-development policy. Most important, perhaps, no organized, vocal constituency pressed the General Assembly to support the commission's recommendations.

In fact, even the commission itself did not encourage the General Assembly to adopt their recommendations. As one business representative on the commission said later: "We had a lot of talent on that commission. But all we did was listen and rubber-stamp recommendations from the committees. We never debated anything or focused in on an approach to dealing with the issues." The commission's co-chair, General Loh, took the position that listening and reporting to the governor was all that the commission was meant to do. He and some commission members rejected the idea that the commission should advocate with the General Assembly to adopt its recommendations. As a result, said another business representative, the commission proved to be "just another layer, without any real substance." Thus, like other conversion- and adjustment-planning processes in Virginia, the Wilder Commission produced some good ideas, but it suffered from lack of political organization and muscle. The commission's key recommendations and their fates are described below.

(1) *Information collection, analysis, and dissemination*: Most of these recommendations were made in November 1992 and focused on continuing the work of the Inter-Agency Task Force, chaired by Robert Griffis, and continuing the role of Griffis and the Virginia Employment Commission (VEC) as staff to the commission. Other recommendations included the monitoring of federal conversion-related programs, monitoring of other states' initiatives, and establishment of a state toll-free hotline on defense and conversion issues.[18] These recommendations were implemented by the Wilder administration, but discontinued in late 1994 by the administration of his successor, George Allen. The commission's January 1994 recommendation to increase funding by $125,000 to accomplish the research agenda was rejected by the General Assembly.

(2) *Business-assistance recommendations*: These included a call for administrative review of environmental regulations that defense and nondefense businesses alike found overly burdensome. The Wilder administration carried out this review. The recommendations also included a proposal to increase the Governor's Opportunity Fund (a pool that typically is tapped to support business-recruitment efforts). Because it supported the goal of business recruitment, the General Assembly passed the measure in 1993, adding $3 million to the fund.

The General Assembly defeated most of the commission's other business-assistance proposals, however, including tax credits for firms that hire displaced defense workers, tax credits for defense contractors who engage in R&D work, establishment of a Defense Conversion Authority to issue below-prime-interest-rate loans to defense-dependent companies diversifying into commercial work, funding of an alternative-use study of the Radford Army Ammunition Plant, establishment of a $1 million Governor's Fund for Defense Conversion, and a loan-guarantee program for nondefense activities pursued by defense contractors. The General Assembly did, however, agree in 1995 to dedicate $600,000 of existing small-business finance monies to capitalize a revolving loan fund for defense-dependent businesses as its match requirement to secure almost $2.1 million in federal Economic Development Administration funds.

The commission endorsed the pursuit of federal defense-conversion funds by state agencies. In addition to the aforementioned Economic Development Administration (EDA) loan fund, the state participated in successful local applications for $560,000 in Office of Economic Adjustment funds and an additional $1.2 million in EDA grants to localities.[19] The most significant grant-funding effort was the state's application for federal Advanced Research Projects Agency (ARPA) Technology Reinvestment Project (TRP) funds during the spring and early summer of 1993. As described in chapter 1, the short-lived federal program awarded funds to private- and public-sector participants to develop so-called dual-use technologies that would help defense-dependent companies develop civilian products and, at the same time, improve the defense industrial base. The Virginia Department of Economic Development coordinated 13 public-sector and 15 private-sector proposals, and Virginia companies submitted 120 proposals independent of the state coordination and review process. The results were impressive. Virginia reportedly received about one-fourth of all TRP funds disbursed in the 1993 program year—about $101 million. Successful projects included a Center for Advanced Ship Repair and Maintenance in Norfolk.

Also successful was a 1993 state proposal to the National Institute of Standards and Technology's Manufacturing Extension Program to fund a Virginia Alliance for Manufacturing Competitiveness, which would facilitate a manufacturing technology-extension service throughout the state. (The technology-extension model is based upon the land-grant university-extension model, which improved agricultural productivity by providing farmers with technical assistance and information throughout the twentieth century.) However, the Allen administration did not agree to its match requirement for the program. The governor's advisors reportedly found the extension idea "socialistic." Indeed, the Allen administration failed to pursue any federal defense-conversion or -adjustment funds.[20]

(3) *Workforce-assistance initiatives also figured prominently in the Wilder commission's deliberations*: A recommendation to increase the Department of Economic Development's workforce training funds (which are used to attract new firms to the state) was passed by the 1993 General Assembly, adding $1.5 million

to the pool of funds. The commission also recommended that the state develop better workforce-education and -training programs. This proposal resulted in a modest amount of additional workforce-training funds being allocated to the Department of Economic Development's Workforce Services program.

The commission also asked the Virginia Employment Commission (VEC) to collaborate with the U.S. Defense Department to develop an inventory of the skills of departing military personnel, which would be translated from military classifications into the standard *Dictionary of Occupational Titles* formats used by employment agencies and economic-development organizations. The Forward Hampton Roads organization requested this action in 1992 to help it market discharged military personnel to potential new businesses in the area. Commission staff suggested that the skills inventory be developed through the VEC's Transition Assistance Program, a three-day seminar that the VEC organized on bases laying off large numbers of workers, in order to acquaint them with the state's employment services. The skills inventory required that departing personnel fill out a survey giving pertinent information. Implementation difficulties proved insurmountable, however. The secretaries of the army and navy reportedly did not support the initiative, and some local base commanders did not like the project either; Governor Wilder did not attempt to convince them otherwise. Those departing personnel who did fill out the forms generally did not do so completely. Thus the data were reportedly of such poor quality that they could not be used to develop the inventory. By 1994 the project had been scuttled.

(4) *The commission made several institutional-development recommendations as well*: The 1993 General Assembly approved the commission's recommendation that a special counsel be hired as a point person on defense-conversion efforts and placed in the office of the Secretary of Economic Development (but the position had disappeared by 1995). The commission also proposed that the state fund the Peninsula Advanced Technology Center (PATC) and encourage the replication of this model throughout the state. The 1993 General Assembly provided funds for the renovation of an office building on the campus of Thomas Nelson Community College for PATC, but it refused to provide more substantial support and did not entertain the prospect of replicating the model throughout the state.[21]

In June 1993 (near the conclusion of the BRAC'93 process) the commission also agreed to "assist as appropriate in the process of developing the position of the commonwealth to respond to base closures" and to develop a "cross-agency rapid-response plan to implement in the case of base-closure announcements."[22] This recommendation was implemented by administrative action. By January 1994 the Secretary of Commerce and Trade (previously Economic Development) had established a Base-Closure Response Team that had visited and been briefed by commanders at several bases.

(5) *The commission's subcommittee on minority- and women-owned businesses made 13 recommendations that were endorsed by the full commission*: In general, those recommendations that called for additional funding or for significant program or policy changes either were not implemented or were deferred for

more study; the other recommendations simply emphasized what were, reportedly, existing practices. Almost half of the recommendations suggested improvements in the services provided by the Small Business Development Centers (SBDCs)—funded by the state, localities, and the federal Small Business Administration. The SBDCs were asked to provide a formal listing of the areas of expertise of staff at the centers, conduct more staff development, initiate a mentoring program whereby retired military and civilian Defense Department staff would assist small minority- and women-owned businesses in applying for government contracts, conduct proactive outreach to assist defense-dependent firms before they experienced crises, organize educational seminars on marketing and other skills, and create mentorships to help small businesses learn how to access new sources of capital. In January 1994 the state reported that, with one exception, either it already provided the services that were recommended or that the SBDCs would be encouraged to do so. However, the implementation of the fourth recommendation—to provide more proactive outreach to defense-dependent firms—was, according to some businesses and even SBDC directors, not aggressively pursued. Indeed, the SBDCs remained chronically under-funded and were thus unable to conduct more extensive outreach.[23]

The commission called for the appointment of an advocate for small minority- and women-owned businesses who would be the state's point person for accessing federal defense-conversion funds for small businesses, but that position was not created. Another recommendation suggested that the Small Business Development Centers program hire additional staff in defense-dependent parts of the state; the state responded by endorsing a successful application by the Hampton Roads, Flory (Northern Virginia), and Radford SBDCs for $300,000 in SBA funds for extra staff to assist small defense businesses.[24]

The Governor's Conference on Defense Conversion

In addition to the work of the commission, the Wilder administration held a statewide conference on defense conversion on March 8 and 9, 1993, in Richmond, attended by about 400 people. Most of the attendees were local and state public officials, with some businesspersons and military officers as well. The conference described conversion programs around the nation and showcased local conversion and adjustment strategies such as the Peninsula Advanced Technology Center in Hampton. Also, local officials and businesspersons met in regional-planning sessions to discuss their communities' situations and strategies to address them. The conference generated substantial enthusiasm among the participants and provided a venue in which a number of productive partnerships could germinate. For example, the idea for the aforementioned Center for Advanced Ship Repair TRP proposal was hatched at the conference when the Secretary of Economic Development's special counsel for defense conversion broached the idea to Hampton Roads representatives.[25] Several local officials later cited the conference as the place where they first learned of federal and state funds for defense conversion or adjustment.

Ironically, the governor's conference met one day before the Pentagon was due to propose its list of bases to be closed or realigned by the 1993 Base Realignment and Closure Commission. In his luncheon speech to conference participants, Senator John Warner stated that his information led him to believe that Virginia would not suffer significant losses in the BRAC'93 round, and he reminded the audience of the need for defense preparedness and sustained military spending. Thus the Pentagon's list of proposed closures and realignments came as a shock to many, for it included the Norfolk Naval Aviation Depot, the Naval Undersea Warfare Center in Suffolk, and Vint Hill Farms Station, as well as the departure of navy office staff from Crystal City. During the course of the BRAC Commission's deliberations, Fort Lee (near Petersburg) and the Oceana Naval Air Station (in Hampton Roads) were briefly added to the list of facilities considered for closure, although they were soon removed from it.

THE CAMPAIGN TO RESIST BASE CLOSINGS, 1993–1995

As described in chapter 3, Hampton Roads perceived the BRAC'93 actions as a "wake-up call." So too did the Virginia General Assembly. In the fall of 1993 the Virginia Senate Finance Committee, chaired by Hampton Senator Hunter Andrews, quietly circulated its own study of the state's defense situation. The study accused the Wilder administration and his commission of failing to defend the Naval Aviation Depot, the Undersea Warfare Center, and Crystal City in the BRAC'93 process, and for generally focusing too little attention on defending the state's bases and too much on defense conversion. As noted above, this criticism clearly reflected a difference in philosophy as well as the Hampton senator's need to defend the jobs of his constituents. It also reflected a general lack of leadership on the part of the Wilder commission.

Defending the Bases: The Allen Commission and Other Activities

In June 1994, about six months after taking office, Governor George Allen created a Commission on Base Retention and Defense Adjustment. The 38-member commission was co-chaired by Robert Skunda, Secretary of Commerce and Trade, and Admiral Harry Train II, U.S. Navy (retired). Six of its members were General Assembly delegates and four were General Assembly senators. Twelve were retired military officers and eleven were businesspersons. The remaining three were the director of the Hampton Roads Planning District Commission and two holdovers from the Wilder commission: a representative from Senator Warner's office and Robert Templin, the new Director of the Virginia Center for Innovative Technology. As the commission's name and its makeup indicate, the primary focus was to be on defending existing military facilities in the BRAC'95 round—a point underscored by Governor Allen in his September 1994 remarks to the Commission.

The commission met twice, in September 1994 and February 1995. It did not hold regional hearings. At its first meeting, the commission established three committees to carry out its work: base retention, defense conversion, and strategic planning. The second and third committees were combined into one in February 1995 and, by all accounts, were not active.[26] Although the base retention committee was stronger than the other two, it did not produce recommendations or tangible products. Instead, its members served as points of contact between the governor's office, the armed services, and communities facing possible base closings. Between September 1994 and March the commission staff, Governor Allen, and the Congressional delegation—particularly Senator Warner's office—visited almost every base in Virginia to reemphasize Virginia's desire to be a good host for the military. Each base commander was asked how the commonwealth could help to facilitate the base's mission.

To support the commission's work, the Democratic General Assembly appropriated approximately $1 million.[27] Of this amount, approximately $500,000 was spent on consultant fees in the defense of Hampton Roads bases, and lesser amounts were spent on defending other facilities such as Fort Lee, the Defense General Supply Center (near Richmond), and Fort Pickett. Except for the funding and visits though, neither state staff nor the commission played active roles in the base-defense efforts. They stood by, ready to assist as needed, but much of the defense work involved local and federal officials.

By August 1995 the BRAC'95 process had been concluded and the commission's director had been reassigned to other activities in the governor's Office. Although the deputy director remained on duty, her role consisted of serving as a point of state contact for base-reuse planning efforts at Vint Hill Farms and Fort Pickett. In the meantime, the Inter-Agency Task Force on Defense Conversion and Economic Adjustment, which had been created in 1990 to monitor the defense economy, was quietly dissolved.[28]

In addition to establishing the Base Retention Commission, Governor Allen revived the Virginia Military Advisory Council, a body that is comprised of the commanders of major bases in Virginia. The council's purpose is to facilitate ongoing communications between state government and military installations so that issues can be addressed and problems solved before they become serious.[29] Formed under the Baliles administration (1985–1989), the council met twice yearly in a festive atmosphere. Under the Wilder administration, meetings of the council were low-key affairs, with only attorneys and other staff persons meeting occasionally. Governor Allen reestablished the council in the fall of 1994, and met with the council again in May and November of 1995.

CONCLUSION

The Commonwealth of Virginia engaged in considerable activity in response to defense cutbacks from 1990 to 1995. From 1990 to 1992 the primary focus of this activity was research and monitoring. During 1992 and 1993 research and monitoring continued, but the primary focus shifted to conversion and adjustment planning. During 1994 and 1995 the focus shifted to resistance to cutbacks through retention and enhancement of existing military facilities.

Some of these efforts proved more effective than others. The research and monitoring efforts, by all accounts, were quite valuable to state and local officials, and they compare very well with other states' information services. Indeed, the only significant gap in the research record was the absence of a list of defense subcontractors located in the state.[30] In its conversion- and adjustment-assistance efforts, however, the state's record was unimpressive. On the plus side, Governor Wilder's Commission on Defense Conversion and the governor's conference in March 1993 focused public attention on the issue and brought people together to develop community responses to defense cuts, and the state's aggressive organization of the application process for first-round federal Technology Reinvestment Project funds garnered over one-fourth of the total TRP funds allocated nationwide. Still, most of the applications received very little state assistance or even direct state involvement.

Ultimately, Virginia accomplished very little in the area of defense conversion and adjustment assistance because the state's dominant interests did not support it. The General Assembly refused to authorize funds to support company-conversion efforts or local development models such as the Peninsula Advanced Technology Center. Nor did the state agree to support individual company requests for conversion assistance. As noted in chapter 3, when Metro Machine Corporation asked the state to help defray a portion the $100 million cost to build a plant to produce commercial tankers through a small grant and guaranteed loan, the Wilder administration and the General Assembly declined to support the request. Yet a few years later, the Allen administration found $98 million to underwrite Newport News Shipyard's Carrier Innovation Center.[31] Even some administrative efforts that did not require General Assembly approval did not work out well. The aforementioned Economic Development Administration–funded revolving loan fund to support conversion began as an application in March 1993. However, the EDA did not approve the application until 1995, and then only with numerous strings attached as lending requirements. By August 1995 only two firms had received loans. A few other defense firms had expressed interest, but they needed far more than the $200,000 loan limit. Judging by the reports of small businesses in Hampton Roads and Northern Virginia as well as some state and local officials, many small businesses were not able to get help when they needed it and they ceased operations prior to 1995. The state also failed in its efforts to develop an effective labor-skills inventory of departing military personnel to be used for economic-development purposes. Indeed, in the area of dislocated-worker retraining and job-placement generally, state and local efforts were marred by lack of information and follow-through, as well as, reportedly, lack of appropriate career counseling and training.

In some aspects of the local adjustment process the state was cited for its helpfulness. For example, local growth interests commended the state for the work of its Department of Environmental Quality in getting water permits to redevelop the Vint Hill Farms station. But some local officials opined that the state could have provided far more support for local strategic-adjustment planning in the New River Valley and Hampton Roads. In fact, it provided none of this type of support.

The base-retention effort, on the other hand, was a smashing success. Local and state officials argued that the strong defensive push during the Pentagon's planning stage in the fall of 1994, rather than during the BRAC deliberation stage in the spring of 1995, contributed to the success of the campaign. It also accounted, they claimed, for the difference between the 1993 BRAC outcome in which several Virginia facilities were closed, and the 1995 outcome in which no major facilities were closed, only one installation (Fort Pickett) was realigned and downsized, and one base—Oceana Naval Air Station—was expanded significantly.

Thus the chief legacy of the commonwealth's efforts in the defense-restructuring process from 1990 to 1995 is that the state enhanced its portion of the nation's decreasing military employment and reaffirmed its ties to the military. To be sure, there was a defense-conversion policy interest in Virginia: The companies that diversified their production to civilian markets, the small businesses that went bankrupt because they could not convert quickly enough, the advocates for high-technology development as an alternative to defense work, and the public officials who administered the state's dislocated worker and small-business-assistance programs. But this interest never became organized so that it could pressure the General Assembly to pass conversion-assistance legislation. Moreover, neither the peace movement nor the labor movement was strong enough to articulate, much less organize support for, a conversion agenda in Virginia.[32] Nor did anyone publicly oppose the campaign to defend the bases. Thus Virginia did indeed move into position as the Defense Department's East Coast "megabase," as some Virginia officials predicted it would at the beginning of the cutback period. The assumption of this role resulted not just from Pentagon planning, but also from state and local choices not to support defense conversion and to fall back on a century-long tradition of courting the military.

NOTES

1. Lobbying Congress to get more work is a time-honored tradition at Newport News Shipyard. See, for example, Kenneth R. Mayer, *The Political Economy of Defense Contracting*. New Haven, CT: Yale University Press, 1991; see also Sanford Gottlieb, *Defense Addiction: Can America Kick the Habit?* Boulder, CO: Westview Press, 1997.

2. In conservative states such as Virginia, however, officials are only expected to take action to save public jobs, such as those at bases. Private-business layoffs are not opposed because they are held to be the prerogative of businesses. Officials are required to show concern for the workers, but not to intervene with the company to avert the layoffs.

3. In many communities, chambers of commerce were the primary organizers of campaigns to resist base closures. As part of their efforts to save Fort Lee during the 1993 Base Realignment and Closure round, for example, local chambers of commerce even paid to have charter buses transport hundreds of area residents to BRAC Commission hearings—almost 50 miles away.

4. Defense Department procurement spending in Virginia grew by 135 percent from

1980 to 1990, mostly in the services, electronics, and communications industries. By 1990 Virginia ranked first in the nation in defense-procurement spending per capita. Commonwealth of Virginia, *Governor's Commission on Defense Conversion and Economic Adjustment, First Report to the Governor*, November 1992.

5. Stephen S. Fuller, "Federal Contractors in the Washington Area: Who Are They? How Have They Been Affected by Reductions in Federal Procurement? What Is Their Future Outlook?" Washington, DC: George Washington University, Department of Urban Planning and Real Estate Development, unpublished paper presented at the Association of Collegiate Schools of Planning Conference, Austin, TX, November 1990; John W. Whaley et al., "Hampton Roads Military Impact." Chesapeake: Southeastern Virginia Planning District Commission (now Hampton Roads Planning District Commission), January 1989; William Porter, "A Study of the Impact of Defense Cuts on Northern Virginia's Economy." Commonwealth of Virginia, Secretary of Economic Development, 1990 (unpublished).

6. Nestor E. Terlekyj, "Defense Spending and the Virginia Economy." Washington, DC: NPA Data Services, unpublished paper presented at the Richmond Association of Business Economists Meeting, November 16, 1990; Charlotte Kerr et al., "Issue Paper: Possible Impacts of Defense Cutbacks on Virginia's Economy." Richmond: Commonwealth of Virginia, Joint Legislative Audit and Review Commission, January 8, 1991; John Knapp, "The Impact of Defense Spending on Virginia's Economy." *Virginia News Letter* 68, no. 9 (October/November, 1992).

7. The following agencies were represented: The Virginia Employment Commission, the Department of Housing and Community Development, the Department of Minority Business Enterprise, the Department of Economic Development, the Department of Taxation, the Port Authority, and the Department of Planning and Budget.

8. After it was taken off the BRAC list in 1993, Fort Lee (near Petersburg, south of Richmond) presented Griffis with a plaque and commended him for helping save the base. Throughout the 1990–1995 period, especially from 1991 to 1993, Griffis was widely known as the expert on Virginia's military economy. His advice was sought by the governor's office, by General Assembly committees, and by Virginia localities.

9. One commission participant found no discrepancy in the shipyard's behavior and asserted that the Shipyard participated in the Wilder commission primarily to ensure that the state took no actions that would adversely affect the shipyard, not because it wished to promote defense conversion.

10. See, for example, the remarks of Economic Development Secretary Lawrence Framme in *Proceedings: Public Service Forum*, Virginia Polytechnic Institute and State University, Norfolk, May 21, 1992.

11. Examples include the Joint Committee to Study the Measures Necessary to Assure Virginia's Economic Recovery, created by House Joint Resolution No. 433, February 22, 1991.

12. Framme, "Defense Cuts: State and Local Action for Economic Adjustment."

13. National Governors' Association, *A Governor's Guide to Economic Conversion.* Washington, DC: National Governor's Association, 1992.

14. Inter-Agency Task Force on Defense Conversion and Economic Adjustment, "The Virginia Economic Conversion and Adjustment Plan" (draft), January 30, 1992.

15. The commission was created through Executive Order No. 43 (92), March 1992.

16. Commonwealth of Virginia, Governor's Commission on Defense Conversion and Economic Adjustment, *First Report to the Governor*, November 1992.

17. The companies represented were Newport News Shipbuilding and Drydock Company, IBM Federal Systems Company, C&W Associates, Computer Sciences Corporation, IBES, Inc., Metro Machine Corporation, Stevi Nicolaus and Company, Systems Engineering and Management Associates, PMI Technologies, and Vector Data Systems.

18. In January 1994 the commission recommended that the hotline be discontinued due to lack of activity during 1993.

19. Commonwealth of Virginia, Governor's Commission on Defense Conversion and Economic Adjustment, *Final Report to the Governor*, January 1994, p. D5.

20. The NIST grant went unused for over two years due to the Allen administration's philosophical opposition to the manufacturing extension concept. Finally, in 1996 the Virginia secretary of commerce and trade quietly asked the already-established A. L. Philpott manufacturing extension center in Martinsville, Virginia, to expand into a statewide organization and to accept the NIST grant. By 1999, the center (now called Virginia's Philpott Manufacturing Extension Partnership) had developed a statewide network of affiliated service providers, including the Manufacturing Technology Center at Wytheville Community College and Technology Applications Center at Old Dominion University. However, the Commonwealth has not funded the partnership as generously as have other states and it did not place it in an economic-development agency that might have a stake in its continued funding. As one staff person explained the partnership's position: "We're a bastard, and we have to fight for every penny we get." Thus, despite the partnership's achievements in enhancing the technical sophistication of Virginia's small manufacturing businesses on a modest budget, as federal funds predictably decrease, it will have to work hard to remain viable.

21. It is noteworthy that the General Assembly declined to provide more substantial support for PATC, despite the fact that Hampton's representative was Hunter Andrews, one of the most powerful legislators in the General Assembly and chair of the Senate Finance Committee until his electoral defeat in November 1995. An explanation lies partly in the General Assembly's criticism of the Wilder commission's focus on conversion rather than base retention and perhaps also in Newport News Shipyard's public opposition to PATC.

22. Commonwealth of Virginia, Governor's Commission on Defense Conversion and Economic Adjustment, *Interim Report to the Governor*, June 1993, pp. 7–8.

23. However, the Hampton Roads, Flory (Northern Virginia), and Radford SBDCs did receive a total of $300,000 in Small Business Administration funds in 1995 to improve their services to defense-dependent businesses.

24. The commission also recommended the development of two new programs: a Women's Business Enterprise Certification program, which, as of January 1994, was reportedly being developed; and new capital-access programs, which the state claimed to be developing in January 1994. Finally, the commission recommended that the governor appoint a government acquisition committee to study procurement policies and regulations that harm small minority- and women-owned businesses. It suggested that this committee establish a working relationship with the Office of Federal Procurement Policy and the Defense Acquisition Regulatory Council to change procurement policies to help small minority- and women-owned businesses. The General Assembly responded with Senate Joint Resolution 314, which established a commission to study these issues. The results of that commission are not known.

25. Likewise, the aforementioned Economic Development Administration-funded Revolving Loan Fund for businesses wishing to diversify or convert to civilian produc-

tion resulted from discussions at the conference between staff of the Virginia Department of Housing and Community Development and the regional representative of the federal Economic Development Administration.

26. One committee member indicated that his group had worked on a list of activities that communities faced with a base closure could undertake, but the list was never completed.

27. Political-party affiliations are noted to show that support within the General Assembly for base-retention activities was bipartisan, as was opposition to many defense-conversion initiatives.

28. The staff director to the Governor's Commission on Base Retention and Defense Adjustment called meetings of the task force in the fall of 1994, but the purpose of the meetings was only to explain to agency heads what the commission was doing to defend the bases. By this time, Governor Allen's team had discontinued the monitoring function that Robert Griffis of the Virginia Employment Commission had established.

29. This is similar to the way that a civilian business-retention committee operates at the local government level.

30. This information is not collected by the Defense Department, so it could only be produced via analyses of defense prime-contractor vendor lists or surveys of local firms. Although the state did not conduct such surveys or analyses, others did some of this work at the local level. In Hampton Roads, the Peninsula Advanced Technology Center included questions on these issues in its survey of technology firms; the New River Valley Planning District Commission asked about subcontracting in its survey of manufacturing and related firms; and economist Stephen Fuller included subcontracting in his surveys in Northern Virginia. Nevertheless, a number of subcontractors may have slipped through the cracks when program-intervention strategies were being developed. In all other respects, the Virginia Employment Commission produced a clear picture of defense dependency in Virginia.

31. The Newport News Carrier Center subsidy was an exception, however. As a number of state-agency staffers explained: "That was Newport News. There's no way that was going to be turned down." Like U.S. Steel in Pittsburgh, Newport News Shipyard commands great respect in the halls of government in Virginia. The ship-repair industry, however, which consists of much smaller firms, has no such clout. And, despite a well-established business-call program (whereby state officials visit existing businesses and ask how the state can be helpful), ship-repair companies in Hampton Roads perceive that the state continues to focus its economic-development resources on traditional business recruitment, not on assistance to existing businesses.

32. Even the Charlottesville–Albemarle Taskforce on Economic Conversion did not promote conversion so much as recommend it as a response to what it believed were probable defense cutbacks.

7

Conversion Advocacy in Other States and Localities

In Virginia, the response to defense-spending cutbacks came primarily from businesses, business organizations (particularly chambers of commerce and high-technology interests), and elected and appointed officials. Labor unions played negligible roles and, with the exception of Charlottesville, peace-advocacy groups played no role whatsoever. In other states with defense-dependent communities, however, peace-advocacy groups played more active roles in stimulating community- and state-wide defense-conversion and -adjustment activities. These roles included those of public-policy advocate, organizer and facilitator of community-wide planning and adjustment programs, and, in some cases, service provider. In a couple of regions, organized labor also joined conversion-advocacy efforts.

As discussed in chapter 2, grass-roots organizations can sometimes influence the direction of state and local economic-development policy, particularly in times of economic crisis or uncertainty. This chapter explores the nature, extent, and limits of such influence by peace- and conversion-advocacy groups in San Diego, Tucson, St. Louis, Maine, Connecticut, and Washington State. It describes the factors that enhanced their influence and those that undermined it. As the discussion shows, these groups significantly influenced public- and private-sector responses in their communities, but their ability to do so was limited by the same forces that limited conversion in Virginia. Moreover, as in Virginia and, indeed, the U.S. Congress, some states and localities experienced a backlash against defense cutbacks after the BRAC'93 process, which resulted in the election of pro-military, or at least anticonversion, officials in November 1993.

SAN DIEGO

Like Hampton Roads, San Diego is a military metropolis. Described by some as "the largest military complex in the free world,"[1] "San Diego was home to U.S.

Navy ships and planes, [General Dynamics'] Tomahawk and advanced cruise mis-sile plants, naval shipbuilding yards, hundreds of small defense firms, and a heavy concentration of military retirees."[2] But it was also home to a local chapter of SANE and the Nuclear Freeze campaign. (Although grass-roots peace-advocacy groups have existed for at least a century in the United States, the arms build-up of the 1980s stimulated a new wave of peace advocacy. Between 1982 and 1984 many local groups participated in a national nuclear-freeze campaign, whose goal was to stop the production of, and eventually abolish, nuclear weapons.) While picketing the General Dynamics missile plant in the early 1980s, SANE/Freeze members were confronted by workers who charged that the peace advocates were insensitive to the defense workers' jobs. (Similar concerns across the country led many peace advocates to embrace the defense-conversion ideas articulated by Seymour Melman, Lloyd Dumas, and others described in chapter 1.)

In 1985 San Diego SANE/Freeze and other community organizations invited Seymour Melman and Lloyd Dumas as well as retired Admiral Eugene Carroll of the Center for Defense Information to discuss defense conversion.[3] Out of that conference, the San Diego Economic Conversion Council (SDECC), which included peace, labor, and religious groups, was formed. After the Berlin Wall fell in 1989, SDECC director Marcia Boruta persuaded Congressman Jim Bates (D-Cal.) to hold a hearing on defense conversion in San Diego, which was attended by San Diego City Councilman and Deputy Mayor Bob Filner. Boruta convinced Filner to introduce a resolution in the city council that called upon the federal government to replace each dollar of military-spending cutbacks with a dollar of expenditures on conversion and adjustment assistance. Filner also con-vinced the city council to establish a subcommittee to plan San Diego's "smooth transition . . . to a peace-based economy."[4]

The council subcommittee established a 29-member Economic Conversion Advisory Group, whose members included the commander of the naval base and representatives of defense contractors, universities, labor, government, and the SDECC. The SDECC used its position in the advisory group to promote the con-cept of conversion to sustainable development—economic activities that do not pollute or deplete natural resources and that pay at least living wages to workers. The work of this advisory group led the city council, in 1991, to establish an Economic Development Task Force that completed an economic-development plan for the city. This plan recommended a study of the impact of defense spend-ing on the San Diego community, which was conducted in 1992 with funding from the U.S. Defense Department's Office of Economic Adjustment. Based upon the recommendations of this study, in 1993 the city secured a portion of the State of California's $6 million grant from the U.S. Economic Development Administration. It used the funds to pay part of the costs of establishing a high-technology resource center, a technology incubator to assist fledgling high-tech businesses, a regional technology alliance to help companies bid on federal grants, a world trade center, and a small-business seed-capital fund.

But by this time the SDECC had lost its direct access to decision-makers in city government. In 1992 Filner was elected to Congress and moved on to other issues. In 1993 San Diego's new mayor, Susan Golding (a rival of Filner), abolished the advisory committee and task force. In their stead, she appointed a High Technology Advisory Committee comprised of business representatives, with no community-group representation. (Golding had run on a platform of transforming San Diego into a high-technology city.[5]) The SDECC responded by holding a series of "town meetings" designed to "democratize" conversion by informing citizens about national, state, and especially local policies and by encouraging citizens to express their views to elected officials.[6] The town meetings were so successful that, when the city received a Defense Department Office of Economic Adjustment grant in 1995, SDECC secured a portion to hold five more town meetings on conversion, worker retraining, and sustainable development. In 1997 SDECC received a small portion of the aforementioned Economic Development Administration grant to conduct a community-wide study and recommend ways to involve community and labor groups in high-technology economic development.

As an SDECC organizer mused in 1999: "[C]onversion [of a sort] did happen. We used to be known as a sleepy navy town. Now we're high tech." Some defense contracting had declined. General Dynamics had disappeared, taking 12,000 jobs out of the economy as it sold its missile division to Hughes (which moved the operation to Tucson), its space systems division to Martin Marietta (which moved it to Colorado), and its other San Diego divisions to other companies. Thousands of additional defense jobs were lost as smaller contractors downsized. And the 1993 BRAC process had slated the San Diego Naval Training Center for closure and the Miramar Air Station for realignment.[7]

But the new high-tech image did not, for the most part, derive from conversion to high-tech civilian production by defense contractors. Rather, it was due to the meteoric rise of the telecommunications industry, especially industry giants like Qualcomm, a software firm employing 9,000 persons by 1997, and the rise of new software developers, most of them employing fewer than 100 workers.[8] To be sure, some of the new firms employed laid-off defense workers and a few used technologies developed in the defense sector.[9] But if the remaining defense contractors were part of the new high-tech economy it was because they were doing high-tech defense work, since, as in Northern Virginia, Department of Defense demand for this work remained high and proved far more lucrative than defense-conversion funds. Indeed, as in Virginia, most San Diego defense contractors reportedly downsized and continued to do defense work.

In addition to high-tech development, San Diego's growth interests had convinced the city to spend large sums on an ambitious agenda of downtown development, including convention-center expansion and construction of new hotels, a new football stadium, and a new baseball park. Ironically, high-tech and downtown development were not sufficient to reduce the community's overall defense dependency, since the loss of General Dynamics was offset by consolidation of navy commands from other parts of the nation. Both in 1989 and 1999, one out of four San Diegans was employed in defense work. Nor had the community changed its attitudes about the defense economy. In 1991, 1993, and 1995 the chamber of commerce led aggressive efforts to defend local military installations against BRAC actions. One local congressman, like his counterparts in Virginia, had worked hard to increase overall defense spending and to shift it to San Diego. And community leaders celebrated the arrival of the new commands from other states as a result of the BRAC process. As one observer noted in 1999, patriotic fervor is still equated with military activity in San Diego.

Thus, despite its initial success in stimulating conversion planning in San Diego, the SDECC ultimately found its efforts limited by local traditions as well as by the lack of sustained federal commitment to defense downsizing and the withdrawal of federal support for conversion. Nevertheless, conversion planning in the early 1990s spurred the community to think about what else it could do besides defense contracting, paving the way for high-tech-development policies. Conversion planning helped the SDECC to refine its thinking as well. As an SDECC organizer explained in 1999: "I got frustrated in the discussions about high-tech company conversion because human needs and the environment were never discussed." After struggling through the latter half of the 1990s with little or no funds, the SDECC adopted the Perma Culture Center, an organization that designs sustainable-development strategies for a variety of clients.

MAINE

During the 1980s defense spending in Maine increased tenfold, making the state fourth in the nation in defense-spending per capita. By 1989 defense was the state's third largest employer, after paper products and tourism. The defense sector's primary employers were the Bath Iron Works shipyard, whose 11,950 workers (as of 1990) make Arleigh Burke-class guided-missile destroyers. Other large employers included Loring Air Force Base with 900 employees (which closed in 1994) and Brunswick Naval Air Station, with 900 employees. Also, many Mainers worked at two installations located nearby in New Hampshire— Pease Air Force Base (now closed) and the Portsmouth Naval Shipyard, with about 4,500 workers in 1994. The state also had a significant number of smaller defense prime contractors and subcontractors, which employed a total of about 3,800 workers in 1989.[10]

As in San Diego, the nuclear-freeze movement of the early-to-mid-1980s was the catalyst for defense conversion in Maine. By 1989 the campaign had evolved into the Peace Economy Project, which sought to educate the public about the high costs of military spending and the need for defense budget cuts and conversion planning. Led by its energetic volunteer executive director, Susie Schweppe, the group took its case to churches and civic groups, state, local, and federal officials, and defense contractors. By 1989 the Peace Economy Project had already won the support and encouragement of Buzz Fitzgerald, president of Bath Iron Works. Fitzgerald, whose company had not built a commercial vessel since 1977, agreed that defense spending would have to be reduced.[11] His company developed an ambitious diversification plan that was implemented with the help of a federal Technology Reinvestment Project grant to work with foreign commercial shipbuilders, a Pentagon grant to design rapid-transit ships, and a labor–management cooperation agreement to improve shop-floor efficiency.[12] Fitzgerald also worked with Schweppe in state and national forums to promote community and state-wide conversion planning.

In the meantime, the Peace Economy Project (later renamed the Maine Economic Conversion Project [MECP]) retained economists Marion Anderson and Greg Bischak to conduct a study of how a 7 percent shift in federal spending from defense to civilian production could help the Maine economy.[13] The MECP used this study to promote conversion across the state. It drafted a resolution asking the federal government to cut military spending; 150 municipalities endorsed it. The MECP also became a founding member of Sustainable Maine, an organization promoting sustainable economic-development policies, and it initiated a "Sustainable Stars" program that recognized companies for taking actions that reduced environmental degradation and promoted sustainability.

In the 1990 gubernatorial campaign, the MECP persuaded both candidates to promise to create a state-wide task force that would study the nature of the state's defense dependency and make recommendations for state policies to respond to job losses resulting from defense-spending cutbacks. The winner, Governor John McKernan, created such a task force, albeit without state funding. Later, the task force received $150,000 from the U.S. Economic Development Administration to prepare a conversion and adjustment plan. The task force issued a report in 1993 calling for the creation of regional teams to plan and implement local conversion, state-funded retraining for laid-off defense workers, and innovative state financing to assist in the creation of new, environmentally friendly industries. The report also called for the establishment of a state office of economic conversion. The state obliged this request, creating an office with $100,000 per year in 1994 and 1995.

The state also developed a Manufacturing Extension Partnership to assist small-manufacturing businesses, supported by the National Institute of Standards and Technology's Manufacturing Extension Program in 1995. Also, four regional conversion teams were established with modest amounts of planning support from the U.S. Department of Housing and Urban Development. In addition to these conversion efforts, the state also allocated substantial funds to assist with the closure and adjustment process at Loring Air Force Base.

Nevertheless, state support was less than optimal. No funds were allocated for dislocated defense-worker retraining outside of the Loring Air Force Base. Other than its support for the Office of Economic Conversion, the state provided very little funding of conversion efforts per se. On the other hand, the state contributed $100,000 to an effort to defend Brunswick Naval Air Station in the BRAC'95 process, and in 1993 it made a major, six-year funding commitment to the tourism industry. (Although tourism is an important Maine industry, it provides mostly seasonal, low- to moderate-wage jobs.)

Although the MECP won praise from many quarters for its style of so-called consensus organizing that brought together a wide variety of business, government, and community leaders who had never worked together before, support was not universal.[14] As Gottlieb (1997) noted, a "whispering campaign" in some state government and business circles impugned the motives of director Susie Schweppe.[15] But more serious damage was done by the cessation of federal defense cutbacks and federal funds to support conversion and adjustment. By 1995 the MECP's foundation support had ceased as well, and in 1996 the organization officially folded. At about the same time, the General Dynamics Corporation purchased Bath Iron Works, thereby, reportedly, discouraging the latter's economic-conversion efforts.[16]

WASHINGTON STATE

As home to the Boeing Company, to a network of military bases, and to a declining shipbuilding industry, the Puget Sound area of Washington State ranks high in defense dependency. The state was fifth in Department of Defense purchases in 1992. Boeing, the Seattle-based maker of the B-2 Stealth Bomber as well as commercial aircraft, employed 106,000 in 1989 and 98,000 in 1993.[17] Bases include the Puget Sound Naval Shipyard in Bremerton, the Keyport Undersea Warfare Center, the Bangor Submarine Base, and the Whidbey Island Naval Air Station.[18] Shipbuilding declined from 11,000 workers in 1982 to 4,000 in 1987. The largest of the remaining yards—Todd Pacific and Lockheed—were in declining health in the early 1990s.[19]

Grass-roots opposition to the area's military economy took shape as early as the 1970s with the formation of the Puget Sound Conversion Project. An active nuclear-freeze campaign during the 1980s set the stage for aggressive and successful conversion organizing. As a result, Washington became the first state to pass conversion legislation. It created a Community Diversification Committee comprised of defense contractors, state and local economic-development officials, labor unions, military representatives, and peace activists to develop a state-wide conversion plan.[20] It also created a Community Diversification Program with one staff member housed in the Department of Community Development, charged with helping communities plan for defense downsizing. Thanks in large part to the aggressive organizing of SANE/Freeze, the program was funded with a base budget of $120,000 that, in some years, was supplemented by as much as $350,000.

The diversification program conducted surveys of defense contractors to ascertain their plans and needs and began organizing conversion and adjustment projects in defense-dependent communities. In 1993 the state allocated $293,000, which leveraged $1.6 million in federal funds and $535,000 in local and private investment, to support community conversion in four geographic or thematic areas. Each initiative faced local opposition and required continuous organizing by state program staff and local leaders, but over time some proved quite successful. One early initiative sought to develop a defense-diversification strategy in the highly vulnerable Kitsap/Bremerton area surrounding the Puget Sound Naval Shipyard, the Keyport Undersea Warfare Center, and the Bangor Submarine Base. Although the local business community did not initially warm up to the idea of diversification planning, a leader on the local economic-development council who was also a retired submarine commander convinced them to do so. The strategy resulted in the creation of a technology and business center to assist small companies wishing to convert, an incubator to support fledgling businesses, entrepreneurial and business training for erstwhile defense workers, and revitalization of the town of Bremerton's downtown.

Federal, state, and local funds also supported an industrial-conversion project in Kitsap County, led primarily by the International Association of Machinists (IAM) and affiliates of SANE/Freeze. The IAM had organized a consortium of passenger ferryboat designers, a small private shipyard, an architect, and several unions to use parts of the Puget Sound Naval Shipyard to build passenger ferryboats. Although the project stalled when the navy refused to lease its unutilized facilities to the IAM–SANE/Freeze consortium, the group eventually found another site not far away and used it to employ 25 persons assembling light railcars for the Washington Department of Transportation.

A third project entailed planning for the economic diversification of the community surrounding the Whidbey Island Naval Air Station. Here the state program and local conversion organizers ran into significant opposition from the local chamber of commerce, which opposed diversification planning and, like communities across the country, paid a lobbyist to save the base.

Last but not least, the Washington Diversification Program established a Manufacturing Network Initiative, funded in part by the National Institute of Standards and Technology's Manufacturing Extension Partnership program. Under this initiative, nine networks were established to improve the commercial competitiveness of defense-dependent firms in the aerospace, electronics, composites, shipbuilding, metalworking, and related industries.[21] Some, such as the Aerospace Alliance, which found ways to lower costs through joint purchasing and other arrangements, were still performing well as of 1999. However, Shipnet, a consortium of shipyards, attempted to focus mostly on winning more defense contracts and disintegrated after a couple of years.

Although some of the diversification program's projects were quite successful, conversion efforts in Washington faced the same barriers that they did in other states. Most significantly, perhaps, the Boeing Company refused to discuss the possibility of conversion of its defense-production facilities. To be sure, Boeing sent a representative to meetings of a regional conversion group organized by the state's economic-conversion program and, unlike many defense prime contractors, it willingly furnished a list of its subcontractors to the planning group. Boeing also provided financial support to the Aerospace Alliance. But it made it clear that its own future would not be part of the regional conversion discussions. Rather, it focused on maintaining its relationship with the Pentagon, even going so far as asking the diversification program to tone down its pro-conversion rhetoric early in its organizing work so that the community did not send the wrong message to Washington. With its purchase of McDonnell Douglas and Rockwell International's defense aerospace division, by 1997 Boeing increased its defense dependency from 21 to 50 percent.[22]

The election of a conservative, Republican-majority legislature in 1994 further undermined support for conversion. The new legislature slashed funding for economic-development programs by $1.5 million.[23] Indirectly, the cutback in economic-development funding ended the diversification program as well. Although the diversification program's $130,000 annual cost had become an accepted part of the Community Development Department's budget, the Manufacturing Network Program, which was perhaps the most lasting achievement of the diversification program, had not. Because it focused mostly on small- to mid-size businesses and helped them to develop competitive strength as clusters, rather than as individual firms, it was not well appreciated by the legislators.[24] When, in 1997, the legislature refused to renew its required match for the federally funded program, the Community Development Department responded by shifting the diversification program's funds to the Manufacturing Network Program.

In the meantime, however, employment in the Puget Sound area had exploded, thanks to the meteoric rise of the software industry, especially Seattle-based Microsoft, as well as Boeing's continued health.[25] City and state subsidies for downtown development, including support for the construction of new baseball and football stadiums, further boosted local development.

CONNECTICUT

Connecticut's vulnerability to defense-industry layoffs exceeded that of Washington. In 1992 almost one-third of its manufacturing jobs—about 7.5 percent of its total workforce—were in the defense sector. Major employers included General Dynamics' Electric Boat facilities in southeastern Connecticut (and Rhode Island), which produced the Polaris, Trident, and, later, Seawolf submarines. Other contractors included United Technologies, whose defense subsidiaries included Pratt and Whitney (aircraft engines), Hamilton Standard, Norden, and Sikorsky. In New London County, a somewhat rural area that is, nevertheless, the home of General Dynamics' Electric Boat Division as well as a Naval Underwater Warfare base and many retired naval officers, 60 percent of the county's 110,000 jobs were in defense companies. Between 1989 and 1995 Connecticut's defense employers laid off 25,000 workers due to declining orders for military products. Another 20,000 layoffs were projected to occur by the end of the decade.[26] These losses came on top of the loss of 45,000 nondefense manufacturing jobs between 1984 and 1989 due to industrial restructuring in the Rustbelt.[27]

Therefore, as a Connecticut peace advocate pointed out: "Peace is not welcome here in the 'Submarine Capitol of the World.'"[28] Indeed, when President Bush announced the end of the Seawolf program in 1992, after only one of a projected 29 submarines had been contracted, the community went into a state of shock. "Save the Seawolf" and "Save the Shipyard" campaigns sprang up, as Electric Boat began laying off workers almost immediately after the announcement.[29] State officials followed the crowd. The State Commissioner of Economic

Development announced: "Our number one strategy is not to diversify the economic base. It is to make absolutely certain that we're getting our share of defense contracts, as well as nondefense contracts, for Connecticut companies."[30] The commissioner's statement was certainly in tune with the behavior of the giant General Dynamics Electric Boat Division, which refused to consider conversion, even spurning a public invitation by *The Day* newspaper of New London to discuss the topic. Like many other defense prime contractors, Electric Boat chose to shed workers and focus on its military market rather than attempt to diversify. It convinced Congress to let it build two more Seawolf submarines, but by 1999 its employment had shrunk to under 6,000 jobs as it finished the third and last in the series. At decade's end it was reportedly conducting R&D for the navy's new attack submarine and proposing to retrofit Trident submarines with cruise missiles. Throughout the decade, state officials (joined by defense contractors and unions) continued to lobby for more contracts. The state also attempted to keep defense contractors satisfied by cutting their costs of doing business. For example, the state granted Pratt and Whitney a sizable package of tax abatements and other incentives, even as the company laid off thousands of workers.[31]

The state did take some actions to support adjustment to defense-spending cuts. In 1991 the legislature passed a defense-diversification act that earmarked $22.5 million in loan guarantees and loans to defense firms. The state added another $10 million to the fund in 1994. Between 1991 and 1994 it implemented additional initiatives. It invested in the University of Connecticut's Institute for Industrial and Engineering Technology to help small defense companies improve their technology. It created oceanographic and technology research centers to develop new products and energy technologies. It also established a network of Procurement Technical Assistance Centers through its Seatech economic-development organization. The centers assist firms both in identifying and bidding on government contracts and in exploring new markets. Seatech also provides services to start-up companies and makes loans to marine science and fishing enterprises. And in New London County, the state funded a new marine-science center and project called Ocean Quest, which features an undersea learning center, a school, a museum, a hotel, and a conference center. Laid off General Dynamics workers were employed to construct the complex. Another promising initiative is Techconn, a private, nonprofit corporation that leverages federal, state, and private funds to develop new products in the environmental, energy, transportation, and marine-science industries. One project sought to convert municipal waste into electric power for motor vehicles.[32]

But the state developed no comprehensive plan for absorbing laid-off defense workers into commercial ventures, much less a plan to convert to a peacetime economy. And the bulk of its efforts did not support defense-company diversification or alternative technologies, but rather entertainment, tourism, and port development.[33] Thus the new jobs found by most laid-off defense workers were not in high-wage manufacturing or high-technology services; rather, they were at the Foxwoods Casino in southeastern Connecticut, which opened in 1992 with 2,300 employees. By 1995 the Foxwoods and Mohegan gaming resorts had become the area's largest employers with 11,000 low- and moderate-wage workers.[34]

In 1994 Connecticut labor unions persuaded the Connecticut legislature to require that all firms with Defense Department contracts exceeding $1 million who also received state aid establish alternative-use committees. Alternative-use committees, as discussed in chapter 1, are labor–management teams within companies that develop plans for commercial products that a plant could produce in the event that defense contracts cease. Organized labor also convinced the Connecticut legislature to pass a law requiring the state's grant-making agencies to add job creation and retention to their goals.[35] But community organizers maintained in 1999 that neither initiative had had any impact on company or state-agency behavior.

Peace and labor advocates attempted to stimulate a more aggressive response. As early as 1960, a Community for Nonviolent Action had organized to stop production of the Polaris submarine and to promote defense conversion. In the 1970s the group opposed production of the Trident submarine and again proposed economic conversion as an alternative. In 1992 Connecticut Peace Action, the War Resisters League, and other community and labor groups organized a Community Coalition for Economic Conversion. The coalition sponsored a "listening project survey" in 1993 to elicit the views of 75 Connecticut residents, defense workers, business persons, clergy, local government officials, and community activists on the southeastern Connecticut community's problems and needed solutions. The respondents suggested that the area needed a shared vision of the future, based upon a creative, regional economic-development plan that included defense conversion. Although the project did not immediately induce political leaders and dominant businesses to develop a plan, it generated more support for defense-diversification planning and expanded the peace group's network of supporters.[36]

In 1995 the Community Coalition for Economic Conversion accepted an invitation from the nonprofit Corporation for Regional Economic Development to join a manufacturing cluster group to develop strategies to help defense manufacturers in the area. The coalition suggested that a manufacturing-needs-assessment survey be conducted. This process identified a labor-skills shortage in small- and mid-size manufacturing firms, despite the glut of laid-off Electric Boat workers with industrial skills.[37]

In the meantime, the Community Coalition had begun working with unions at Electric Boat through an initiative called "A Call to Action: Labor's Agenda for Economic Conversion." For the unions, this marked a departure from their previous strategy of lobbying Congress for more submarine contracts. Through "A Call to Action," the Community Coalition for Economic Conversion began to make the links between small businesses' needs for skilled labor and defense workers' needs for good jobs. Working with the Private Industry Council (which administers EDWAA dislocated worker-training funds in southeastern Connecticut) and the Metal Trades Council (which represents workers at Electric Boat), in 1997 the coalition secured a $4.3 million grant from the U.S. Department of Labor's special Defense Conversion Adjustment Demonstration fund to support a three-part innovative project.[38] The project built upon the initial manufacturing-needs-assessment survey, an improved worker-counseling service, and a skills-profiling effort. It sought to help workers ascertain what skills they could market to nondefense employers, to describe the skills in terms that would be understood by nondefense employers, and to identify areas where they could find good jobs after brief retraining. For example, the skills-profiling process determined that Electric Boat workers had many skills that were useful in the building trades, so the project worked with the Connecticut Department of Labor to certify workers in construction. Other workers took short courses in computer-numeric machining and fiber-optics installation (skills that were in high demand), which built upon their skills in metalworking and electrical work.[39]

These projects became part of the Community Coalition's Good Jobs Campaign, designed to push state and local officials to take more constructive action for defense workers than just lobby for more submarine contracts, grow more entertainment and tourism jobs, and focus on recruiting a big, new company that might not even employ laid-off workers. By 1999 the campaign seemed to be gathering steam. After almost a decade of resistance to defense cutbacks and mostly traditional growth solutions, Connecticut was taking a step toward the difficult but important work of labor-based defense adjustment, thanks in large part to the work of its peace and labor advocates.

TUCSON

In 1950 Tucson was a sleepy desert town with a population of 45,000. But after local growth interests (a real estate developer and the chamber of commerce) convinced Hughes Aircraft Company to build its new missile-production facilities in Tucson, the population skyrocketed, reaching 400,000 persons by 1990. In that year, the Hughes complex employed 5,500 persons (down from 9,000 in 1986) who made Tow Phoenix and Maverick air-to-ground missiles. In addition to Hughes, defense employment in the area included a Lockheed plant, hundreds of defense subcontractors (200 companies supplied military components to Hughes alone), and the Davis-Monthan Air Force Base.[40]

As the Cold War came to a close, Hughes laid off large portions of its workforce and, coincidentally, an IBM plant that had set up shop in the early 1980s closed. By the mid-1990s Hughes had cut its payroll to 1,300 workers and severed its contracts with all but a small handful of Tucson suppliers. These dislocations and the prospect that more might follow led Tucson Mayor John Volgy to organize the Greater Tucson Economic Council, comprised of representatives of local governments, the chamber of commerce (banks, land developers, large retail companies), Hughes Company, and the University of Arizona's Community Economic Development Office. The purpose of the council was to devise appropriate responses to defense downsizing. However, it was far from clear that the Tucson business establishment would pursue conversion.

Roz Boxer made it her business to convince the community that conversion was, indeed, the appropriate response. After hearing a speech on defense conversion by Lloyd Dumas in 1989, Boxer, then a part-time staff person for the Tucson chapter of Physicians for Social Responsibility, organized the Tucson Council on Economic Conversion (later changed to Arizona Council on Economic Conversion [ACEC]). Like conversion-advocacy groups in other communities, ACEC spent its first year publicizing the idea of conversion and seeking support from the Greater Tucson Economic Council and from defense businesses, including Hughes. Management at the Hughes plant expressed some support and undertook a few minor in-house initiatives to develop commercial products.

Unlike most conversion groups, however, ACEC quickly concluded that it could not succeed simply through advocacy and information dissemination. It would have to provide services that made it, and the path of conversion, valuable to local businesses. Its first project was a Technology Exchange Forum—a series of breakfasts that brought together defense and nondefense companies, politicians, and other community leaders to hear and discuss expert presentations on new technologies and environmentally friendly industries. The forum also fostered networking among companies that resulted in a number of new business relationships.[41] The Technology Exchange Forum convinced some small defense contractors, local officials in Pima County (which includes Tucson), and participants at the University of Arizona College of Engineering that ACEC could play a useful role in the community. Next, ACEC teamed up with Pima County on a $456,000 grant from the U.S. Department of Labor to help Sargent Controls, a maker of valves for the Seawolf submarine, compete in commercial markets. The ACEC received $30,000 for designing a management-assessment process and worker-training program and for monitoring the implementation of the effort.

Success on the Sargent Controls project led to a second federal grant—this one from the Department of Defense's Office of Economic Adjustment—to work with seven small defense companies in four counties surrounding Tucson. The ACEC helped the companies to assess their capabilities, identify commercial-product alternatives, and find capital to finance the conversion. It also designed a training program to help each company's workers learn new skills and techniques. But the grant included no funds for the worker training itself, so ACEC went back to the U.S. Department of Labor for funds to train the companies' workers. By 1995 ACEC had trained workers in 14 former defense companies to make commercial products. In the meantime, Roz Boxer and the ACEC had campaigned for state funds to support defense conversion for small firms. In April 1996 the conservative Arizona legislature finally passed what had become known as the "Roz Boxer bill," which earmarked $250,000 for small-business conversion.

Nevertheless, the overall climate for conversion in Tucson and the state of Arizona was not friendly. Arizona's governor vetoed the above-mentioned Boxer bill on the advice of his Commerce Department and some business leaders that the bill catered to special interests, but this was a code word for a more fundamental concern. The ACEC had found it impossible to overcome its roots in the peace movement, particularly the Physicians for Social Responsibility that, in the

1980s, had called for closure of the Davis-Monthan Air Force Base. Although the ACEC stated numerous times that it did not advocate closure of the base, the leaders of the Tucson Chamber of Commerce did not believe it. "We were a lightning rod for liberalism and communism and everything that's wrong," said one ACEC staff member. The leaders of the chamber of commerce—bankers, land developers, a hospital CEO, and a beer distributor—formed the "Davis-Monthan 50" group to save the base (which did not appear on any BRAC closure list). They received widespread support in Tucson city government, and also at the state level and from Arizona's congressional delegation.

In the meantime, the Greater Tucson Economic Council and the Greater Phoenix Economic Council, both comprised of growth interests and politicians, chose not to pursue conversion or to support small-business-development generally. Instead, they reportedly hired a consultant to lobby Congress for more defense contracts. They also pushed a sizable tax-credit bill through the Arizona legislature to help attract the General Dynamics missile-production operation from San Diego after Hughes bought it in the mid-1990s. (Hughes later sold its defense operations in Tucson to Raytheon.[42]) The bill provided a tax cut and worker-training funds to any Arizona company doing more than $10 million in business annually. Only Hughes and McDonnell Douglas qualified under that criterion and the subsidy would apply only to new, out-of-state workers hired by the company. In effect, the bill subsidized Hughes for moving the General Dynamics operation and its workers from San Diego to Tucson. Thus the bill did not encourage Hughes or any other company to hire laid-off workers from Hughes' Tucson plant or from other defense companies in the area. Many of those workers reportedly left Tucson by the late 1990s. (The ACEC publicly opposed the Hughes subsidy bill, as did others. The bad publicity resulting from this episode helped to convince the legislature, a few years later, to designate $6 million in annual lottery proceeds for businesses hiring new workers or training existing workers to work on new production processes. The state pays 75 percent of the training costs and the company pays the remainder. Eligible companies include those converting from defense to civilian production. By 1999, however, few firms were left that were interested in converting.)

Although ACEC was not able to win over Arizona's established growth interests and military boosters, its attempt to work with defense contractors alienated it from other peace-advocacy groups. As an ACEC staff person said: "[Peace groups] wanted us to picket Hughes, not ask for a free computer. They didn't want us to work with small defense contractors because these companies pollute and don't pay everyone living wages." Nevertheless, the ACEC managed to survive and even thrive after conversion funds dried up by setting up entrepreneurship centers and providing training in home-based business-management and other skills to persons losing welfare benefits. It continued to provide some services to small defense contractors wishing to enter commercial markets through the aforementioned state program that used lottery funds for workforce recruitment and training.

ST. LOUIS

In 1993 St. Louis was the second most-defense-dependent region in the nation due to the presence of McDonnell Douglas Corporation, maker of the F-15 jet fighter, the F-18 Super Hornet, and the T-45 missile. By 1989 McDonnell Douglas employed all but 2,000 of the region's 42,300 aerospace workers.[43] But McDonnell Douglas' robust employment growth in the 1980s had been overshadowed by steep declines elsewhere in St. Louis's manufacturing sector—in the automotive, primary metals, and brewing industries.[44] Between 1989 and 1993 McDonnell Douglas shed 15,000 workers, adding further stress to the local economy.

The economic dislocations of the 1980s led to the creation of state and local economic-development programs to help retain manufacturing industries and revitalize the region's economy. Therefore the community was somewhat experienced in dealing with industrial restructuring and unemployment. Nevertheless, defense cutbacks posed more problems than existing economic-development institutions could handle, so in 1989 St. Louis County officials organized the St. Louis Economic Adjustment and Diversification Committee (EADC). The committee comprised local economic-development officials from a number of localities in the St. Louis area (including the states of Missouri and Illinois), businesses (including McDonnell Douglas), labor representatives, academicians, and the St. Louis Economic Conversion Program, a conversion-advocacy group. The EADC worked for six years developing responses to defense downsizing. It started by conducting an extensive survey of defense contractors in the St. Louis area. With help from the U.S. Commerce Department's Economic Development Administration and local governments, the EADC then raised $15 million to fund worker retraining, community adjustment, and business assistance.

Over a half of these funds supported the Midwest Technology Manufacturing Center (Mid Tec). Mid Tec was designed as a teaching factory where small defense-dependent metalworking shop owners and their workers could become acquainted with new machinery and develop new production techniques. Like the Peninsula Advanced Technology Center in Hampton Roads, Mid Tec did not pursue conversion per se, just technology upgrading to improve competitiveness. But the organization's mission was unclear and political problems undermined its effectiveness. By 1999 it had been scaled back to a small welfare-to-work-assistance project.

Most of the EADC's efforts were successful, however. It established two new small-business incubator facilities to stimulate new business formation and, in 1992, it used Defense Logistics Agency funds to establish a Procurement Assistance Center to help St. Louis firms bid on federal contracts. The EADC supported the establishment of a St. Louis world trade center to provide information and networking assistance to small businesses wishing to enter export markets. Using $1.3 million in U.S. Economic Development Administration funds as seed capital, it established a revolving loan fund to provide capital to former defense workers starting new nondefense businesses, and to small companies (including defense contractors) seeking to convert to commercial markets.[45]

But local officials associated with the EADC expressed most pride in the job-retraining system they established for laid-off defense workers. By carefully coordinating economic-development and job-training agencies, the community was able to reemploy 80 percent of the workers laid off in the early 1990s in the St. Louis area, including 5 percent who started their own businesses (9 percent retired and 10 percent remained unemployed as of 1999). Unlike most other job-training programs, which do not supplement EDWAA with their own funds, St. Louis conducted longitudinal studies at one-, two-, and three-year intervals to track workers' statuses after being retrained.

Although local officials, especially local economic-development staff, provided the spark that started defense-adjustment programming in the St. Louis area, the peace movement played a role as well. Peace advocacy in St. Louis started in the 1970s with the Institute for Peace and Justice's St. Louis Economic Conversion Project (SLECP). In 1988 Sr. Mary Ann McGivern, a Roman Catholic nun who had organized a coalition of religious groups to introduce defense-conversion resolutions at McDonnell Douglas shareholder meetings, revived the moribund SLECP. The group actively participated in the work of the EADC. It also wrote successful federal-grant proposals to fund conversion projects, including a $500,000 Department of Labor grant to fund a Management Assistance and Technology Transfer program (MATT). From 1993 through 1994 this demonstration project provided 20 small defense-dependent companies with assessments of their production and management practices, as well as 50 percent of the costs of consultants who helped the companies develop and implement conversion plans.[46] As of 1999 the MATT program was still operating and had been incorporated into the Middle America Manufacturing Technology Program, which was funded by the National Institute of Standards and Technology's Manufacturing Extension Partnership program.

The SLECP also continued to publicly call for conversion at McDonnell Douglas and to advocate a regional industrial policy that would stimulate light manufacturing in the envirotechnology and commercial-transportation industries. It advocated worker participation in conversion planning and called for public assistance to workers wishing to buy out defense-dependent companies and convert them to civilian production. In these endeavors, however, SLECP was not successful. Moreover, its advocacy of conversion and industrial policy and its outspoken criticism of McDonnell Douglas did not endear it to established political and business interests, even though SLECP and McDonnell Douglas worked cooperatively on the EADC. As Gottlieb noted, the mayor of the city of St. Louis did not invite SLECP to important meetings on local economic-development policy. These were dominated by corporate CEOs.[47] Thus, notwithstanding many significant and successful initiatives, defense conversion and adjustment in St. Louis faced some of the same limitations that other communities experienced. McDonnell Douglas refused to consider significant diversification initiatives, having decided as a result of previous commercial ventures that it could not do so profitably. However, the company did embark on a project to build fatigue-resistant bridge and highway components by using the composites technology it had designed for the A-12 attack plane. McDonnell Douglas also explored ways to commercialize its high-speed machining and process-integrating software, as well as a technique to remove aircraft paint in an efficient and environmentally friendly way. Neither project would create many jobs, however.[48]

In the meantime, the St. Louis Civic Progress organization, a downtown chamber-of-commerce–sponsored consortium of the community's 25 largest local-growth-oriented businesses, convinced local governments to spend very large sums on the entertainment and tourism industries. These included $128 million to expand the St. Louis Convention Center, $265 million for a new football stadium to attract the NFL Rams, and additional funds for another new sports arena and other public improvements.[49] None of these activities, of course, could replace the high-wage jobs that McDonnell Douglas was shedding, but they fit the growth machine's vision of an appropriate response to manufacturing decline and defense cutbacks in St. Louis. In the meantime, many of the community's 120–130 defense-dependent suppliers to McDonnell Douglas reportedly went out of business.

On a more positive note, in 1993 the Civic Progress downtown-development organization, whose chairman appreciated high technology, asked the EADC to join it in organizing a Critical Technologies Task Force comprised of business, government, and university leaders. Its purpose was to stimulate development in the areas of advanced materials, manufacturing processes, energy and the environment, biotechnology and life sciences, information and communications, and aeronautics and surface transportation.[50] This effort marked the first time that traditional growth interests joined with industrial-development interests in St. Louis. (Neither labor nor peace-advocacy groups were invited to participate on the task force, however.) By 1999 this task force had created a Center for Emerging Technologies to stimulate R&D in a variety of fields, including the genetic manipulation of plants and other health-sciences-related endeavors.

Thus in St. Louis peace-advocacy groups did not play the catalytic leadership roles that they played, to some extent, in Washington, Maine, San Diego, and eventually Connecticut. Nevertheless, EADC staff referred to the St. Louis Economic Conversion Council as a "moral voice" that continuously reminded the group of the impacts of defense downsizing on workers, small businesses, and families. But in St. Louis it was the community's prior experience with industrial dislocation that created the public-program infrastructure and professional staff that made it possible to respond to defense downsizing without the prodding of a grass-roots movement.[51] Although these efforts purposely did not challenge McDonnell Douglas (later purchased by Boeing) to engage in more conversion efforts, and although the growth machine's focus on downtown recreation and tourism development limited the community's effectiveness in developing high-wage, commercial-employment opportunities, the efforts were very important. They improved local economic performance and fostered community confidence that defense downsizing could result in new, commercial activities.

A NOTE ON MASSACHUSETTS

St. Louis was not the only community to benefit by its previous experience with industrial restructuring and economic-development capacity-building. Other Rustbelt states such as Michigan, New York, and Massachusetts also had institutions in place that were used to mount sophisticated, labor-based conversion and adjustment responses. In Massachusetts, for example, the Machine Action Project (introduced in chapter 2) provided its state funding-agency sponsor, the Industrial Services Program, with an early warning of the effects of defense downsizing on small companies. The Industrial Services Project responded with workshops and seminars on company conversion and provided production-modernization assistance to companies that later evolved into a manufacturing extension effort funded by the National Institute for Standards and Technology's Manufacturing Extension Partnership program. But, thanks to its experience in the area of industrial restructuring, the Industrial Services Project recognized that company technology upgrading alone would not ensure conversion. Like its counterparts in Tucson and southeastern Connecticut, the Industrial Services Project applied for a U.S. Department of Labor demonstration grant to fund so-called incumbent-worker training so that existing workers could be prepared to make new products in commercial markets.[52]

CONCLUSION

The foregoing cases illustrate the point made in chapter 2, that economic crises can create political spaces in which unconventional economic-development ideas, even those championed by groups that are not generally known for their economic-development expertise, can get a hearing in the community. In Virginia, the peace and labor movements were too weak to advance an economic-conversion agenda. But in San Diego, Washington State, Maine, and to some extent Tucson, southeastern Connecticut, and St. Louis, these groups exerted significant influence. In some areas, especially St. Louis (as well as Massachusetts and New York State), prior experience with industrial restructuring and dislocation had created an infrastructure of public agencies and programs that could be quickly focused on conversion or adjustment. This infrastructure also included a cadre of public officials who understood the benefits that conversion and adjustment initiatives could bring.

The end of the Cold War presented peace advocates with a unique opportunity to advance their goal of bringing about a peace economy by embracing the conversion model articulated by Seymour Melman, Lloyd Dumas, and others. As the foregoing cases attest, some peace groups were able to influence their communities' responses in ways that promoted conversion. But the effort stretched them in uncomfortable ways. Most had to work hard to develop the expertise to speak convincingly about the economy, defense dependency, conversion planning, and federal funds that were available to support the effort. Even after they did so, most still struggled to get businesses and politicians to take them seriously.

Even most labor unions provided, at best, passive support. It was primarily through their ability to access federal funds to support conversion initiatives that conversion groups, in most communities, won a measure of respect and support.

When federal conversion funds were cut in FY95 and even more in FY96 it "cut the rug out from under us," as one local conversion staff person put it. The end of the BRAC process in 1995 as well as the increases in Defense Department spending after 1994 convinced many defense contractors and local military boosters that the shake-out was over. By 1999 most state and local conversion groups had either dissolved or shifted focus. Those that remained had decreased staff to a couple of persons, as had the national conversion clearinghouse and technical-assistance organizations, the Center for Economic Conversion in Mountain View, California, and the National Commission on Economic Conversion and Disarmament in Washington, D.C. Within defense-dependent communities some conversion and adjustment initiatives continued, although they were gradually being incorporated into more generic small-business assistance, worker-retraining, and technology-development programs.

Thus, although conversion-advocacy groups were able to push their states or communities toward conversion and adjustment, the fate of their efforts hinged upon the same factors that influenced events in Virginia: The availability of federal funding to support such efforts, the nature and magnitude of defense cuts, and the power and influence of traditional growth interests and prime defense contractors.

NOTES

1. Marcia Boruta, "San Diego Prepares for a Peace Economy." *Positive Alternatives* 1, no. 4 (summer 1991), p. 2.

2. Sanford Gottlieb, *Defense Addiction: Can America Kick the Habit?* Boulder, CO: Westview Press, 1997, p. 98.

3. Ibid.

4. Ibid., p. 99.

5. Hedrick Smith, *Surviving the Bottom Line, Part 3: San Diego.* South Carolina Educational Television, 1997, distributed by Films for the Humanities and Sciences.

6. San Diego Economic Conversion Council, "Traveling Town Meeting Report, Prepared by the San Diego Economic Conversion Council, June 1994," unpublished document.

7. *The Planning Journal*, "Navy Base Closure and Realignment Process in the San Diego Region: Two Early Impressions." San Diego: American Planning Association San Diego Section, April 1994, pp. 1–4.

8. Smith, *Surviving the Bottom Line, Part 3.*

9. For example, Callaway Golf, which grew from a staff of five in 1983 to 2,000 by 1997, produced a golf club with an enlarged head of titanium, an ultralight composite material that was initially developed for the defense-aerospace industry. See William Charland, "Conversion Happens: Scenes from San Diego's Defense Industry." *Positive Alternatives* 7, no. 3 (spring 1997), pp. 13–14.

10. Gregory N. Stone, "At Bath Iron Works, a Rare Attitude." *Day* 112, no. 131 (November 9, 1992), pp. A1–5; Jo Josephson, "Economic Conversion: From Defense to Domestic Spending." *Maine Townsman: The Magazine of the Maine Municipal*

Association (May 1991), pp. 25–28; John MacDougal, "Economic Conversion without Military Doctrinal Debate: The Case of Maine, USA." Unpublished paper, October 1994; *Maine Economic Conversion Project, Defense Dependency—Its Impacts and Conversion Efforts in Maine, Summary*. Portland: Maine Economic Conversion Project, June 1994.

11. Unlike most other defense prime contractor CEOs, Fitzgerald had grown up in Bath and had worked at the shipyard since he was a youth. Thus he was concerned about the future of the community and the workforce. See Stone, "At Bath Iron Works, a Rare Attitude."

12. On the labor–management agreement, see Sanford Gottlieb, "Teamwork for a Change: Bath Iron Works' Labor–Management Partnership." *Positive Alternatives* 5, no. 3 (spring 1995), pp. 4–5.

13. Marion Anderson and Greg Bischak, "A Shift in Federal Spending: What the Peace Dividend Can Mean to Maine." Maine Peace Economy Project, 1990.

14. MacDougal, "Economic Conversion without Military Doctrinal Debate."

15. Gottlieb, *Defense Addiction*, p. 94.

16. Greg Bischak, *Brief 9: U.S. Conversion after the Cold War, 1990–1997: Lessons for Forging a New Conversion Policy*. Bonn: Bonn International Center for Conversion, July 1997, p. 11.

17. Gregory N. Stone, "In Seattle, Boeing Doesn't Like to Discuss Conversion." *Day* 112, no. 130 (November 8, 1992), pp. A1–6.

18. Paul Knox, "Washington State Community Diversification Program Report, January 1993–May 1994." Olympia: Washington State Community Development Department, Community Diversification Program, May 1994.

19. Stone, "In Seattle, Boeing Doesn't Like to Discuss Conversion."

20. Gottlieb, *Defense Addiction*, p. 105.

21. Knox, "Washington State Community Diversification Program Report."

22. Bischak, *Brief 9*, p. 11.

23. Gottlieb, *Defense Addiction*, p. 107.

24. Indeed, although manufacturing and other business networks are prolific in some Western European countries, they have had difficulty taking root in the United States, both because American economic-development policies tend not to favor small businesses and because the network idea goes against the individualist grain of most American businesses.

25. Business at Boeing boomed in the mid-'90s because of plentiful commercial-aircraft orders. By 1999, however, orders had slowed and a "little bust," as one observer called it, had set in.

26. Community Coalition for Economic Conversion, "Defense Jobs Are Down. What's Up?" Hartford: Connecticut Peace Action, January 1995.

27. Connecticut SANE/Freeze, "Connecticut Calls for New Priorities: Economic Conversion: Vital to the State's Economy," November 1992.

28. Joanne Sheehan, "Making a 'Penalty' Positive." *New England WRL News* (spring 1993).

29. Joanne Sheehan, "Community Coalition for Economic Conversion." Unpublished history by the Community Coalition for Economic Conversion, Uncasville, CT, 1997. Sheehan maintains that Electric Boat's immediate layoff of 2,000 workers was designed to stir up community opposition to the ending of the Seawolf program. Observers in Virginia ascribed the same motives to Newport News Shipyard in the early '90s.

30. Quoted in Gottlieb, *Defense Addiction*, p. 101.

31. This practice, of course, was not unique to Connecticut. See Laura Powers and

Ann Markusen, *A Just Transition? Lessons from Defense Worker Adjustment in the 1990s.* Washington, DC: Economic Policy Institute Technical Paper No. 237, April 1999, p. 17.

32. Gottlieb, *Defense Addiction*, pp. 102–4.

33. Ibid., p. 103; Community Coalition for Economic Conversion, "Defense Jobs Are Down."

34. *Boston Sunday Globe*, "High-Stakes Gambling" (February 11, 1996), p. B10.

35. Gottlieb, *Defense Addiction*, pp. 103–4

36. Sheehan, "Community Coalition for Economic Conversion."

37. Ibid.

38. The Department of Labor established the $11-million Defense Conversion and Adjustment Demonstration fund because it recognized the fact that the EDWAA program was not meeting the needs of middle-aged dislocated defense workers with specialized skills. In particular, the failure of EDWAA to link worker retraining with appropriate jobs was addressed in several demonstration projects funded by the demonstration fund. See Powers and Markusen, *A Just Transition?*, pp. 20–21.

39. Sheehan, "Community Coalition for Economic Conversion"; see also Powers and Markusen, *A Just Transition?*, pp. 20–22.

40. Gregory N. Stone, "In Tucson, the Community Helps Encourage Conversion Efforts." *Day* 112, no. 123 (November 1, 1992), pp. A1–6; Gottlieb, *Defense Addiction*, p. 89.

41. Beth Delson, "Making Waves in Arizona: A Discussion with Rosalyn Boxer." *Positive Alternatives* 3, no. 2 (winter 1993), p. 9; Gottlieb, *Defense Addiction*, p. 90.

42. Bischak, *Brief 9*, p 11.

43. Michael Oden et al., *Changing the Future: Converting the St. Louis Economy.* Piscataway, NJ: Rutgers University Center for Urban Policy Research, November 1993.

44. Employment in health care, education, and retail increased during the same period.

45. Oden et al., *Changing the Future*, pp. 52–55.

46. Ibid., p. 51.

47. Gottlieb, *Defense Addiction*, pp. 97–98.

48. Gregory N. Stone, "Defense Workers Seek Applications for Technology: McDonnell Douglas Process Could Yield Stronger Bridges." *Day* 112, no. 127 (November 5, 1992), pp. A1–8; Oden et al., *Changing the Future*, pp. 17–18; Gottlieb, *Defense Addiction*, p. 95.

49. Oden et al., *Changing the Future*, p. 57.

50. Ibid., p. 56.

51. Indeed, the EADC effort further increased local capacity to respond to economic dislocation. When production of the F-15 ended in 1999 and Boeing (which purchased McDonnell Douglas in 1997) began to lay off 7,000 workers, the EADC was quickly and easily revived to develop worker-assistance initiatives.

52. Powers and Markusen, *A Just Transition?*, pp. 29–32.

8

Transforming the Politics
of Defense Conversion

SUMMING UP: STAKEHOLDERS AND OTHER INFLUENCES

Chapter 1 posed the question of how communities would respond to the federal government's mixed signals on defense-spending cutbacks. The evidence from Virginia and other regions shows a variety of responses: resistance, adjustment, and conversion. Because defense-spending cutbacks take place within a context of ongoing economic-development issues and interests, the response to defense cutbacks is determined by many of the same factors that affect other aspects of state and local economic-development policy. These include:

- Regional industrial structure and the nature and magnitude of perceived cutbacks and impacts on the economy;
- Established interests: defense contractors; growth interests and elected officials; peace advocates; technology-development interests; labor unions; and appointed officials and staff, especially those working with displaced workers and small businesses;
- Public-sector capacity to deal with the impacts, specifically (a) prior experience with economic dislocation and the existence of agencies, staff, and programs to address it, and (b) community-planning capacity, generally reflected in local government structure and intergovernmental relations;
- Leadership—the ability to organize disparate or even opposing interests effectively and surmount institutional barriers;
- Assistance from higher levels of government, both financial and organizational.

Some of these factors were predicted in chapter 2; others were not but emerged clearly in the cases discussed in chapters 3 through 7. This chapter summarizes the roles that these factors played in the regional response to defense-spending cutbacks in the 1990s. Following that discussion, the chapter concludes with an assessment of the possibilities for achieving a peacetime economy in the United States and a discussion of paths towards that goal.

Regional Industrial Structure and the Nature and Magnitude of Cutbacks

In the cases reviewed in this volume, industrial structure exerted less influence than might have been predicted. Defense prime-contractor willingness to convert, as opposed to simply downsizing or exiting the defense business, did not appear to be determined by the magnitude of cutbacks they were experiencing or expected to experience. Nor did the *type* of community-wide response seem to vary in accordance with the type of private industrial structure there; the *intensity* of the community-wide response was greater in manufacturing regions such as Hampton Roads, Radford, St. Louis, and western Washington than in Northern Virginia, whose information-technology industries grew after 1990. To some extent, the type of community-wide response varied according to whether military bases were present or not. Radford and St. Louis, for example, accommodated the cutbacks more readily than did Hampton Roads, Tucson, San Diego, or southeastern Connecticut where large military-retirement communities and aggressive defense of local bases undermined the willingness to accept cutbacks. In all regions, doubts about the federal government's will to make lasting cuts, especially after 1994, dampened the enthusiasm for conversion, or at least the will to search for alternatives to the military.

Established Interests: Elected Officials

As discussed in chapter 2, state and local elected officials perceive that they have two primary responsibilities in economic matters: to increase jobs and tax revenues, or, more importantly, to be perceived to be doing so during their terms of office. When it came to defense downsizing, almost all state and local elected officials aggressively defended their bases and bemoaned the loss of jobs at shipbuilding, aerospace, and other defense-related firms. The few who were perceived as failing to do so—Arlington, Virginia's economic-development staff director in 1993 and Virginia's Governor Douglas Wilder later that same year, for example—were publicly chastised by other politicians or growth interests. Popular opinion generally supported the critics.

Although job retention is generally good economic policy, the economic logic of aggressively retaining bases and ignoring development alternatives is somewhat flawed. Most research on the subject shows that communities usually recover from base closings within seven to ten years and moreover do better than they did with the base.[1] The closure creates new economic opportunities, as chamber of commerce leaders and a few local elected officials in Hampton Roads recognized. Moreover, since military bases do not pay real estate taxes, a community could potentially improve its fiscal health by replacing a base with a commercial activity. Still, as Hampton Roads officials stated and as they and their counterparts in other communities demonstrated, it would be political suicide to allow a base to close without a fight. Officials were also expected to resist because base closings were seen as "merely" political acts that lacked the assumed authority of a market-based closure decision such as that made by a company in the commercial market. Thus it was unacceptable for a politician to say: "I'm going to let this base close without a fight and then we'll figure out how to find new jobs." Exceptions such as Cameron Station in Alexandria, Virginia, which employed relatively few local residents and which was highly coveted by real estate developers, proved the rule.[2] Moreover, because, over time, civic pride becomes bound up with local bases, a politician who allows a base to depart without a public fight may be perceived as lacking respect for the community itself. This is shortsighted, of course, but election cycles are short. Few politicians can build careers on future plans that are perceived to sacrifice the present. State and local politicians had fewer avenues through which to retain defense-contractor jobs in the post–Cold War period, but those they had, they used. In Newport News, southeastern Connecticut, Tucson, and elsewhere, they deferred to contractors' wishes not to develop community-conversion initiatives or they and their congressional representatives helped lobby Congress for more defense-related orders.

Once cuts or closures occurred, however, local, state, and congressional politicians had to demonstrate concern for those who were losing their jobs and take measures to reemploy them. Such measures often took the form of quick-fix, high-profile solutions such as recruitment of new branch plants or development of sports stadiums or other entertainment facilities. These efforts not only added jobs (albeit not very good ones) relatively quickly, they also promised to increase real estate tax revenues and were supported by growth interests. Company conversion, on the other hand, which takes three to five years under good circumstances, could not make such a dramatic statement, especially since it occurred mostly in small firms and addressed technical or mundane issues that do not interest most politicians or growth boosters. (Conversion in larger companies would have made better press headlines, but even these efforts would have lacked the drama and land-value increases of new real estate development.)

In addition to job and tax-base concerns, ideology and political-party affiliation played minor roles in elected officials' responses to defense-spending cutbacks. Generally, Democrats were more likely to support community-wide conversion planning, small-business assistance, and worker-retraining initiatives. Several state and local conversion initiatives were halted or lost funding support after conservative Republicans came into office. When Republicans became the majority party in Congress after the 1994 elections, they immediately began to attack the Clinton administration's weak conversion programs. By 1996 they had done away with them and increased defense spending. Nevertheless, at the state and local levels, neither political party nor ideology outweighed the imperative to champion jobs.

Growth Interests

Chambers of commerce and other growth organizations played significant roles in state and local responses to defense-spending cutbacks. Their vision of the good community is built around population and land-value growth. Thus, growth interests in Hampton Roads, Northern Virginia, Tucson, San Diego, and Puget Sound often spearheaded efforts to defend local bases from BRAC cuts. Once the cuts came, however, growth interests usually were among the first to begin planning the adjustment process, since it was in their interests to ensure a quick recovery. Indeed, in large urban areas, growth interests are looked upon as stewards of the local economy.[3] Therefore growth interests occupied prominent places on many base-reuse committees. As the Hampton Roads case shows, they had several redevelopment ideas for Hampton Roads bases in case the BRAC process targeted them. But traditional growth interests did not promote company conversion, diversification, or worker retraining. They promoted the types of projects that they were already working on: downtown commercial and office development, construction of new entertainment and tourism facilities, and the recruitment of new branch plants. Such strategies bring job and population growth and increases in land values. And the results—new structures—are easier to see and understand than esoteric company conversion and worker-retraining initiatives.

Prime Contractors

Contractors also influenced state and local responses to cutbacks. As is true of export-oriented companies in the nonmilitary sector, defense prime contractors focused on their export markets—the Pentagon and foreign arms buyers, not on the community. For reasons described in chapter 1, few prime contractors in the manufacturing sector chose the path of diversification or departure from the defense business. Having concluded that they could not diversify into commercial markets profitably, they took the path of least resistance, shedding labor and capital assets and focusing on their core military competencies. Only one manufacturing contractor described in this volume, Bath Iron Works, pursued diversification using its existing workforce, in part because its CEO grew up in the Bath area and cared about the well-being of the community and workforce. Although other prime contractors (e.g., Hughes Electronics Corporation, Westinghouse Electric, Tenneco, General Electric, and Loral) exited the defense industry by selling off their defense divisions, none attempted to help their defense workforces convert to civilian production.[4] Of course, where the Pentagon mandated diversification, as in the case of the Radford Army Ammunition Plant, the contractor worked to make it happen, albeit by recruiting new operations, not by converting existing defense workers.[5] However, as discussed in chapters 3 and 4, prime- and subcontractors in business, engineering, and management services found it easier to diversify, not into commercial markets, but into other government markets.

Some defense manufacturers such as McDonnell Douglas and Boeing assisted in local conversion and adjustment planning, providing subcontractor lists and workforce-transition facilities and even helping to capitalize some new, small commercial ventures. By and large, however, contractor resistance to conversion or diversification had a chilling effect on community-planning efforts. In several cases, such as those of Newport News Shipyard in Hampton Roads, Electric Boat in Connecticut, and Hughes/Raytheon in Tucson, contractor resistance to conversion undermined state and local political support for it as well. Like export-oriented companies in the civilian sector, the size and power of most defense prime contractors intimidates elected officials.

Unions

Few labor-union locals openly contradicted their company's stance on conversion. In the few cases where they did, such as at Unisys in Minnesota, management rebuffed them.[6] Defense workers are hostages of their well-paying jobs and the lack of comparable opportunities elsewhere, especially for middle-age persons. Powerless to stop the massive layoffs, most workers consented to the company strategy of getting as large a share of the remaining defense contracts as possible. Workers at McDonnell Douglas, Electric Boat, and Newport News Shipyard even joined management in seeking more defense work; petitioning the federal government for export licenses or lobbying Congress to buy more of their company's products.

Peace Advocates

Peace and conversion advocates played important catalytic roles in most of the communities that developed conversion and adjustment initiatives. But their influence derived from their appeal to conversion and diversification as a pragmatic necessity, not as a normative one. Defense-worker opposition to their campaigns in the 1970s and '80s had convinced them to avoid discussion of philosophical principles and focus on providing practical solutions and federal funds to solve the problems of dislocation wrought by defense downsizing. In Washington State, San Diego, and Maine, conversion organizers provided the spark that ignited community-wide conversion and adjustment planning. In St. Louis, they were a continuous and, to some extent, respected voice in the regional adjustment-planning process. Through their knowledge of and, sometimes, ability to secure federal grants to support conversion and adjustment, conversion advocates were able to provide a useful service that increased local receptivity of their message. In southeastern Connecticut and Tucson, however, conversion proponents were not able to overcome resistance by contractors, growth interests, and elected officials. Nevertheless, in both communities, conversion advocates established sophisticated, labor-based conversion and retraining programs. Still, even where they were successful, conversion advocates found that their influence began to wane as established interests reasserted control over the local policy agenda and as federal conversion support diminished. By the time federal funding stopped in the latter half of the 1990s, conversion advocacy had disappeared in most communities.

Technology Interests

Although "technology interests" are difficult to describe in a way that is entirely consistent across communities, there are persons at the local, state, and federal levels who subscribe to the view that technology development is the key to economic prosperity. There are two variants of this view: A "high tech" variant, and a so-called "appropriate technology" one. Although the boundary between them is blurry, the former is more supply side in focus, while the latter is more demand driven. High-tech advocates consider technological innovation to be the engine of the economy. They promote commercialization of basic scientific research at universities and federal research labs as well as the spin-off of exotic defense technologies into the commercial sector. Many of the Clinton–Gore administration's economic-policy ideas are rooted in this philosophy, and the administration's Technology Reinvestment Project is a good example. At the local level, proponents of the high-tech solution included the founders of the Peninsula Advanced Technology Center in Hampton Roads: engineering professors at Old Dominion University, the commander of NASA/Langley Research Lab, a technology-transfer agent with the Virginia Center for Innovative Technology, and a community college president. It also included industrialists such as Franklin Moreno in Northern Virginia and the chamber of commerce president in St. Louis as well as engineering professors at Washington University in St. Louis. Like the Technology Reinvestment Project, the high-tech solution is, at least in theory, neither pro-conversion nor pro-military. This is both a strength and weakness. In conversion-hostile climates such as Hampton Roads, it could, to some degree, manage to slip some conversion in the back door, so to speak—providing a defense company with a new technology might help it to break into commercial markets. And in communities that were more open to conversion such as St. Louis, it could lay the foundation for new industries. In San Diego the high-tech telecommunications and biotechnology industries did, to some degree, become the replacements for defense manufacturing. But as the Technology Reinvestment Project showed, high-tech development could just as easily (actually more easily) be used to enhance military production as conversion in defense firms. Moreover, the high-tech solution, as a San Diego peace activist noted, ignored sustainable development and human needs. It also tended to ignore some existing business needs, as some critics of the Peninsula Advanced Technology Center in Hampton Roads charged.

Manufacturing extension services, on the other hand, such as the Southwest Virginia Manufacturing Technology Center near the New River Valley, the manufacturing extension programs in Washington, St. Louis, and Maine, and the business-assistance services of the Arizona Council for Economic Conversion took an "appropriate technology" perspective. Although engineers were associated with most of these efforts as well, the projects were organized by conversion advocates and community developers. Like high technology, there is nothing inherently peaceful about appropriate technology, but the programs mentioned here explicitly sought to help companies convert to civilian markets, not by commercializing a new, advanced technology, but by solving problems and moving into civilian markets using technologies appropriate to the company's stage of development. In short, appropriate technology tends to be market driven and worker based, whereas high technology tends to be technology driven.[7]

Appointed Officials

Professional staff in community- and economic-development offices, small-business development, and job-training centers comprised another important set of actors. Although they were limited by political directives that were influenced by the other actors mentioned above, public professionals, especially those whose work brought them into contact with dislocated workers or struggling businesses, became advocates for public conversion and adjustment assistance. In St. Louis, economic-development professionals, with the strong support of elected officials, initiated and guided the adjustment and conversion process. In Washington, aggressive leadership by state staff produced a number of successful local initiatives. In Virginia, professional staffpersons at Forward Hampton Roads were the first to realize the need for the Plan 2007 process, professionals in Fairfax County initiated the study of defense-contractor responses to downsizing, and the New River Valley Planning District Commission staff worked hard to make the ARMS Initiative a workable facility-reuse program. Small-business-development center directors in Hampton Roads and Northern Virginia sought increased federal funding to assist defense businesses. Job-training professionals in Northern Virginia, Hampton Roads, and the New River Valley sought more funding to better serve and track displaced workers, and in Hampton Roads and the New River Valley they sought to improve the links between their work and that of economic developers. In Tucson, job-training professionals and small-business-development staff were among the few public officials who advocated for the Arizona Council on Economic Conversion.

Institutional Capacity

Responses to defense downsizing were more extensive in states and localities that already had an infrastructure of agencies and programs to deal with economic dislocation and restructuring. St. Louis County, which, in the 1980s had suffered widespread manufacturing downsizing, provides the best example of preexisting local-restructuring capacity, manifested not only in its professional staff but in the supportive attitudes of its elected officials. Massachusetts and

New York State also had established programs for addressing industrial dislocation that they applied to the defense sector in the 1990s.[8] At the other end of the
spectrum, Virginia and Arizona lacked previous experience with industrial
decline and therefore were not prepared to introduce conversion and adjustment.

Local Political and Fiscal Structures

American communities are fragmented into multiple political jurisdictions,
each of which relies to a significant degree upon real estate property taxes to
finance local services. Since the most lucrative sources of property-tax revenues
are commercial and industrial properties, individual jurisdictions compete for
these "ratables." This competition undermines the very thing that community
defense-conversion requires—region-wide planning. Moreover, the fixation on
property-tax revenues exaggerates the importance of land development, which,
as discussed earlier, eclipses company conversion and labor-force development
as economic-policy alternatives.

Under these conditions, only a crisis may be able to bring about serious
interjurisdictional cooperation, and then only for a limited time. Thus some
regions like St. Louis managed to develop regional responses to dramatic
employment losses at McDonnell Douglas (albeit at first without strong support
from the growth coalition in the city). Hampton Roads's warring localities managed to cooperate to mount a spirited defense against BRAC'95—a short-term
effort against a clear "enemy." But interjurisdictional competition in Hampton
Roads undermined the Plan 2007 process and the Peninsula Advanced Technology Center—longer-term efforts with less clear goals than the BRAC defense.

Leadership

The ability to organize effectively, especially across established interest-
group and local government lines, also proved important in successful conversion. Often, effective leadership resulted mainly from the work of a single individual. In Maine, Susie Schweppe convinced Buzz Fitzgerald of Bath Iron Works
to engage in conversion, and she brought many groups, such as businesses and
environmentalists, together for the first time. In Washington, Paul Knox was able
to use his positions on the board of the local SANE/Freeze peace-advocacy chapter and on the staff of the Washington Community Development Department to
help channel SANE/Freeze's energy into objectives that would achieve wider
acceptance. The result was state legislation that created the Community Diversification Program. In St. Louis, Dennis Coleman, director of the Economic
Adjustment and Diversification Committee, supported by county officials, managed to draw the city, counties, the states of Missouri and Illinois, the International Association of Machinists union, and even McDonnell Douglas and the
St. Louis Economic Conversion Project—who clashed in other arenas—into a
cooperative planning and implementation relationship that lasted six years and
produced several successful initiatives. Coleman eventually won over the St.

Louis city-based chamber of commerce as well, partly because of its president's interest in technology development. The failure of Hampton Roads's chamber of commerce to organize across established local-government boundaries and the failure of the Arizona Council on Economic Conversion (not for lack of trying!) to make inroads into the established political and economic leadership stalled community-wide conversion and adjustment planning there.

Federal Assistance

Financial and organizational aid from the federal government proved to be one of the most important determinants of the state and local response to defense-spending cutbacks. Given the paucity of state and local funds, few conversion and adjustment efforts would have gotten off the ground without funds from the Commerce Department's Economic Development Administration and National Institute of Standards and Technology, the Department of Labor, and the Defense Department's Office of Economic Adjustment. Indeed, the state matching funds required for some of these grants constituted the only state funds expended for conversion or adjustment.[9] As noted above, in some communities conversion advocates were able to achieve a measure of public legitimacy through their success in attracting federal funds or by helping public agencies to do so. And when federal funds began to dry up after 1994, so did conversion efforts in most communities.

THE UPSHOT

Out of this mix of regional contexts and interests came a number of successful conversion and adjustment programs, some of which still existed in 1999, sometimes having evolved from their initial forms and purposes. Virtually all of these programs focused on small-business conversion and diversification and worker retraining. Notable examples include Washington's Manufacturing Extension Partnership and its constituent industry alliances, St. Louis' Middle America Manufacturing Technology Program, and the St. Louis and southeastern Connecticut worker-retraining and job-development systems. The Arizona Council on Economic Conversion had evolved from a defense-conversion retraining program into a welfare-to-work program, but its core values and approach remained intact. In Hampton Roads, the Peninsula Advanced Technology Center had been incorporated into the Peninsula Economic Development Council (a chamber-led group), but it continued to serve small businesses, as did the Southwestern Virginia Manufacturing Technology Center.

In many communities, defense conversion and adjustment planning marked the first time that some organizations had worked together. Examples include Maine's regional alliances and St. Louis' Economic Adjustment and Diversification Council. These experiences paved the way for future cooperative efforts. For example, when, in 1999, production of the F-15 came to an end and Boeing began to lay off 7,000 workers, the Economic Adjustment and Diversification

Council was reconstituted to develop appropriate responses. Even some BRAC defense efforts helped to lay a foundation for possible future cooperation. In Hampton Roads, the community's successful BRAC'95 defense, which involved the business community, political leaders, and retired military from the entire 13-jurisdiction metro area, served as a springboard to further region-wide economic-development ventures. Most importantly, conversion happened. Several large contractors—Hughes, Westinghouse, Tenneco, and others—sold their defense operations and shifted focus to civilian production. Hundreds of smaller companies diversified or exited defense markets entirely, some entering the growing environmental market, others entering health, transportation, and other technology-intensive industries.[10]

Nevertheless, the overall impact of defense conversion and adjustment efforts bears a strong resemblance to that of mammals in the Mesozoic period: Energetic and thriving, to some extent, but still dominated by the dinosaurs. As described in chapter 1, annual military spending is again approaching the $290 billion mark (in current dollars) and after the early-to-mid-1990s reduction from its Reagan-era high watermark, defense employment is stabilizing. The base review and closure process has ceased, pending presidential and congressional resolve to resume it.

State and local economies that suffered defense cutbacks rebounded very well, but not primarily because of conversion or diversification in small companies. Rather, the comeback is due to the effects of the national economic boom of the mid-to-late–1990s, fueled by explosive growth in information technology-related industries, services, and even, in some cases, manufacturing. To be sure, this represents a shift of some resources from defense to civilian uses. But the manner in which it occurred bears little relation to the conversion model promoted by Melman, Dumas, and others (discussed in chapter 1). Nor has it resulted in the widespread development of sustainable industries such as alternative energy production and electric vehicles (notwithstanding the ambitious CAL-START project in California).[11] The conversion model calls for the deliberate, planned process of shifting workers and equipment from military to civilian pursuits, with minimum waste of human and physical capital. The core of the model is the alternative-use committee, a cooperative labor–management effort to apply the company's existing capabilities (human and physical) to the production of commercial products and services. To make conversion a practical alternative, the federal government would stimulate demand for sustainable goods and services in environmental mitigation, transportation, housing, and alternative-energy production, while lowering defense spending. Where conversion was not feasible or for those workers whom a converting company could not employ, the federal government would provide adequate training and support to move into good jobs that utilized their skills.

Although conversion happened in many small companies, it could not succeed on the scale envisioned in the model because crucial pieces of the puzzle were missing. Although the defense budget was cut substantially from its peacetime high in 1985, it remained at 80 to 85 percent of its Cold War average. The two-regional-war scenario envisioned in the 1993 Bottom-Up Review meant that most existing weapon platforms and many systems would be retained, although fewer units would be built. This, coupled with high spending levels, drove many contractors to downsize rather than get out of the defense business. Companies could easily shed workers because workers had no power to resist layoffs. Weak labor unions and decades of cyclical defense employment had convinced many workers that this was their lot. Attempts to mandate alternative-use committees had failed in Congress. Even if such mandates had become law, it is not clear that the committees would have become viable corporate-planning tools. Decades of experience with labor–management cooperation programs in the United States have shown that such efforts do not last unless management has a stake in the outcome.[12] Unless management wanted to get into new markets, it is not likely that it would have made a strong commitment to the alternative-use committees.

But the federal government failed to generate enough demand in new markets to induce defense companies to undertake the costly and time-consuming process of converting to serve them. Nor did the federal government use other tools to encourage defense contractors to shift into commercial markets. The government did reinstate the maritime subsidy (cancelled during the early years of the Reagan administration) that, in effect, subsidizes sales by U.S. shipyards to foreign buyers. But it chose not to incentivize American participation in the huge and growing global environmental-protection market. Instead, it increased subsidies to help defense firms export arms to foreign buyers.[13]

Under these inauspicious circumstances, local barriers stymied conversion in some communities and limited its prospects in others. Because defense prime contractors were not interested in diversification or conversion and because communities have little leverage over large export-oriented companies, conversion efforts could only involve small businesses. But as one conversion organizer said: "Small business is small potatoes" to elected leaders and growth interests. Indeed, despite political rhetoric to the contrary, in most communities small business is treated as a stepchild. Small business does not make good newspaper headlines. Elected officials who need to demonstrate their commitment to growing jobs with eye-catching events over a short time frame get little political mileage from small-business development. Therefore small-business-development programs, whether their focus is conversion or cosmetology, usually are starved of state and local resources. Thus few if any of the successful small-business-conversion initiatives discussed previously would have begun, let alone survived, without federal-funding support, short-lived as it was. Even some of the more successful initiatives such as Washington's Manufacturing Extension Program almost died for lack of state support. Only the Community Development Department's ability to use the diversification program budget for the Manufacturing Extension Program kept it alive.

But much defense conversion is not just small-business development—it is business development that requires technological change, entry into new markets, and well-designed worker retraining, all of which are difficult to achieve and difficult for lay persons to understand. Although Americans generally are fascinated with whiz-bang technology, their interest in the difficult process of developing new products and production methods remains undeveloped. Nor are Americans sufficiently committed (yet) to the ideals of sustainable industry, agriculture, and human settlement to devote significant public resources towards realizing them (although knowledge and appreciation of the harmfulness of traditional industrial and development patterns and the importance of sustainable technologies is expanding). Thus the goals of many conversion advocates to convert defense businesses to eco-friendly, sustainable industries received only a modest public hearing in the early 1990s and certainly were not widely embraced.[14]

On the other hand, high-profile efforts to defend against base closures, to attract new branch plants, or to build new stadiums for professional sports teams or new downtown waterfront shopping centers make great newspaper headlines and offer seemingly tangible employment benefits. As one state economic-development official said: "More people follow sports than follow DOD budgets." And because they tend to substantially increase land values and population, such developments are embraced by growth interests.[15] It is not surprising that politicians tend to favor them. As discussed previously, local political fragmentation and reliance on real estate taxes favor this kind of response also.

ENDING THE COLD WAR CAPTIVITY

The foregoing account has shown some of the potential for conversion as well as some important regional and federal political barriers.[16] As the end of the Cold War and the expectation of a peace dividend now become a dim memory and the nation sinks back into acquiescence with the Pentagon's $290 billion military budget, it is necessary to ask how we might escape the shackles of the Cold War economy. The cases reviewed in this book have shown that states and localities will be able to do little without a supportive national conversion policy. The dominant interests in most communities will ensure that communities respond to federal spending priorities, whether they be for military hardware, mass-transit vehicles, or ocean thermal-energy production. But national conversion policy must emanate from a supportive national security policy. The tragic flaw in defense downsizing and conversion policy in the 1990s is that it had little foundation in America's national security policy. Advocates tried to sell conversion as a rational way to deal with inevitable defense downsizing, but the argument had little foundation because defense downsizing was not as inevitable as advocates maintained.

A Real New-World Order

When the Berlin Wall came down and the Soviet Union disintegrated, President Bush called for "a new world order." And indeed, the end of the Cold War provided the opportunity for the nation to truly ponder the role it could play in bringing about a new, peaceful world order and the implications that might have for national security policy. But America wasted that opportunity. No thorough debate on the U.S. role in the post–Cold War world took place. The nation came no closer to such a debate than the 1993 Bottom-Up Review. This exercise focused narrowly on military policy, not on the broader set of considerations that concern U.S. trade policy, foreign aid, diplomacy, and cooperative security arrangements. Indeed, the Bottom-Up Review, in assuming the need for military forces capable of fighting two regional wars simultaneously, on short notice, without allies, and to decisive victory, kept the nation locked in the offensive force-projection model of national security that characterized its Cold War policy. This model fails to account for most of the likely threats to peace in the twenty-first century: ethnic conflicts within nation-states, international terrorism, natural-resource shortages (e.g., lack of potable water), and mass refugee migrations.[17] But more importantly, as Forsberg (1995) persuasively argues, this model becomes a self-fulfilling prophecy. By continuing the arms race and aggressively selling weapons abroad, by failing to establish strong, cooperative international security arrangements, by alienating former adversaries but potential future allies such as Russia (through, for example, NATO expansion), and by failing to develop viable nonviolent solutions to regional crises, the United States is itself creating future threats to peace.[18]

There are alternatives to the offensive military philosophy that undergirds American national-security strategy. But because the United States failed to engage in a thorough debate of these alternatives, it established no clear national consensus for the future of military spending. The federal government simply began to cut the Defense Department's budget. Therefore greater uncertainty surrounded the cutbacks than might have occurred under a clearer policy. And when the Clinton administration accelerated the cuts begun by President Bush, a backlash occurred that Congressional hawks exploited. As a result, both cutbacks and defense-conversion spending ceased.

It is not too late to have a national debate on security policy. Indeed, it is more necessary now than ever. The debate could consider the prospects for nuclear arms reduction in the aftermath of the U.S. Senate's October 1999 rejection of the Comprehensive Nuclear Test Ban Treaty, the lack of an international code of conduct in foreign arms sales, the high level of U.S. subsidies for American arms exports, and whether the nation truly needs the National Missile Defense System (aka Star Wars). Such a debate might also entertain suggestions for ending international war, such as Randall Forsberg's 1998 proposal for a convention limiting nations to defensive military actions and committing them to stopping aggression through standing U.N.-led police forces, not U.S.-led bombing campaigns or ad hoc U.N. forces. (Under such an arrangement, Forsberg argues, the United States could eventually reduce its military to a defensive force costing less than $100 billion per year and freeing up funds for developing the civilian economy.[19]) Agreements such as these would require stronger international institutions than those that presently exist.

The United States is uniquely positioned to help create these institutions and it is in its own self-interest to do so. Another 20 years of military spending at the expense of the commercial economy will further weaken the United States with respect to its trading partners and further undermine even the basis for a strong military. (See the discussion of the U.S. defense-industrial base in chapter 1.) Over the long term, the United States cannot win the military game that its policies perpetuate. As America's relative economic dominance continues to recede, its military hegemony will be questioned as well. Unless the United States begins now to build a stronger cooperative international security system it may be superseded by the next superpower, just as the rest of the world defers to the United States now.

And What of Conversion?

Should the nation find the political will to adopt a defensive rather than offensive national security policy, we would be able to reduce defense spending by one-half to two-thirds of current amounts. Then it would be appropriate to speak of conversion and make use of the lessons of the 1990s in designing effective policies. In the best-case scenario, the United States would divert military expenditures to investments in some combination of education, a modern infrastructure, alternative-energy production, environmental mitigation, mass transit, affordable housing, and health care. With a sustained federal commitment to such activities, defense prime contractors would be able to plan their transition from military to civilian production. Under this scenario, it would not be necessary to *mandate* the alternative-use committees envisioned in early conversion models. Nor would such a mandate be workable, as discussed above. However, since cooperative, labor–management alternative-use planning is likely to improve the total, social efficiency of the transition process by saving human capital and other resources, federal and state governments could incentivize it. They could offer planning grants or give preference to companies bidding on federal or state nonmilitary contracts that use former or current defense workers. Federal and state governments could also use incentive grants to encourage defense prime contractors to spin off divisions or new operations to do nonmilitary work. Both federal and state governments have also stimulated markets and could do so much more, through regulations. For example, federal and state (as well as foreign country) air- and water-pollution regulations have helped to create a huge and growing global environmental-mitigation industry.[20] Such regulations also have spurred development of alternative-transportation technologies. It is no coincidence that CAL-START, an ambitious effort to develop electric-automobile technology, started in California, the state with the most stringent automobile-emissions standards.[21] However, the ultimate motivation to convert a company from defense to nonmilitary work must come from defense-contractor management, not from government or labor. The company conversion and diversification examples cited in this volume show that if demand for nonmilitary goods and services is created and sustained, management will supply it.

It is doubtful that "dual-use" programs such as the Clinton administration's Technology Reinvestment Project (TRP) would be appropriate under this defense-downsizing scenario. A primary purpose of those programs was not conversion but enhancement of the defense industrial base by infusing state-of-the-art commercial technology into outmoded military products and services. Even a defense-oriented military must have a healthy industrial base, but it is disingenuous to promote that as a conversion policy. The bigger flaw in TRP, however, is that it was technology driven, not demand driven, so even its impact on the defense industrial base is dubious. It should be noted that some local "conversion" programs such as the Peninsula Advanced Technology Center in Hampton Roads were based on the Technology Reinvestment Project model. Without this model and the possibility of federal funds, Hampton Roads might not have attempted even this modest amount of public conversion support. But if a shift in national security policy were followed by a forthright defense-downsizing program and some alternative government markets, there would be no need to sneak conversion in the back door.

Worker-retraining policies are equally if not more important than company-conversion incentives. There is ample evidence from the experience of Virginia communities and others that America's worker-retraining system is inadequate.[22] The best programs integrate incumbent workforce retraining with the development of new products and markets; examples include the conversion programs in Tucson, St. Louis, southeastern Connecticut, and Massachusetts, and to some extent the Peninsula Advanced Technology Center's labor policies and the technology-upgrading strategy of the New River Valley's Corporate Roundtable. Such strategies are especially important now, as the economy becomes increasingly polarized into good jobs and bad ones. Efforts that integrate company and workforce development can ensure that workers obtain better jobs. Even if job and worker development are not integrated, current federal/state programs can be improved by lengthening training time, providing stipends so that workers can continue to feed their families while retraining, improving the quality of career counseling, and conducting better follow-up studies of worker-employment outcomes. Such efforts might appear to be more expensive than current programs, but America has wasted untold billions in productivity because of its failure to properly retrain dislocated workers and link them with appropriate jobs.[23]

The integration of workforce retraining and conversion would be smoother if relevant federal conversion and adjustment agencies were coordinated. At a minimum, workforce-retraining programs of the Department of Labor should be coordinated with the Defense Department's Office of Economic Adjustment and the Commerce Department's Economic Development Administration. It would be better still if all economic-adjustment programs were consolidated under the Commerce and Labor Departments. And better coordination is needed between the armed services and federal, state, and local civilian agencies so that the base-closure and reuse-planning process as well as the discharge and reemployment of military personnel in civilian occupations proceeds more smoothly. Also, worker participation should be added to the base- and facility-reuse-planning process. The base-reuse planning problems encountered in Hampton Roads, Vint Hill Farms Station, and at the Radford Army Ammunition Plant in Virginia were experienced elsewhere as well.[24]

Although interagency coordination was lacking, the assistance of the Office of Economic Adjustment, the Department of Labor, and the Economic Development Administration was crucial to regional conversion and adjustment efforts during the 1990s. Without it very little conversion would have occurred, since states and localities were unwilling to spend much of their own money on these tasks. Under any future defense-downsizing scenario, federal support for company-conversion and community-adjustment planning would be necessary. Indeed, it should be increased and sustained over a longer period of time than it was during the 1990s if it is to be maximally effective. Furthermore, communities should receive assistance in proportion to the impact of downsizing on their economies, and in proportion to their unemployment rates and per capita incomes as well.[25]

Local Reforms to Enhance Regional Planning

Under any imaginable defense-downsizing scenario, communities may resist cutbacks. The most defense-dependent communities, especially those with military bases and retirees, can be expected to put up the greatest resistance, even if, as suggested above, they were to receive greater federal adjustment assistance and if their contractors were to enter government-stimulated markets for non-military goods and services. It is part of the unwritten job description of state and local elected officials as well as their congressional delegations that they be perceived as defending existing jobs. Thus the BRAC process, despite its perverse effect of driving communities to reinforce their ties to the military, is probably the most rational and equitable way that can be devised to close military installations, and it should continue.

The same forces that drive communities to resist defense-spending cutbacks—the protection of existing jobs and the requirements of local growth interests—equip them to adjust to downsizing, albeit through the attraction of new branch plants and the development of flashy recreation and tourism facilities, not through company conversion. However, if the federal government were to stimulate demand for new products and services and subsidize worker retraining, some defense contractors would convert to supplying that demand and local growth interests would have new industries to recruit. Therefore some of the resistance-to-conversion problem would take care of itself.

Nevertheless, certain reforms could improve community planning and development in general and thus improve the community response to defense-spending cutbacks. American communities are fragmented into multiple competing jurisdictions, a situation that has prevailed despite decades of effort by various interests to achieve regional cooperation or regional government. Across the country, a number of different arrangements have been tried and many more have been recommended to overcome the problem of local fragmentation.[26] One reform that might be easier to achieve, albeit less far-reaching in its consequences than the more ambitious regional-governance proposals often proffered, is tax reform. As discussed previously, the average American locality still relies upon the real-property tax for about one-third of its revenue base; an antiquated tax that no longer accurately reflects wealth, but which fuels interjurisdictional competition for businesses. States could deflate some of these conflicts and thus make regional cooperation and planning easier to achieve by replacing the local real-property tax with state aid derived from higher progressive income taxes.[27] Replacing or severely restricting the real-property tax would not only make it easier to carry out regional planning and adjustment efforts, it would also moderate the influence of growth interests on local development policy, since one rationale for local land-development and business-recruitment policies is to increase real-estate tax revenues. With that rationale gone or diminished, local governments might be somewhat more inclined to focus attention on sustainable development policies that do not increase growth, such as company-conversion assistance.[28]

Reforms are also needed to curb the irresponsible use of state and local subsidies to support business recruitment. Although most analysts, and even economic-development practitioners, understand the problems inherent in this approach to economic development, elected officials and growth interests have a vested interest in continuing it. As the cases in this volume illustrate, the practice of business recruitment often marginalizes business retention, small-business development, and company-conversion assistance. Some scholars have recommended that the federal government limit the practice of interstate recruitment, or at least limit the public subsidies that fuel it.[29] Such reforms might help, but the larger question is one of accountability: What net benefits, or net costs, does a footloose branch plant bring to a community over time? What are the opportunity costs of courting such plants, as opposed to nurturing locally owned businesses and, if necessary, helping them to shift from military to commercial markets? Although the federal government cannot ensure that states and localities make wise economic-development decisions, it could conduct studies of the long-range impacts of business-recruitment policies and disseminate the results widely. This would improve local decision-making and, no doubt, shift attention and resources away from recruitment and toward better economic-development policies, including conversion assistance.[30]

Those are not the only public-policy changes that would improve local planning and economic health and also foster defense conversion. For example, improvements in U.S. labor law and its interpretation by the National Labor Relations Board as well as higher labor and environmental standards in developing countries would improve labor and community bargaining power vis-à-vis global corporations in the United States. With more bargaining power, labor and communities could discourage corporations from simply shedding labor whenever markets (including defense markets) contract. This would induce corporations to search for new markets and develop new products using existing labor. Though important, such changes are not the most important ones if the main objective is to achieve a peacetime economy in the United States.

First Things First

The most well-designed defense-conversion policies will be useless until the nation finds the will to develop a new, defense-oriented national security policy that makes the need for meaningful defense-spending reductions obvious to the vast majority of Americans. It seems unlikely that such a wholesale policy change will come about in the near future. America has a long tradition of aversion to global affairs and ignorance of its impact on the world, despite its economic and political dominance.[31] Indeed, Americans sometimes seem willing to pay the Pentagon almost any price to keep the world at bay, as it were, despite the ultimate futility of that goal. And recurrent regional crises in the 1990s have undoubtedly convinced many that we need more guns, not more international cooperation.

However, there is reason to be hopeful. The peace movement is alive and well at the national, state, and local levels, as many Americans see the need to move from a global system based upon fear to one rooted in mutual respect and cooperation. At the national level, think tanks such as the Center for Defense Information, the Institute for Defense and Disarmament Studies, Women's Action for New Directions, and coalitions such as Global Action to Prevent War focus on alternative security policy, dismantling the U.S. nuclear arsenal, and canceling expensive and unnecessary weapon systems.[32] At the local level, groups such as Peace Action (successor to SANE/Freeze) and a multitude of local peace-education centers address Americans' fears of violence in schools and workplaces and on the streets. They then link those concerns with larger issues of international violence and war. As one local Peace Action organizer said:

I used to think we needed to focus all of our attention on national issues like defeating the MX missile and ratifying the Comprehensive Test Ban Treaty. But it was always hard to get people interested in that. Now we spend half of our time dealing with security issues that people care about, like school violence. Then when we ask them to sign a petition to ratify the Comprehensive Test Ban Treaty, we get lots of support. People see the connection.

Peace advocates are not the only ones working for a new national security policy. Many others see how military spending saps energy from the commercial economy and from civil society in general. For example, in the spring of 1999 a national group called Business Leaders for Sensible Priorities announced plans to participate in the 2000 election campaign by challenging presidential candidates to support a 3-percent cut in the defense budget, to be used for health care and education. Step by step, national and local initiatives such as these can create a peace constituency in the United States until it becomes politically feasible for national leaders to take bolder steps to create a global security system based upon peace and defensive, not offensive, military establishments.[33]

The conversion success stories of the 1990s can help to make the case for a peacetime economy. For the 1990s have furnished valuable lessons, not only on the barriers to conversion, but on some ways to overcome them. Nevertheless, the primary barrier to conversion is not technical or even economic, but political. Those who want conversion and those who want a healthy economy should join the peace advocates and work for a national security policy that makes conversion necessary.

NOTES

1. Andy Isserman and Peter Stenberg, "The Recovery of Rural Economies from Military Base Closures: Control Group Analysis of Two Decades of Experience." Paper presented at the Southern Regional Science Association Meeting, Orlando, Florida, April 1994, cited in Michael Brzoska and Ann Markusen, "The Regional Role in Post–Cold War Military–Industrial Conversion." *International Regional Science Review* (January 2000).

2. The community seemed to find it easy to ignore the adjustment needs of Cameron Station's low-wage, Hispanic commissary workers, however. Whether ethnic insensitivity played a role here is not known.

3. This seems to be less true in rural areas and even in some suburban counties, however. For example, Pima County, which surrounds Tucson, St. Louis County, which surrounds St. Louis, and both the New River Valley and Fort Pickett/Blackstone rural areas in Virginia developed responses to defense-spending cutbacks without strong chamber influence.

4. Greg Bischak, *Brief 9: U.S. Conversion after the Cold War, 1990–1997: Lessons for Forging a New Conversion Policy.* Bonn: Bonn International Center for Conversion, July 1997.

5. Actually, the Hercules Corporation did not work very hard to make it happen, but Alliant TechSystems, which bought the business in 1994, did.

6. Gregory N. Stone, "Workers Offer Conversion Plans." *Day* 112, no. 128 (November 6, 1992), pp. A1–4. Managements' refusal to consider workers' conversion ideas is nothing new. Perhaps the most famous case of this sort is that of Lucas Aerospace, a British company that went out of business in about 1980 rather than attempt to produce the commercial products that skilled workers and engineers proposed. See Dave Elliott and Hilary Wainwright, "The Lucas Plan: Roots of the Movement," in ed. Suzanne Gordon and Dave McFadden, *Economic Conversion: Revitalizing America's Economy.* Cambridge, MA: Ballinger Publishing, 1984, pp. 89–107.

7. Some practitioners distinguish between *technology development* and *technology deployment*, where the former connotes new "high-tech," and the latter, "appropriate technology." The Manufacturing Extension Partnership programs funded by NIST generally fall into the deployment category, while the R&D work of federal research labs such as NASA/Langley, as well as the St. Louis Center for Emerging Technologies and Connecticut's Techconn and, to a large degree, the Peninsula Advanced Technology Center, fall into the technology development category. In practice, however, sometimes the lines between the two may blur somewhat.

8. See Laura Powers and Ann Markusen, *A Just Transition? Lessons from Defense Worker Adjustment in the 1990s.* Washington, DC: Economic Policy Institute Technical Paper No. 237, April 1999.

9. Other federal agencies and programs, including the Technology Reinvestment Project, the Department of Housing and Urban Development, and the Department of Energy, also provided funds.

10. Organizations such as the Center for Economic Conversion in Mountain View, California, and the National Commission for Economic Conversion and Disarmament in Washington, DC, kept good records on conversion progress across the country.

11. See, for example, the account in Sanford Gottlieb, *Defense Addiction: Can America Kick the Habit?* Boulder, CO: Westview Press, 1997, chap. 13.

12. See, for example, John J. Accordino, "Quality of Working Life Systems in Large Cities: An Assessment." *Public Productivity Review* (summer 1989).

13. See Miriam Pemberton, "Doing Well by Doing Good." *Positive Alternatives* 8, no. 4 (summer 1998), p. 1.

14. There were, of course, exceptions. A number of Technology Reinvestment Projects used the funds to develop environmentally benign technologies. One example is the Center for Advanced Ship Repair in Hampton Roads, which sought, among other things, to develop environmentally benign methods of sandblasting and painting ship hulls. McDonnell Douglas won a TRP grant to develop similar technologies for aircraft. Moreover, many new industrial technologies are more environmentally friendly than their predecessors, thanks in large part to environmental regulations that have stimulated such innovations.

15. This approach is not entirely unreasonable either. As discussed chapter 2, the logic of expending public resources on large firms (if they are export-oriented establishments) is that they will draw supplier firms and create other positive multiplier effects on the economy. The problem is that big, export-oriented establishments are increasingly footloose branch plants with no commitment to the community, so they bring about instability rather than local economic health. A less flashy but better way to develop a local economy is to stimulate and nurture locally owned businesses and create business-location advantages other than public tax incentives such as clusters or networks of companies. This philosophy underpins much of Washington State's conversion efforts.

16. The account is by no means complete, however. Gottlieb (1997) and others have described many conversion successes that are not described here. See Gottlieb, *Defense Addiction*; see also *Positive Alternatives*, published by the Center for Economic Conversion in Mountain View, California, which published numerous accounts of conversion successes (as well as problems) throughout the 1990s.

17. See, for example, the remarks of Admiral John J. Shanahan, Ret., of the Center for Defense Information Testimony at the National Defense Panel Quadrennial Review, April 29, 1997: <http://www.defenselink.mil/topstory/0429_ndp.html>.

18. Randall Forsberg, "Force Without Reason." *Boston Review* 20, no. 3 (summer 1995); Elise Boulding and Randall Forsberg, *Abolishing War.* Boston: Boston Research Center for the 21st Century, November 1998.

19. Forsberg, "Force Without Reason"; Boulding and Forsberg, *Abolishing War.*

20. Interagency Environmental Technologies Exports Working Group, *Environmental Technologies Exports: Strategic Framework for U.S. Leadership.* Washington, DC: U.S. Commerce Department, November, 1993; Roger H. Bezdek and Robert M. Wendling, "Environmental Market Opportunities," in ed. Thomas F. P. Sullivan, *The Greening of American Business.* Rockville, MD: Government Institutes, 1992; Pemberton, "Doing Well by Doing Good."

21. Gottlieb, *Defense Addiction*, chap. 13.

22. Elizabeth Mueller, "Retraining for What? Displaced Workers and Federal Programs in Two Regions," in ed. Lloyd J. Dumas, *The Socio-Economics of Conversion from War to Peace.* Armonk, NY: M.E. Sharpe, 1995; Powers and Markusen, *A Just Transition?*

23. In recent decades America has also failed to develop the mid-range jobs and career ladders within companies that can utilize more skilled workers. See Commission

on the Skills of the American Workforce, *America's Choice: High Skills or Low Wages?* Rochester, NY: National Center on Education and the Economy, 1990.

24. This recommendation does not take other defense-downsizing operations into account such as cutbacks or diversification of the Department of Energy's nuclear-research labs or diversification of other federal military-oriented labs.

25. However, a "dollar-for-dollar" policy of replacing each lost federal defense dollar with a federal dollar for assistance or nonmilitary spending, as called for in a 1990 San Diego ordinance, is probably not feasible and not necessary.

26. See, for example, Myron Orfield, *Metropolitics: A Regional Agenda for Community and Stability.* Washington, DC: Brookings Institution Press, 1997.

27. States determine which taxes localities are allowed to levy. Thus states would have to enact policies to restrict the use of real property taxes (to levels much lower than current restrictions) and would have to increase state income taxes and pass the revenues back to localities. Note that if local property taxes were simply replaced with other local taxes, such as sales taxes (as happened in California), the problem of interlocal competition would not disappear but grow worse.

28. Growth interests would continue to function, of course. Wealth could still be increased through investment in land development and local growth-oriented industries would still push for local policies that increased growth. And particular growth interests would continue to advocate for local policies that allocate that growth to areas where those growth interests would most benefit. The change that would come about as a result of elimination of the real property tax would be a modest one, but it would be better than the status quo.

29. See, for example, Melvin L. Burstein and Arthur J. Rolnick, "Congress Should End the Economic War among the States." Federal Reserve Bank of Minneapolis, *1994 Annual Report* 9, no. 1 (March 1995).

30. For discussion of these and related ideas see Timothy Bartik, *What Should the Federal Government Be Doing About Urban Economic Development?* Kalamazoo, MI: W.E. Upjohn Institute for Employment Research, April 1994.

31. Forsberg, "Force without Reason."

32. The Center for Defense Information is located in Washington, DC; the Institute for Defense and Disarmament Studies is located in Cambridge, MA; and the Women's Action for New Directions is located in Arlington, MA. The Global Action to Prevent War coalition is sponsored by the Global Action International Network at <www.globalactionpw.org>.

33. Women's Action for New Directions reported in the fall of 1999 that an estimated 82 percent of Americans support the Comprehensive Test Ban Treaty that the U.S. Senate rejected in October 1999. Perhaps Americans will express their disagreement with the Senate in the November 2000 elections. See Women's Action for New Directions, *WAND Bulletin* 18, no. 4 (fall 1999), p. 1.

References

Accordino, John J. *Community-Based Development: An Idea Whose Time has Come.* Richmond: Federal Reserve Bank of Richmond, 1997.

———. *The United States in the Global Economy: Challenges and Policy Choices.* Chicago: American Library Association, 1992.

———. "Quality of Working Life Systems in Large Cities: An Assessment." *Public Productivity Review,* summer 1989.

Anderson, Courtney. "Capturing a Labor Force for Virginia's Growth Industries." *Virginia News Letter* 75, no. 5, May 1999.

Anderson, Marion, and Greg Bischak. "A Shift in Federal Spending: What the Peace Dividend Can Mean to Maine." Maine Peace Economy Project, 1990.

Anderson, Marion, Greg Bischak, and Michael Oden. *Converting the American Economy: The Economic Effects of an Alternative Security Policy.* Lansing, MI: Employment Research Associates, 1991.

Arlington Journal. "Navy Rethinks Move." November 2, 1994.

ARMS National Marketing Program. "Operation Enterprise. Facility Amenities" <http://www.openterprise.comarms/armover.html>, 1996– 1998.

———. *The Arms Program: Opportunity for Business Growth and Expansion,* 1996– 1998.

Aronson, J. Richard, and Eli Schwartz. *Management Policies in Local Government Finance.* Washington, DC: International City Management Association, 1987.

Arthur, Robert. *History of Fort Monroe.* 1930. Reprint, Ann Arbor, MI: University Microfilms International, 1979.

Ashby, Charles. "Army Lab Site Set to Become Wildlife Refuge." *Potomac News* (August 1994): A1–A4.

Bacque, Peter, and Jamie C. Ruff. "State Guard Studies Taking Over Pickett." *Richmond Times-Dispatch*, March 3, 1995.

Bartik, Timothy. *Who Benefits from State and Local Economic-Development Policies?* Kalamazoo, MI: W.E. Upjohn Institute for Employment Research, 1991.

———. *What Should the Federal Government Be Doing About Urban Economic Development?* Kalamazoo, MI: W.E. Upjohn Institute for Employment Research, April 1994.

Bates, Steve. "Homeless Groups Favored in Army Base Duel." *Washington Post,* July 4, 1994.

———. "Charity Loses Bid for Army Post in VA." *Washington Post,* August 5, 1994.

———. "Cameron Station Plans Submitted." *Washington Post,* February 1, 1996.

Becker, Karen L. "Community Economic Disaster Planning: Dynamics of Perception and Response to Economic Threat." Master's thesis, Department of Urban Studies and Planning, Virginia Commonwealth University, 1994.

Behr, Peter. "Federal Cuts Give the Private Sector a Paramount Role." *Washington Post,* April 4, 1995.

Bertelli, Domenick. "Military Contractor Conversion in the United States," in ed. Lloyd J. Dumas, *The Socio-Economics of Conversion from War to Peace.* Armonk, NY: M.E. Sharpe, 1995.

Bezdek Roger H., and Robert M. Wendling. "Environmental Market Opportunities," in ed. Thomas F. P. Sullivan, *The Greening of American Business.* Rockville, MD: Government Institutes, 1992.

Bischak, Gregory A., ed. *Towards a Peace Economy in the United States.* New York: St. Martin's Press, 1991.

———. *Brief 9: U.S. Conversion after the Cold War, 1990–1997: Lessons for Forging a New Conversion Policy.* Bonn: Bonn International Center for Conversion, July 1997.

Blair, John P. *Local Economic Development: Analysis and Practice.* Thousand Oaks, CA: Sage Publications, 1995.

Blakely, Edward J. *Planning Local Economic Development: Theory and Practice.* Thousand Oaks, CA: Sage Publications, 1994.

Boruta, Marcia. "San Diego Prepares for a Peace Economy." *Positive Alternatives* 1, no. 4, summer 1991.

Boston Sunday Globe. "High-Stakes Gambling" (February 11, 1996): B10.

Boulding, Elise, and Randall Forsberg. *Abolishing War.* Boston: Boston Research Center for the 21st Century, November 1998.

Bradley, Paul. "Manassas to Get IBM–Toshiba Deal." *Richmond Times-Dispatch,* August 8, 1995.

———. "Chips Outshine Magic Kingdom." *Richmond Times-Dispatch,* August 9, 1995.

Bridgman, Jim. *Foul Play.* Washington, DC: Peace Action, n.d. <http://www.webcom.com/peacact/foulplay.html>.

Brzoska, Michael, and Ann Markusen. "The Regional Role in Post–Cold War Military–Industrial Conversion." *International Regional Science Review,* January 2000.

Bureau of Labor Statistics. *Employment and Earnings, 1979.* Washington, DC: U.S. Department of Labor, 1979.

———. *Employment and Earnings, 1989.* Washington, DC: U.S. Department of Labor, 1989.

———. *Employment and Earnings, 1993.* Washington, DC: U.S. Department of Labor, 1993.

———. *County Business Patterns for Virginia 1988.* Washington, DC: U.S. Census Bureau, 1998.

Burstein, Melvin L., and Arthur J. Rolnick. "Congress Should End the Economic War among the States. Federal Reserve Bank of Minneapolis, *1994 Annual Report* 9, no. 1, March 1995.

Butt, Marshall W. *Portsmouth Under Four Flags, 1752–1961.* Portsmouth, VA: Portsmouth Historical Association, 1961.

Calhoun, Martin. *U.S. Military Spending, 1945–1996.* Washington, DC: Center for Defense Information, July 9, 1996.

Canan, Timothy F. *Economic Trends in Metropolitan Washington.* Washington, DC: Metropolitan Washington Council of Governments, August 1991.

Cassidy, Kevin, and Gregory Bischak, eds. *Real Security: Converting the Defense Economy and Building Peace.* Albany: State University of New York Press, 1993.

Center for Defense Information. "Base Realignment and Closure Statistics." bracstat.html at <www.cdi.org>, April 1999.

Chapman, Gary, and Joel Yudken. *Briefing Book on the Military–Industrial Complex.* Washington, DC: Council for a Livable World, December 1992.

Charland, William. "Conversion Happens: Scenes from San Diego's Defense Industry." *Positive Alternatives* 7, no. 3, spring 1997.

Charlottesville–Albemarle Taskforce on Economic Conversion. "Preparing for Reduced Military Spending." Unpublished report, February 12, 1991.

Choate, Pat, and Susan Walter. *America in Ruins: Beyond the Public Works Pork Barrel.* Washington, DC: Council of Planning Agencies, 1981.

Clark, Gordon L. "Pittsburgh in Transition: Consolidation of Prosperity in an era of Economic Restructuring," in ed. Robert A. Beauregard, *Economic Restructuring and Political Response.* Newbury Park, CA: Sage Publications, 1989.

Clauser, Laura L., and John L. Knapp. *Virginia's Local Economies 1998 Edition.* Charlottesville: University of Virginia, Weldon Cooper Center for Public Service, 1998.

Clavel, Pierre. *The Progressive City: Planning and Participation, 1969–1984.* New Brunswick, NJ: Rutgers University Press, 1986.

Clinch Powell Sustainable Development Forum. "Sustainable Development for Northeast Tennessee and Southwest Virginia." Abingdon, VA, April 1994.

Commander, U.S. Army, Armament Munitions and Chemical Command. "Armament Retooling and Manufacturing Support Initiative." Brochure, circa 1993.

Commission on the Skills of the American Workforce. *America's Choice: High Skills or Low Wages?* Rochester, NY: National Center on Education and the Economy, 1990.

Commonwealth of Virginia. House Joint Resolution No. 433, February 22, 1991.

———. Commission on Local Government. *Report on the Comparative Revenue Capacity, Revenue Effort, and Fiscal Stress of Virginia's Counties and Cities 1988/89,* September 1991.

———. Inter-Agency Task Force on Defense Conversion and Economic Adjustment. *The Virginia Economic Conversion and Adjustment Plan.* Draft, January 30, 1992.

———. Executive Order Number 43(92), creating the Governor's Commission on Defense Conversion and Economic Adjustment, March, 1992.

———. Governor's Commission on Defense Conversion and Economic Adjustment, *First Report to the Governor,* November 1992.

———. "Southwestern Virginia Advanced Manufacturing Technology Center." *Technology Reinvestment Program Applications,* May 1993.

———. Governor's Commission on Defense Conversion and Economic Adjustment. *Interim Report to the Governor,* June 1993.

———. Governor's Commission on Defense Conversion and Economic Adjustment. *Final Report to the Governor,* January 1994.

———. Commission on Local Government. *Report on the Comparative Revenue Capacity, Revenue Effort, and Fiscal Stress of Virginia's Counties and Cities 1995/96,* July 1998.

Community Coalition for Economic Conversion. *Defense Jobs Are Down. What's Up?* Hartford: Connecticut Peace Action, January 1995.

Connecticut SANE/Freeze. "Connecticut Calls for New Priorities: Economic Conversion: Vital to the State's Economy." November 1992.

Crenson, Matthew A. *The Un-Politics of Air Pollution: A Study of Non-Decisionmaking in the Cities.* Baltimore: Johns Hopkins University Press, 1971.

Cusack, Thomas. "On the Domestic Political–Economic Sources of American Military Spending," in ed. Alex Mintz, *The Political Economy of Military Spending in the United States*. London: Routledge, 1992.

Delson, Beth. "Making Waves in Arizona: A Discussion with Rosalyn Boxer." *Positive Alternatives* 3, no. 2, winter, 1993.

Dertouzos, Michael L., Richard Lester, Robert Solow, and the MIT Commission on Industrial Productivity. *Made in America: Regaining the Productive Edge*. Cambridge: MIT Press, 1989.

Dinsmore, Christopher. "Shipyard Takes First Steps into Global Market—Frigates." *Virginian-Pilot*, March 19, 1995.

Dorsey, Jack, and Dale Eisman. "Oceana Comes Out a Winner." *Virginian-Pilot*, March 1, 1995.

Dumas, Lloyd J. "Finding the Future: The Role of Economic Conversion in Shaping the Twenty-first Century," in ed. Lloyd J. Dumas, *The Socio-Economics of Conversion from War to Peace*. Armonk, NY: M.E. Sharpe, 1995.

Edwards, Greg. "ITT Makes Deal: Begins New Product Line." *Roanoke Times and World News*, August 24, 1994.

Eisman, Dale. "N.C. Plans a Dogfight This Week for Navy Jets." *Virginian-Pilot*, May 2, 1995.

Elkin, S. *City and Regime in the American Republic*. Chicago: University of Chicago Press, 1987.

Elliott, Dave, and Hilary Wainwright. "The Lucas Plan: Roots of the Movement," in ed. Suzanne Gordon and Dave McFadden, *Economic Conversion: Revitalizing America's Economy*. Cambridge, MA: Ballinger Publishing, 1984.

Feldman, Jonathan. "Constituencies and New Markets for Economic Conversion: Reconstructing the United States' Physical, Environmental, and Social Infrastructure," in ed. Gregory Bischak, *Towards a Peace Economy for the United States*. New York: St. Martin's Press, 1991.

———. "Public Choice, Foreign Policy Crises, and Military Spending," in ed. Lloyd J. Dumas, *The Socio-Economics of Conversion from War to Peace*. Armonk, NY: M.E. Sharpe, 1995.

First U.S. Citistate Regional Flag, <http://www.citistates.com/hampton.htm>.

Fitzgerald, Joan. "Labor Force, Education, and Work," in ed. Richard D. Bingham and Robert Mier, *Theories of Local Economic Development: Perspectives Across the Disciplines*. Newbury Park, CA: Sage Publications, 1993.

Fitzgerald, Joan, and Louise Simmons. "From Consumption to Production: Labor Participation in Grass-Roots Movements." *Urban Affairs Quarterly* 26, no. 4 (June 1991): 512–31.

Forsberg, Randall. "Wasting Billions," in ed. Randall Forsberg and Alexei Arbatov, "Cooperative Security: The Military Problem." *Boston Review* 19, no. 2, April/May 1994.

———. "Force Without Reason." *Boston Review* 20, no. 3, summer 1995.

Framme, Lawrence. "Defense Cuts: State and Local Action for Economic Adjustment," in *Proceedings: Public Service Forum*, Virginia Polytechnic Institute and State University, Norfolk, May 21, 1992.

Freis, Robert. "A Stern Necessity." *Roanoke Times On-Line* <http://www.newrivervalley.com/news/features/raap1.html>, circa 1997.

———. "Behind the Gates." *Roanoke Times On-Line* <http://www.newrivervalley.com/news/features/raap3.html>, circa 1997.

―――. "Swords into Plowshares." *Roanoke Times On-Line* <http://www.newrivervalley. com/news/features/raap4.html>, circa 1997.

Fuller, Stephen S. "The Internationalization of the Washington, DC, Area Economy," in ed. Richard V. Knight, *Cities in a Global Society*, vol. 35, *Urban Affairs Annual Reviews*. Newbury Park, CA: Sage Publications, 1989.

―――. *Federal Purchases in Greater Washington*. Washington, DC: Greater Washington Research Center, December 1989.

―――. "Federal Contractors in the Washington Area: Who Are They? How Have They Been Affected by Reductions in Federal Procurement? What Is Their Future Outlook?" Washington, DC: George Washington University, Department of Urban Planning and Real Estate Development. Unpublished paper presented at the Association of Collegiate Schools of Planning Conference, Austin, TX, November 1990.

Garreau, Joel. *Edge City: Life on the New Frontier*. New York: Doubleday, 1991.

Gaventa, John, Barbara Ellen Smith, and Alex Willingham, eds. *Communities in Economic Crisis: Appalachia and the South*. Philadelphia: Temple University Press, 1990.

Gittell, Ross J. *Renewing Cities*. Princeton, NJ: Princeton University Press, 1992.

Gottlieb, Sanford. "Teamwork for a Change: Bath Iron Works' Labor–Management Partnership." *Positive Alternatives* 5, no. 3, spring 1995.

―――. *Defense Addiction: Can America Kick the Habit?* Boulder, CO: Westview Press, 1997.

Green, Constance McLaughlin. *American Cities in the Growth of the Nation*. New York: Harper & Row, 1957.

Griffis, Robert J. *Listing of Virginia's Prime Defense Contractors Ranked by Contract Amount, 1991*. Richmond: Virginia Employment Commission, February 1993.

―――. *Estimated Private Sector Defense Employment by Industry and Region in Virginia*. Richmond: Virginia Employment Commission, February 1993.

Griffis Robert J., and Timothy O. Kestner. *Department of Defense Employment Military and Civilian, by Service Branch and Region, 1989–92*. Richmond: Virginia Employment Commission, September 1993.

Griffis, Robert J., Ann D. Lang, and Michael A. Thacker. *Listing of Virginia's Prime Defense Contractors Ranked by Contract Amount, 1993*. Richmond: Virginia Employment Commission, September 1994.

Griffis, Robert J., Ann D. Lang, and Timothy O. Kestner, *Defense Expenditures in Virginia*. Richmond: Virginia Employment Commission, June 1995.

―――. *Department of Defense Employment Military and Civilian, by Service Branch and Region, 1993–94*. Richmond: Virginia Employment Commission, July 1995.

Hall, Peter, and Ann R. Markusen. "The Pentagon and the Gunbelt," in ed. Andrew Kirby, *The Pentagon and the Cities*. Newbury Park, CA: Sage Publications, 1992.

Hampton Roads Planning District Commission Staff. "The Hampton Roads Military Complex." Unpublished paper, November 21, 1994.

―――. "Selected Impacts from the 1996–1999 Oceana Expansion." June 1996.

Harding, Alan. "Elite Theory and Growth Machines," in ed. David Judge, Gerry Stoker, and Harold Wolman, *Theories of Urban Politics*. London: Sage Publications, 1995.

Hardy, Michael, and Mike Allen. "Allen Offers Plan to Offset Pickett Closure." *Richmond Times-Dispatch,* July 15, 1995.

Harrison, Bennett. "The Return of the Big Firms." *Social Policy* 21, no. 1 (summer 1990): 7–19.

Hatcher, Patrick Lloyd. *Economic Earthquakes: Converting Defense Cuts to Economic Opportunities*. Berkeley, CA: Institute of Governmental Studies Press, 1994.

Herndon, James R. "Local Shipyards Should Survive." *Virginian-Pilot,* March 13, 1995.

Higgins, Kelly Jackson. "A New Vision for Virginia's Defense Industry." *Virginia Business*, May 1993.

Hill, Isabel, and Betsy Newman. *Made in Brooklyn*. Hohokus, NJ: New Day Films, 1993.

Hoerr, John. *And the Wolf Finally Came: The Decline of the American Steel Industry*. Pittsburgh: University of Pittsburgh Press, 1988.

Hooks, Gregory. *Forging the Military–Industrial Complex: World War II's Battle of the Potomac*. Urbana: University of Illinois Press, 1991.

Hsu, Spencer. "Army Facility Could Become Office Park." *Washington Post*, November 15, 1994.

Interagency Environmental Technologies Exports Working Group. *Environmental Technologies Exports: Strategic Framework for U.S. Leadership*. Washington, DC: U.S. Commerce Department, November, 1993.

Isserman, Andy, and Peter Stenberg. "The Recovery of Rural Economies from Military Base Closures: Control Group Analysis of Two Decades of Experience." Paper presented at the Southern Regional Science Association Meeting, Orlando, Florida, April 1994.

Jacobs, Jane. *The Economy of Cities*. New York: Random House, 1969.

Jick, Todd D. "Mixing Quantitative and Qualitative Methods: Triangulation in Action." *Administrative Science Quarterly* 24, December 1979.

Johnson, Thomas G., et al. "An Economic Opportunity Analysis for the New River Valley." Report to the New River Valley Planning District Commission. Virginia Polytechnic Institute and State University, Program in Agricultural Economics, March 1994.

Josephson, Jo. "Economic Conversion: From Defense to Domestic Spending." *Maine Townsman: The Magazine of the Maine Municipal Association*, May 1991.

Kerr, Charlotte, et al. "Issue Paper: Possible Impacts of Defense Cutbacks on Virginia's Economy." Richmond: Commonwealth of Virginia, Joint Legislative Audit and Review Commission, January 8, 1991.

Kinsley, Michael J. *Economic Renewal Guide: A Collaborative Process for Sustainable Community Development*. Snowmass, CO: Rocky Mountain Institute, 1997.

Knapp, John. "The Impact of Defense Spending on Virginia's Economy." *Virginia News Letter* 68, no. 9, October/November, 1992.

Knox, Paul. "Washington State Community Diversification Program Report, January 1993–May 1994." Olympia: Washington State Community Development Department, Community Diversification Program, May 1994.

Kutay, Aydan. "Prospects for High-Technology-Based Economic Development in Mature Industrial Regions: Pittsburgh as a Case Study." Unpublished paper, Carnegie Mellon University, Department of Engineering and Public Policy, November 1988.

LeRoy, Greg. *No More Candy Store: States and Cities Making Job Subsidies Accountable*. Washington, DC: Federation for Industrial Retention and Renewal, 1994.

Levy, John M. *Economic Development Programs for Cities, Counties, and Towns*. New York: Praeger Publishers, 1990.

———. *Contemporary Urban Planning*. Englewood Cliffs, NJ: Prentice-Hall, 1991.

Little, Robert. "Blackstone's Fort Pickett: A Town, a Fort, a Future?" *Virginian-Pilot*, March 12, 1995.

Logan, John R., and Harvey L. Molotch. *Urban Fortunes: The Political Economy of Place*. Berkeley: University of California Press, 1987.

Lotchin, Roger, ed. *The Martial Metropolis: U.S. Cities in War and Peace*. New York: Praeger Publishers, 1984.

Luke, Jeffrey S., Curtis Ventriss, B. J. Reed, and Christine M. Reed. *Managing Economic Development: A Guide to State and Local Leadership Strategies.* San Francisco: Jossey-Bass, 1988.

MacDougal, John. "Economic Conversion without Military Doctrinal Debate: The Case of Maine, USA." Unpublished paper, October 1994.

Maine Economic Conversion Project: Defense Dependency—Its Impacts and Conversion Efforts in Maine, Summary. Portland: Maine Economic Conversion Project, June 1994.

Mangalindan, Mylene. "Hampton Roads, Hoping for Best, Braces for Worst." *Virginian-Pilot,* February 14, 1995.

Markusen, Ann. "How We Lost the Peace Dividend." *American Prospect,* no. 33 (July–August 1997): 86–94.

Markusen, Ann, Peter Hall, Scott Campbell, and Sabina Deitrick. *The Rise of the Gunbelt: The Military Remapping of Industrial America.* New York: Oxford University Press, 1991.

Mayer, Kenneth R. *The Political Economy of Defense Contracting.* New Haven, CT: Yale University Press, 1991.

McManus Brian P., and John L. Knapp. *Piedmont Planning District Number 14.* Charlottesville: University of Virginia, Weldon Cooper Center for Public Service, 1998.

Melman, Seymour. "From Private to State Capitalism: How the Permanent War Economy Transformed the Institutions of American Capitalism." *Journal of Economic Issues* 31, no. 2 (June 1997): 311.

———. "Profits without Production: Deterioration in the Industrial System," in ed. Suzanne Gordon and Dave McFadden, *Economic Conversion: Revitalizing America's Economy.* Cambridge, MA: Ballinger Publishing, 1984.

Mintz, Alex. *The Political Economy of Military Spending in the United States.* London: Routledge, 1992.

Mintz, John. "Another Addition to the Loral Corral." *Washington Post,* March 22, 1995.

———. "Raytheon to Acquire E-Systems, $2.3 Billion Merger Continues Trend." *Washington Post,* April 4, 1995.

Mueller, Elizabeth. "Retraining for What? Displaced Defense Workers and Federal Programs in Two Regions," in ed. Lloyd J. Dumas, *The Socio-Economics of Conversion from War to Peace.* Armonk, NY: M.E. Sharpe, 1995.

National Governors' Association. *A Governor's Guide to Economic Conversion.* Washington, DC: National Governor's Association, 1992.

National Guard Association of the United States. "Washington Focus" <http://www.ngaus.org/washfoc/99brac.html>.

New River Valley Planning District Commission. "New River Valley News & Views," October–November 1998 <http://crusher.bev.net/blacksburg/pdc/octo98.html>.

———. "New River Valley Vision 2020," April 1995.

Oden, Michael, et al. *Changing the Future: Converting the St. Louis Economy.* Piscataway, NJ: Rutgers University Center for Urban Policy Research, November 1993.

Orfield, Myron. *Metropolitics: A Regional Agenda for Community and Stability.* Washington, DC: Brookings Institution Press; Cambridge, MA: Lincoln Institute of Land Policy, 1997.

Osborne, David, and Ted Gaebler. *Reinventing Government: How the Entrepreneurial Spirit Is Transforming the Public Sector.* New York: Penguin Group, 1993.

Pages, Erik R. *Responding to Defense Dependence: Policy Ideas and the Defense Industrial Base.* Westport, CT: Praeger Publishers, 1996.

Parker, Robert E., and Joe R. Feagin. "Military Spending in Free Enterprise Cities: The

Military–Industrial Complex in Houston and Las Vegas," in ed. Andrew Kirby, *The Pentagon and the Cities*. Newbury Park, CA: Sage Publications, 1992.

Parramore, Thomas C. *Norfolk: The First Four Centuries*. Charlottesville: University Press of Virginia, 1994.

Pemberton, Miriam. "Doing Well by Doing Good." *Positive Alternatives* 8, no. 4 (summer, 1998): 1.

Petrie, Timothy. "A Reuse Plan for Fort Pickett Army Base." Department of Urban Studies and Planning, Virginia Commonwealth University, April 1992.

Piedmont Planning District Commission. "Restoration and Enhancement of the Blackstone–Fort Pickett Army Air Base: Assessment and Recommendations," February 25, 1985.

———. "Fort Pickett: The Economic Impact on the Piedmont Planning District," December 15, 1988.

Planning Journal, The. "Navy Base Closure and Realignment Process in the San Diego Region: Two Early Impressions." San Diego: American Planning Association San Diego Section, April 1994, pp. 1–4.

Porter, William. "A Study of the Impact of Defense Cuts on Northern Virginia's Economy." Richmond: Commonwealth of Virginia, Secretary of Economic Development, October 12, 1990 (unpublished).

Powers, Laura, and Ann Markusen. *A Just Transition? Lessons from Defense Worker Adjustment in the 1990s*. Washington, DC: Economic Policy Institute Technical Paper No. 237, April 1999.

Raffel, James. "Economic Conversion Legislation: Past Approaches and the Search for a New Framework," in ed. Lloyd J. Dumas, *The Socio-Economics of Conversion from War to Peace*. Armonk, NY: M.E. Sharpe, 1995.

Richmond Times-Dispatch. "Gains Top Losses" (March 1, 1995): A1, A8.

———. "Alexandria Can't Wait for This Base to Close." March 12, 1995.

———. "Making Prosperity Blend with the Scenery." July 18, 1995.

———. "Senate Shuts Door on Base Closings" (May 27, 1999): A9.

Roanoke Times and World News. "Montgomery Wants Plan to Ease Arsenal Cuts' Impact." September 26, 1992.

———. "Cuts Hurt Western Virginia Workers Too." March 10, 1993.

Rose, Fred. "Organizing for Conversion: Peace and Labor Coalitions," in ed. Lloyd J. Dumas, *The Socio-Economics of Conversion from War to Peace*. Armonk, NY: M.E. Sharpe, 1995.

Rouse, Parke, Jr. *Endless Harbor: The Story of Newport News*. Newport News, VA: Newport News Historical Committee, 1969.

Ruberry, William. "Personnel at Bases Edgy Over 'Hit List.'" *Richmond Times-Dispatch*, December 1988.

———. "A. P. Hill, Pickett, Put on List of Bases that U.S. May Shut." *Richmond Times-Dispatch*, June 1, 1991.

Rusk, David. *Cities without Suburbs*. Washington, DC: Woodrow Wilson Center Press, 1993.

San Diego Economic Conversion Council. "Traveling Town Meeting Report, Prepared by the San Diego Economic Conversion Council, June 1994." Unpublished document.

Sbragia, Alberta. "The Pittsburgh Model of Economic Development: Partnership, Responsiveness, and Indifference," in ed. Gregory D. Squires, *Unequal Partnerships: The Political Economy of Urban Redevelopment in Postwar America*. New Brunswick, NJ: Rutgers University Press, 1989.

Scampavia, James. "Fairfax County Defense Industry Phase One and Phase Two Survey Results." Executive Summaries. Fairfax County, VA: Fairfax County Economic Development Authority, April and October, 1990.

Schultz, James. "The Great Communicators." *Golden Egg* 1, 1998 (Herndon: Virginia Center for Innovative Technology).

Shanahan, Admiral John J., Ret., of the Center for Defense Information, Testimony at the National Defense Panel Quadrennial Review, April 29, 1997 <http://www.defense-link.mil/topstory/0429_ndp.html>.

Shean, Tom. "Q & A: James F. Babcock Retired Banker: Regionalism Still a Huge Issue." *Virginian-Pilot*, August 2, 1998.

Sheehan, Joanne. "Making a 'Penalty' Positive." *New England WRL News*, spring 1993.

———. "Community Coalition for Economic Conversion." Unpublished history by the Community Coalition for Economic Conversion, Uncasville, CT, 1997.

Silver, Christopher. "Norfolk and the Navy: The Evolution of City–Federal Relations, 1917–46," in ed. Roger W. Lotchin, *The Martial Metropolis: U.S. Cities in War and Peace*. New York: Praeger Publishers, 1984.

Smith, Hedrick. *Surviving the Bottom Line, Part 3: San Diego*. South Carolina Educational Television, 1997, distributed by Films for the Humanities and Sciences.

Squires, Gregory D. "Public–Private Partnerships: Who Gets What and Why," in ed. Gregory D. Squires, *Unequal Partnerships: The Political Economy of Urban Redevelopment in Postwar America*. New Brunswick, NJ: Rutgers University Press, 1989.

Stewart, Thomas A. "The Netplex: It's a New Silicon Valley." *Fortune*, March 7, 1994.

Stone, Clarence N. *Economic Growth and Neighborhood Discontent: System Bias in the Urban Renewal Program of Atlanta*. Chapel Hill: University of North Carolina Press, 1976.

Stone, Gregory N. "In Tucson, the Community Helps Encourage Conversion Efforts." *Day* 112, no. 123 (November 1, 1992): A-1–6.

———. "Defense Workers Seek Applications for Technology: McDonnell Douglas Process Could Yield Stronger Bridges." *Day* 112, no. 127 (November 5, 1992): A-1–8.

———. "Workers Offer Conversion Plans." *Day* 112, no. 128 (November 6, 1992): A-1–4.

———. "In Seattle, Boeing Doesn't Like to Discuss Conversion." *Day* 112, no. 130 (November 8, 1992): A-1–6.

———. "At Bath Iron Works, a Rare Attitude." *Day* 112, no. 131 (November 9, 1992): A-1–5.

Storper, Michael, and Richard Walker. "The Spatial Division of Labor: Labor and the Location of Industries," in ed. Larry Sawers and William K. Tabb, *Sunbelt/Snowbelt: Urban Development and Regional Restructuring*. New York: Oxford University Press, 1984.

Swanstrom, Todd. *The Crisis of Growth Politics: Cleveland, Kucinich, and the Challenge of Urban Populism*. Philadelphia: Temple University Press, 1985.

Temple, David G. *Merger Politics: Local Government Consolidation in Tidewater Virginia*. Charlottesville: University Press of Virginia, 1972.

Terlekyj, Nestor E. "Defense Spending and the Virginia Economy." Washington, DC: NPA Data Services. Unpublished paper presented at the Richmond Association of Business Economists Meeting, November 16, 1990.

U.S. Congress, Office of Technology Assessment. *After the Cold War: Living with Lower*

Defense Spending, OTA-ITE-524. Washington, DC: U.S. Government Printing Office, February 1992.

U.S. Public Law 101-510. Defense Base Closure and Realignment Act of 1990.

U.S. Public Law 102-484, 106 STAT. 2315, FY1993, Defense Authorization Act, Subtitle H, Armament Retooling and Manufacturing Support Initiative, October 23, 1992.

Verhovek, Sam Howe. "Intel's Oregon Deal Includes Limit on Jobs." *New York Times*, June 9, 1999.

Virginia Employment Commission. *Covered Employment and Wages by 2-Digit SIC Industry (ES-202), 1979*. Richmond: Virginia Employment Commission, 1979.

———. *Covered Employment and Wages by 2-Digit SIC Industry (ES-202), 1989*. Richmond: Virginia Employment Commission, 1989.

———. *Employer Information for Defense Contractors as of December 1992*. Richmond: Virginia Employment Commission, 1992.

———. *Employer Information for Defense Contractors as of March 1994*. Richmond: Virginia Employment Commission, 1992.

———. *Virginia Population Projections, 2010*. Richmond: Virginia Employment Commission, June 1993.

———. *Covered Employment and Wages by 2-Digit SIC Industry (ES-202), 1993*. Richmond: Virginia Employment Commission, 1993.

———. *A Revised Impact Analysis of Fort Pickett*. Richmond: Virginia Employment Commission, March 1995.

Virginia Tech Center for Survey Research. "New River Valley Economic Adjustment Strategy Corporate Survey." Prepared for the New River Valley Planning District Commission, October 1993.

Virginian-Pilot. "Everyone's Fighting Base Closing: Suddenly, a Megabase." January 23, 1995.

———. "Base Closing List Galvanizes Support for Fort Pickett; State and Local Leaders Begin a Campaign to Keep the Army Facility from Closing." March 6, 1995.

———. "BRAC Commander to Visit Fort Pickett in Virginia." March 19, 1995.

———. "Newport News Shipbuilding Bids on Kuwait Frigate." May 3, 1995.

———. "Low Wages: What's Holding Us Back? Hampton Roads Still Far Below National Average." Editorial, March 14, 1999.

Washington Post. "Army Solicits Bids for Most of Base." January 26, 1995.

Wertenbaker, Thomas J. *Norfolk: Historic Southern Port*. Durham, NC: Duke University Press, 1962.

Whaley, John W., et al. "Hampton Roads Military Impact." Chesapeake: Southeastern Virginia Planning District Commission (now Hampton Roads Planning District Commission), January 1989.

Wiewel, Wim, David Ranney, and George W. Putnam. "Technological Change in the Graphic Communications Industry: Implications for Economic-Development Planning." *Economic Development Quarterly* 4, no. 4 (November 1990): 371–82.

Winiecki, Susan. "Major Export–Import Center Proposed for Southside." *Richmond Times-Dispatch*, January 17, 1992.

Women's Action for New Directions. *WAND Bulletin* 18, no. 4, fall 1999.

Women's Action for New Directions Education Fund. *Women Take Action: Control U.S. Arms Trade*. Brochure. Arlington, MA: WAND, March 1999.

Woodwell, James, and Adrian Overton. *Economic Trends in Metropolitan Washington*. Washington, DC: Metropolitan Washington Council of Governments, December 8, 1993.

Index

About the Author

John J. Accordino is associate professor of economic-development policy and planning in the Department of Urban Studies and Planning at Virginia Commonwealth University in Richmond. His publications include *The United States in the Global Economy: Challenges and Policy Choices* and *Community-Based Development: An Idea Whose Time Has Come*, as well as articles in a variety of planning and economic-development journals. He and his students assist local governments and community-based organizations through economic-development and revitalization plans and policy analyses. He is a past chair of the American Planning Association's Economic Development Division. He holds a doctorate degree in urban and regional planning from the Massachusetts Institute of Technology.

ISBN 0-275-96561-9

9 780275 965617

90000>

EAN

HARDCOVER BAR CODE